RUPTURING RHETORIC

RACE
RHETORIC
& MEDIA

Davis W. Houck, Series Editor

RUPTURING RHETORIC

The Politics of Race and
Popular Culture since Ferguson

Edited by Byron B Craig,
Patricia G. Davis, and Stephen E. Rahko

University Press of Mississippi / Jackson

The University Press of Mississippi is the scholarly publishing agency of the Mississippi Institutions of Higher Learning: Alcorn State University, Delta State University, Jackson State University, Mississippi State University, Mississippi University for Women, Mississippi Valley State University, University of Mississippi, and University of Southern Mississippi.

Any discriminatory or derogatory language or hate speech regarding race, ethnicity, religion, sex, gender, class, national origin, age, or disability that has been retained or appears in elided form is in no way an endorsement of the use of such language outside a scholarly context.

www.upress.state.ms.us

The University Press of Mississippi is a member of the Association of University Presses.

∞

Library of Congress Cataloging-in-Publication Data

Names: Craig, Byron B, editor. | Davis, Patricia G. (Patricia Gail), 1970– editor. | Rahko, Stephen E., editor.
Title: Rupturing rhetoric : the politics of race and popular culture since Ferguson / Byron B Craig, Patricia G. Davis, Stephen E. Rahko.
Other titles: Race, rhetoric, and media series.
Description: Jackson : University Press of Mississippi, 2024. | Series: Race, rhetoric, and media series | Includes bibliographical references and index.
Identifiers: LCCN 2024014813 (print) | LCCN 2024014814 (ebook) | ISBN 9781496852335 (hardback) | ISBN 9781496852328 (trade paperback) | ISBN 9781496852311 (epub) | ISBN 9781496852304 (epub) | ISBN 9781496852298 (pdf) | ISBN 9781496852281 (pdf)
Subjects: LCSH: Post-racialism—United States. | Racism—United States. | Minorities—United States. | Black lives matter movement. | United States—Race relations.
Classification: LCC E184.A1 R746 2024 (print) | LCC E184.A1 (ebook) | DDC 305.800973—dc23/eng/20240506
LC record available at https://lccn.loc.gov/2024014813
LC ebook record available at https://lccn.loc.gov/2024014814

British Library Cataloging-in-Publication Data available

CONTENTS

Part 3: Postrace Rereleased

Part 4: Crafting Memory in the Postrace Era

Part 5: The Spatial and Social Class Dynamics of Postrace

ACKNOWLEDGMENTS

The seeds of *Rupturing Rhetoric: The Politics of Race and Popular Culture since Ferguson* grew out of a paper session titled "Surviving (Post) Racial Fantasies in American Popular Culture" at the 2019 National Communication Association (NCA) convention in Baltimore, Maryland. The dynamic conversation that unfolded between participants and audience members energized and propelled this project. We thank the Critical and Cultural Studies Division of NCA for sponsoring the original paper session that has now blossomed into this book volume.

The University Press of Mississippi (UPM) has been steadfast in its support, enthusiasm, and encouragement for this project. It has been a joy working with this press, and we especially thank Emily Bandy for her guidance as we navigated each step in our journey.

Our anonymous reviewers provided invaluable advice, especially on the introduction. We are indebted to their insights and careful scrutiny of our work. Our project was deeply enriched by the generosity and support of our colleagues at Illinois State University, Northeastern University, and Indiana University Bloomington. The faculty and student affiliates of the Center for Research on Race and Ethnicity in Society (CRRES) at Indiana University Bloomington enriched this volume through many quotidian conversations over coffee and bagels that helped clarify the direction it ultimately took. We especially thank, from Illinois State University, Dr. Heather Dillaway, dean of the College of Arts and Sciences, and the School of Communication, for providing university funds to support copyediting and indexing.

Most of all, we thank the fantastic contributors to this volume, who believed in this project and made it possible through the brilliance of their observations and insights into the racial politics of our contemporary era.

RUPTURING RHETORIC

TAKING STOCK OF THE
(POST)RACIAL ORDER OF THINGS

BYRON B CRAIG, PATRICIA G. DAVIS, AND STEPHEN E. RAHKO

In his "Theses on the Philosophy of History," Walter Benjamin (1969) famously describes a Paul Klee painting, *Angelus Novus*, for his allegory of history in thesis nine. "This is how one pictures the angel of history," he writes (p. 257).

> His face is turned toward the past. Where we perceive a chain of events, he sees one single catastrophe which keeps piling wreckage upon wreckage and hurls it in front of his feet. The angel would like to stay, awaken the dead, and make whole what has been smashed. But a storm is blowing from Paradise; it has got caught in his wings with such violence that the angel can no longer close them. This storm irresistibly propels him into the future to which his back is turned, while the pile of debris before him grows skyward. This storm is what we call progress. (pp. 257–258)

Benjamin's cherub is a fitting image for the discursive formation we have come to call "postrace" in the United States. Like Benjamin's angel, the popular notion of a "postracial" America looks upon us with numb incapacity while we are promised racial "progress." As an aspiration to declare the "end of history" on matters of race, the notion offers us cold indifference as the carnage of our recent racial past—a past replete with predatory lending, violent hate crimes, white nationalism, gentrification, assaults on voting rights, climate migrations, police brutality, and protofascism—continues to pile up. The notion of the "postracial" suggests that the United States has largely achieved racial equality and that race is no longer a central organizing category in American society. Enabled in part by a confluence of complex shifts in demographic trends—such as marriage, immigration, and emerging attitudes along generational divides—"postrace" evokes a glamorous image of harmonious racial assimilation grounded in the celebration of diversity and difference (Mukherjee et al., 2019). Some scholars trace the discursive rudiments of American discourses of the "postracial" to the late 1960s, but the seminal event that solidified it into a cohesive ideological narrative was indubitably the historic campaign and election of America's first Black president, Barack Obama, in 2008 and 2012 (Glaude, 2014; Mukherjee, 2014; Squires, 2014; Taylor, 2016). In the political arena, the idea of postracialism came into vogue even before Obama was elected, as essays in *The Economist* ("The Cooks," 2008), the *New Yorker* (Boyer, 2008), and other outlets in the wake of his victory in the Iowa caucuses proclaimed the emergence of a "postracial generation" that saw Obama as the embodiment of its hopes that America could transcend the racial divisions that would be relegated to the past.[1]

These assumptions gained greater currency upon his election and continued well into his presidency. The election of the country's first Black president, so the reasoning went, served as proof that the United States had moved beyond racial categories. This idea was eagerly embraced across the political spectrum by mainstream conservatives and liberals alike. The *Wall Street Journal*, for example, described Obama's 2008 victory as a "tribute to American opportunity" and proposed that "perhaps we can put to rest the myth of racism as a barrier to achievement in this splendid country" ("President-Elect Obama," 2008). Echoing these sentiments, John McWhorter (2008), writing in *Forbes*, declared that Obama's election meant that "racism in America is over." Likewise, in commenting on Obama's first State of the Union address, prominent liberal political pundit Chris Matthews proclaimed: "It's interesting, he is postracial, by all appearances. I forgot he was Black tonight for an hour." Though this assertion drew criticism in some quarters, the notion that the election of the first African American president signified incontrovertible evidence of racism's demise remained intact (Graham, 2010). Statements such as these represented a new American *doxa* on race that has pervaded a number of influential—and culturally authoritative—societal institutions well beyond the realm of political discourse.

Despite the seemingly optimistic nature of such pronunciations, postracial assumptions have not functioned as an ideal, but rather served several interrelated rhetorical functions premised on the notion that systemic racism has been confined to the past. To wit, they suggest that racist practices or outcomes are the result of individual rather than systemic biases, that persistent disparities with respect to various societal measures spring from individual or group "deficiencies" rather than programmed inequities, and, most notably, that there is thus no longer any need for structural remedies to address them. These assumptions have operated to preserve white supremacy and other forms of inequality and further enshrine them in the country's social, political, and economic institutions. For example, in the judicial arena, these assumptions provided the primary justification for the Supreme Court to dismantle a key enforcement provision of the Voting Rights Act of 1965 in its landmark *Shelby County v. Holder* decision in 2013, signaling the court's adoption of a new era of race jurisprudence that C. M. Powell (2018) has referred to as "postracial constitutionalism." Postracial constitutionalism was also on full display in the court's 2023 decision in *Students for Fair Admissions v. President and Fellows of Harvard College*, which reversed more than forty years of precedent to effectively ban the consideration of race in college admissions. The Supreme Court's ruling in *Harvard* helps preserve white supremacy since it undermines race as a consideration for college admissions while maintaining other kinds of admission preferences—such as those for athletic recruits and legacy status applicants or children of employees and donors—that often benefit white students (Cineas, 2023).

Discourses of postracialism have also pervaded a number of influential societal institutions, from education (Aleman et al., 2011) to Silicon Valley (Noble & Roberts, 2019) and beyond. Its many usages—most accomplishing the same end of maintaining the status quo—have constructed it as a potent rhetorical force in a society that has yet to come to terms with its history and contemporary realities of racial hierarchy. The postracial discourses that attain widespread circulation within US sociopolitical culture assume the language and actions of multiculturalism, creating the illusion of full inclusion in society while leaving intact the structures that sustain uneven power relations (Sugino, 2019). In the process, they render Blackness "hypervisible as a symbol of a post-race United States" yet "invisible in terms of its own social and cultural relevance" (Cobb, 2011, p. 407). In essence, postracialism as an ideology constitutes a twenty-first-century version of the "colorblind" discourses that characterized American sociopolitical culture in the years after the civil rights movement, revised and revamped to reflect more contemporary assumptions of racial progress or transcendence, race-neutral universalism, moral equivalence, and political distancing (Cho, 2009). Indeed, America's postracial fantasy has served as a basis for the symbolic retelling of American history in a way that has sought to vindicate its violent past of slavery and Jim Crow segregation while affirming the nation's mythic conviction in its own exceptionalism.

(RE)PERIODIZING AND CRITIQUING POSTRACE

Rupturing Rhetoric: The Politics of Race and Popular Culture since Ferguson analyzes and critically responds to the racial rhetorics of American popular culture since the killing of Michael Brown in Ferguson, Missouri, on August 9, 2014. The central argument of the book is that Brown's death and the civic protests that his death engendered have transformed the rhetorical landscape of American racial politics. Like other historical events that immediately capture the cultural mood of an era by the mere evocation of them, such as "Pearl Harbor" or "9/11," we argue that "Ferguson" symbolically stands as an event in our popular political lexicon that summarizes the rupturing of what we shall call America's "postracial fantasy." To be sure, the legitimacy of America's postracial fantasy was the first casualty of the tanks, tear gas, and rubber bullets that met protesters during the sweltering summer heat of August 2014.

The events surrounding the death of Michael Brown have been constructed as a watershed moment in US history. As Louis Maraj (2020) argues, our current period is best defined as a post-Ferguson era. Indeed, one need only invoke "Ferguson," the name of the Missouri town in which the events took place, to evoke the intersection of race, state power, and physical and economic violence. Though this instance of police brutality—and the subsequent acquittal of the perpetrator and the protests that followed—represented only the latest amidst decades of similar patterns pointing to the collaboration of the entire justice system in the killing of African Americans, it resonated with the public in ways that made it stand out as symbolic of state complicity in the deployment of violence to maintain the racial order. In many ways, the script was familiar: a tense encounter between a police officer and an unarmed African American man resulting in the Black man's death, the authorities' initial refusal to hold the officer accountable followed by prosecutorial efforts enacted under pressure that resulted in the miscarriage of justice, and mass protests designed to highlight the failures of the criminal-justice system more broadly. However, in significant ways, the events stood out from those of the past: the protests over the failure to indict the officer, now global in scale, reinvigorated the Black Lives Matter movement while a subsequent Justice Department investigation found widespread, systemic abuses of Ferguson's Black citizens not only in the police department but also within the municipal court system as well.[2] Most importantly, the unrest in Ferguson brought about a dramatic shift in the perception of law enforcement and, having taken place five years after Barack Obama's historic ascendancy to the presidency, occasioned a more critical orientation in thinking about systemic racism, including increased attention to the long narrative of Black political, social, and economic struggle. These shifts, in the popular imaginary, constituted a "seismic moment in American race relations" ("It's Been Five Years," 2019). They have thus positioned Ferguson as both a geographical location and a discursive construction.

It is in this spirit that we locate Ferguson as the starting point for this collection of essays centered on postracial discourses in popular culture. Popular culture represents one of the more influential sites through which postracial discourses are sustained, interrogated, or dismantled. Pop culture is seen not only to influence and reflect the values of those who consume it in its many forms but also to be a political arena wherein particular ideas—especially those either implicitly or explicitly guiding current events—are advanced or contested (Freccero, 1999). In this sense, it not just serves as a form of entertainment or escape but also performs a variety of functions: informational, pedagogical, and sociological, among others. Race, and the ideologies that sustain it as a social category, has historically constituted a significant aspect of pop-cultural production. Its influence in this arena renders pop culture an important location for the various historically situated projects implicated in racial formations, defined as the "sociohistorical processes by which racial categories are created, inhabited, transformed, and destroyed" (Omi & Winant, 2014, p. 6). Beginning with blackface minstrelsy, which, in many respects, represented the earliest form of American popular culture, and continuing with film, radio, television, and other mass-mediated entertainment genres, racialized productions have historically served the specific needs of white Americans by presenting "evidence" that various groups were not quite ready for full citizenship. In broader terms, the pop-cultural realm served up overtly dehumanizing depictions of people of color that offered confirmation for racist beliefs, along with justification for the public policies that sustained white racial domination.

Postracialism presents a mode of racial hegemony that, in contrast to racial domination, operates more subtly and therefore, in many ways, more powerfully. In an era marked by the mainstreaming of hardcore white nationalism, as evidenced by the popularity of the "great replacement" theory, postracialism ideologically offers a softer edge with a more subdued, taciturn, and underhanded tone. It assumes many forms, all of which align with contemporary culture's self-congratulatory emphasis on social progress in all matters of representation, including those inside and outside of popular culture. Its hegemonic reach infuses both "high" and "low" culture, rendering such distinctions virtually meaningless when it comes to the ideal of having moved beyond race and the signifying work that such distinctions are meant to culturally perform. It enables us to look with disdain at the racist texts of the past with their portrayals of defeminized mammies, "yellow peril"–type Asian and Asian American villains, Latino gang members, and other stereotypical renderings and remark upon the progress that has been made in terms of the better-developed, more "diverse" characters who inhabit our more enlightened contemporary pop-cultural landscape. These assumptions, of course, mirror those that pervade our broader culture and suggest the necessity of a "racial reckoning" that includes increased attention to the role of pop culture in fostering a sense of complacency about the continuing pervasiveness of race as the primary social force in American society. A more analytical approach to these texts, particularly one that considers the rhetorical work that postracial assumptions perform within popular culture, is warranted.

Ferguson implores us to not look away. It therefore constitutes the primal scene for a set of racial projects that interrogate "postrace" as a set of guiding assumptions within popular cultural production. As M. Omi and H. Winant (2015) suggest, "every racial project is both a reflection of and response to the broader patterning of race in the overall social system. In turn, every racial project attempts to reproduce, extend, subvert, or directly challenge that system" (p. 125). Just as a multitude of racial projects throughout history led to the abuses in Ferguson and innumerable other locations within and outside of the United States, so may the myriad ways we attempt to address and redress racial inequities be constructed as racial projects. Ferguson, in its dual role as a set of significations for abusive law enforcement and the enactment of the practices of mass resistance that draw our attention to them, may be situated as a racial project. The idea of Ferguson as the social location for critical analyses of popular-cultural texts, especially those that mobilize postracial assumptions to lull us into complacency about the continuing importance of race, constitute a racial project. We thus situate Ferguson as a racial project in the sense that the essays in this book present various cases that draw these connections between postracial discourses and contemporary popular culture.

Through case studies advancing close critical analysis of media texts in American popular culture since 2014, *Rupturing Rhetoric* seeks to map how the fantasy of a postracial America has been ruptured since the Ferguson protests. By "rupture," we claim that the rhetorical boundaries of (post)race have been redrawn since 2014, creating space for both resistance to and the reinscription of the politics of the postracial. To be sure, by "rupture," we do not mean to suggest that the postracial formation is being replaced, but rather, as our chapters demonstrate, that the symbolic landscape of the postracial has come to be marked by a series of "fissures" in a Foucauldian sense that are redrawing the rhetorical boundaries of our racial order of things (Foucault, 1984, p. 82). The aftershocks of Ferguson have been felt across America, especially since 2020, which witnessed the rise of a new civil rights movement replete with massive, nationwide protests and a renewed discourse of social justice around the historical legacy of structures of systemic racism that accompanied the murders of George Floyd, Ahmaud Arbery, Breonna Taylor, and Rayshard Brooks.

The films, television series, and digital media that constitute popular culture are discursive sources of shared political fantasy. By "political fantasy," we mean the narrative and scopic regimes of the visual and symbolic that define the dramatic and ideological boundaries of political expression, performance, and social agency. Rhetoric has long been identified as the quintessential civic art, and given the rise of social tensions and anxieties over race that intensified during the Trump presidency, our project seeks to recognize the complex ways popular culture can serve as a cultural resource not only for reinforcing postracial fantasies but also for resisting them through civic engagement and political contestation within an American landscape of media convergence and social fragmentation.

The chapters collected in this volume employ techniques of close critical analysis to map and critically interrogate how contemporary media texts within American popular culture negotiate the political fantasy underlying the racial project of our time: postrace. We approach "postrace" as an organizing discursive and material force that shapes socioeconomic structures, crafts cultural identities, and informs the assigning of privilege and stigma in American political life. Accordingly, our project is critical in its orientation and seeks to understand discourse and its effectivity, including the complex ways power constitutes sociopolitical relations and subjectivities through its cultural circulation (Lacy & Ono, 2011).

We believe that the critique of "postrace" requires that we not be constrained by disciplinary myopia, perspectives, or approaches; instead, it should be enriched by insights from a multitude of scholarly fields, methods, and styles of critique that unfold from the vibrant interstices of academic fields. As we watch the complex mutations of "postrace" and the novel ways that racial formation is being represented in our public culture, we acknowledge that there is a plethora of ways to approach and analyze discourses and representations of race. We recognize that a critical rhetorical approach to the critique of "postrace" must draw upon multiple methodologies in order to map the changing rhetorical and symbolic landscape of racial politics in the United States. Toward this end, our project advances a transdisciplinary approach that forges methods of critique that cross multiple theoretical and humanistic approaches from different disciplines, including rhetorical theory and criticism, media studies, cultural studies, theater, psychology, film theory, critical race theory, Afropessimism, Asian American studies, history, gender and queer studies, postcolonial criticism, political and social theory, and transnational and diaspora studies.

Our project seeks to contribute to and build upon recent studies of post-race. A growing number of studies have advanced significant discussions of the relationship between popular culture, postracial ideologies, and social change (Jenkins et al., 2020; Kennedy et al., 2017; Mukherjee et al., 2019; Squires, 2014; Terrill, 2017; Watts, 2017). Most of these studies have been firmly located methodologically in media and cultural studies. Our volume is interdisciplinary but rooted in rhetorical approaches to cultural criticism and interpretation. Methodologically, rhetorical analysis can deepen and develop our understanding of the postracial by revealing the rhetorical and symbolic devices upon which the ideological landscape and boundaries of "race" turn in American politics and culture. Arguments about (post)race—whether they take the form of public address, popular film or television shows, Broadway plays, news coverage, or any number of cultural artifacts—are always built contingently from a culture's rhetorical foundations—that is, its *doxas*, commonplaces, figures, genres, and topoi. These cultural resources have histories and are rooted in the speech acts and modes of symbolic action that constitute a discursively shared public culture. *Rupturing Rhetoric*, accordingly, seeks to contribute to this new bourgeoning scholarship by examining recent American popular culture in terms of its emerging rhetorical representations of race with a particular focus on media texts that make the question of "postrace" a direct reference for aesthetic intervention, creativity, critique, and ideological reproduction.

Notably, our volume extends these analyses in three specific ways. First, *Rupturing Rhetoric* includes chapters that depart from previous volumes' analytical focus on whiteness. Our volume includes chapters that critically explore the rise of both "woke" culture and the postracial dynamics of white-grievance politics that have accompanied Trumpism in the United States. However, the postracial project touches all ethnicities and identities, not just whiteness, which means that all racial categories and ontologies must negotiate the terms and conditions of postrace. The politics of postrace often involve a direct negotiation with the hegemonic terms of whiteness, but many of our contributing authors demonstrate that this is not always the case since postracialism also transcends whiteness. Put another way, the politics of postrace are often negotiated in interracial and intraracial terms that may indirectly hinge on whiteness but may also not involve whiteness much at all.

Second, *Rupturing Rhetoric* is the first book to explore and analyze how postracial assumptions infuse "high" culture, namely in Broadway theater and art-house cinema.[3] Attending to the way postrace operates at the level of both "high" and popular culture illustrates the complex ways that postracialism permeates and constitutes taste cultures across all social classes of American life. Finally, it incorporates the reinvigoration of the Black Lives Matter movement since 2020, the public and state responses to it, and its implications with respect to postracial assumptions. The Movement for Black Lives is the most important contemporary social movement advocating against anti-Blackness, and several chapters in our volume explore the relationship between the postracial and anti-Blackness, which puts *Rupturing Rhetoric* in direct correspondence with recent work in rhetorical studies that has explored this nexus (Cobb, 2011; Edgar & Johnson, 2018; Johnson, 2022). *Rupturing Rhetoric*'s contribution thus insists on the necessity of analyzing the intersection of the postracial and anti-Blackness while simultaneously emphasizing that we continue to explore the postracial as a paradigm that operates on its own terms alongside anti-Blackness and other forms of racial domination.

Primarily, *Rupturing Rhetoric* seeks to advance scholarship on postrace by emphasizing a new time signature for understanding how the postracial is culturally negotiated, organized, and dramatized in American life. By foregrounding Ferguson as a rupturing event, we seek to propel scholarship on postrace in a new direction that shifts focus on an emergent and ongoing periodization of cultural production that, at the same time, directly participates in the ideological remaking of American racial discourse and identity formation that is currently unfolding in our public culture. In many ways, *Rupturing Rhetoric* offers an exploration of the manifold afterlives of postrace. The notion of afterlife has become a paradigmatic approach to the study of race that traces the continuities of the past that may be obscured by the narrative of progress (Hartman, 2007; Sexton, 2010; Sharpe, 2016). By exploring the ways that US racial politics are shaped between the historical echoes and tensions of resistance to and reinscription of racial violence and colorblindness, *Rupturing Rhetoric* advances a critique of the postracial that seeks to map the complex terrain on which (post)racial politics is negotiated. By foregrounding previously undeveloped and underdeveloped perspectives, particularly those grounded in rhetorical theory, and by focusing on a topic so central to the political conflicts and controversies that mark our present era, *Rupturing Rhetoric* advances a new periodization of the present that explores the intersections among race, rhetoric, and media in American cultural, political, and social discourse, as well as advances close critical readings of the rhetoric of contemporary media texts that examine how race and ethnicity are ideologically represented, framed, and negotiated with regard to the question of the "postracial."

Our project also seeks to contribute to and build upon recent studies of popular representations of race as well as studies in racial rhetorical criticism. Several recent books focus, for example, on the way historical representations of race flatten the complexities of lived experience to ideological stereotypes, where representation itself serves as a form of racial profiling of African Americans, Latinos, and Asian Americans (duCille, 2018; Erigha, 2019; Flores, 2020; Han, 2020; Hoerl, 2018; Hunt & Ramon, 2010; Lopez, 2020; Lacy & Ono, 2011). Many other recent books have advanced close readings of historical media representations to focus on hermeneutical space for resistance against ideological stereotypes within the text, often emphasizing representations that transgress or undermine ideological expectations for racialized and gendered characters (Beltran & Fojas, 2008; Buonanno, 2017; Francis, 2021; Kaplan, 2010; Konzett, 2019; Washington, 2017). Finally, a third strand of recent scholarship in media representation focuses on the way the ideologies of whiteness contain political expressions of racial self-actualization. These scholars argue that Hollywood remains largely exclusive to white male protagonists to the point that even Black film icons, such as Sidney Poitier, must signify racial reconciliation without threatening whiteness as a dominant racial norm of media culture, thus perpetuating deep hegemonically compromised representations of race, gender, and sexuality (Sisco King, 2011; Willis, 2015). *Rupturing Rhetoric* takes up where these books leave off yet also places emphasis on the rhetorical dimensions of popular culture. Moreover, to this point, rhetorical studies of postrace have been primarily limited to article-length interventions; *Rupturing Rhetoric* is the first book in rhetorical studies to critique recent American popular culture with a focus entirely on the question of postrace.

OVERVIEW OF CHAPTERS

The chapters collected in this volume explore how the rhetorical boundaries of (post)race have been ruptured since 2014 through close textual analyses of texts from mainstream American popular culture. Some texts offer a range of discursive efforts aimed at destabilizing the postracial fantasy, while others affirm, embody, or otherwise reveal its symbolic potency and durability as a dominant discourse of our time. Each chapter offers a case study examining popular texts that negotiate how the boundaries of (post)race are being drawn in our current aporetic era. They offer different approaches to analyzing how race and its intersectional orders of difference are being both challenged and rearticulated into new rhetorical terms and forms that constitute American politics and public affairs. Indeed, the chapters build off each other in an interdiscursive manner that together paint a mosaic of the many forms postracial discourse takes across a range of points of American cultural production, including various types of media (i.e., television, film, radio, newspapers) as well as forms situated as "high" culture (i.e., Broadway theater, art-house cinema, and their adaptation in traditional forms of mass culture, such as film and television). Moreover, each chapter signals deeper and wider intersectional implications of postracialism that link the politics of race to that of gender, feminism, queerness, class, and globalization.

We begin our volume with a series of chapters that address the question of postrace in terms of symbolic violence and cultural appropriation. Patricia G. Davis's chapter "Blackness as Spectral Presence: Postracial Discourses in *Fresh Off the Boat*" argues that the popular television sitcom *Fresh Off the Boat*'s (2015–2020) depiction of the Asian American "model-minority" trope, when situated within its historical context, advances many of the assumptions implicated in a form of anti-Blackness that borrows Black cultural expressions while relegating African Americans to more of a spectral presence than a material one. This form of what she calls "racial poaching" enables the construction of a set of dominant group identifications that, as enacted in *Fresh Off the Boat*, activates a set of postracial discourses in which the context of celebrating differences gives license to appropriate the cultural products of one marginalized group and shift their most useful features onto another, less "threatening" one.

Likewise, Oscar Giner's chapter analyzes postracial symbolic violence in terms of its deeper cultural and mythological roots in American imperialism and empire. Following Bertolt Brecht's "A Short Organum for the Theatre" as an inspired model and Bernard Shaw's (1965) premise that all serious theater should teach a moral lesson, Giner examines the film version of Lin-Manuel Miranda's *Hamilton* on Disney+. His analysis reveals how *Hamilton* expresses the ways American imperialism absorbs the cultural energies of fugitive aesthetic traditions, such as American hip-hop and aesthetic movements throughout the Caribbean, only to then manufacture them into its own postracial image of bland and abstract multiculturalism. His critique of the *Hamilton* phenomenon contextualizes Miranda's commercial success and fame in terms of the everyday struggle for Puerto Rican cultural affirmation. Giner's critique forces us to confront what it means to be political in an era marked by postracial spectacle for, as he argues, *Hamilton* is a play about politics, but it is not a *political* play.

Several chapters address the question of postrace in terms of the rhetorical and identity scripts of whiteness. Stephen E. Rahko and Byron B Craig's chapter examines woke whiteness as a specific articulation of the American postracial fantasy, which informs the discursive terrain of the politics of cinematic representation. They offer a response to this trend by advancing a critique of the Oscar-winning film *Green Book* (2018), a film that outlines a new stock racial trope that they call the "Nuse." Rahko and Craig argue that the "Nuse" (short for Negro muse) is a new figuration of Blackness that enlightens whiteness to its racist misdeeds. Rahko and Craig ultimately argue that films such as *Green Book* ideologically reinforce the legacy of American structural racism by recentering whiteness under the aegis of a moral awakening on its own terms.

Jaclyn S. Olson's chapter examines how postrace informs popular discourses of patriotism and cultural rituals of American nation building. Through an analysis of National Public Radio's 2018–2019 music series *American Anthem*, she critiques what she calls "postracial patriotism" to reveal how the postracial operates as an unstated premise of (white) nation building. She shows how anthems function within an American imaginary already marked as "white" and critiques how the very idea of the anthem is always already politicized and deployed to secure the American nation-state. As the controversy over Colin Kaepernick's kneeling protests illustrate, Olson's chapter underscores the ways the anthem serves as a volatile, urgent site of struggle over national identity in the allegedly "postrace" era.

Likewise, Craig, Rahko, and J. Scott Jordan's chapter addresses the question of postrace in terms of the Trumpian turn in whiteness and America's traumatic legacy of racial violence. Their chapter analyzes the rise of the phrase "All Lives Matter," a slogan that has been circulating as a conservative counterpoint to "Black Lives Matter" since 2014. They understand the phrase "All Lives Matter" to be emblematic of what they call a "postracial discourse of trauma," which they define as a popular rhetoric of race that strategically seeks to undermine race-specific claims to historical and systemic injustices. They advance an analysis of the HBO series *Lovecraft Country* (2020), specifically the series' depiction of the Tulsa Race Massacre of 1921, as a discursive response to the phrase "All Lives Matter" that disrupts America's postracial political condition.

Several chapters address the question of postrace through an analysis of historical films that were either rereleased or remade after Ferguson. Christopher Gilbert's chapter, for example, examines Spike Lee's classic *Bamboozled*

(2000), which was rereleased in 2020 as part of the Criterion Collection. Gilbert argues that Lee's portrayal of Blackness as commodified caricature bespeaks a systemic practice of realizing fascinations with Black culture and fantasies about Black Otherness in the consignment of race relations to the rhetorical spaces of entertainment, festivity, and amusement. Originally a comic satire of dark pasts made present, Gilbert understands the film's rerelease during the Trump years as a cautionary tale about the institutional and cultural frameworks for a postracial minstrelsy and argues that audiences should view *Bamboozled* as a satire of the follies that undercut the false promises of postracialism.

Likewise, Arthur D. Soto-Vásquez's chapter examines Disney's recent remake of three classic animated films from its catalogue—*Dumbo* (1941), *The Lion King* (1994), and *Lady and the Tramp* (1955)—into live-action films. Through a close reading of each film, Soto-Vásquez argues that the live-action remakes attempt to construct what he calls a "postracial fantasyland" where multiculturalism was always the norm and racial violence and strife never existed. Much like the use of historical theming at Disney parks, Soto-Vásquez argues that Disney's postracial fantasyland simultaneously sanitizes and obscures race as it commodifies racial progress into a consumable good. He identifies three rhetorical strategies that underlie the postracial fantasyland—racial remembering and forgetting, multicultural representation, and racial Imagineering—that are indicative of a corporatized response to racial injustice that was on full display during 2020.

In a similar vein, several chapters address postrace in terms of the question of memory. A. Susan Owen and Peter Ehrenhaus's chapter examines the rhetorical construction of memory in Spike Lee's film *BlacKkKlansman* (2018). In particular, they map four intertwined strategies used by Lee to (re)construct memory of the history of racism in the United States: (1) intertextuality, (2) ironic juxtaposition, (3) subversive comedy, and (4) stylistic pastiche. They show how the film resists the postracial fantasy through its construction of critical Black memory, the subversion of white gazes, and the film's invitation to audiences of all races to embody a critical Black gaze on the history of violence and anti-Blackness.

Likewise, Euni Kim's chapter critiques the representational politics of the film *Crazy Rich Asians* (2018). Drawing on the work of A. Mbembe, Kim theorizes postrace as necropolitical and demonstrates how the postracial fantasy relies on symbolically violent memory practices that at once erase yet affirm racial identity and subjectivity. By positing memory as necropolitical, she traces the cultural production of "Asian America" as a racialized signifier that rhetorically floats between practices of memory and amnesia and presence and absence, as well as intentional acts of preservation and destruction that implicate the discursive as a condition of the material. Through a close analysis of the rhetoric surrounding the film, she argues that the film risks Southeast Asian American erasure through rhetorical amnesia within the broader signifier of "Asian American" as a racial term of identification.

Moreover, Erika M. Thomas and Maksim Bugrov's chapter examines postracial memory through an Afropessimistic reading of Quentin Tarantino's film *The Hateful Eight* (2015). Set during the failed period of Reconstruction, *The Hateful Eight* offers an allegorical critique of the Obama years that counters the postracial aspiration of (Afro)optimistic conditions of possibility. The film illustrates deeply embedded racist relationships that constitute American politics and ultimately reveals society's exploitive and structural ontological dependency on Black suffering. Their analysis demonstrates how Tarantino's allegory of our postracial times critically uses the era of Reconstruction as a historical reference for mapping the way postracial rhetorics remain inherently parasitic on Blackness in an era when mainstream culture has declared that racial "progress" has been achieved.

Finally, we conclude our volume with two chapters that examine the postrace in terms of the spatial dynamics of social class, solidarity, and economic inequality. Whitney Gent and Melanie Loehwing's chapter examines the film *The Public* (2018), which tells the story of a multiracial group of homeless men who stage a peaceful occupation of the public library in downtown Cincinnati, Ohio. Gent and Loehwing argue that the film constructs a postracial fantasy of protest and solidarity in which racial difference is limited to the visual depictions of characters and plays no meaningful role in the narrative, thus suggesting that racial difference pertains only to superficial distinctions among the characters and does not correspond with fundamental and far-reaching disparities that continue to plague contemporary American society. Gent and Loehwing argue that the film embodies what they call a "postracial enthymeme" since the film leaves it up to the audience to see how race is either emphasized or not within the story of collective struggle.

Likewise, Nick J. Sciullo's chapter addresses the question of postrace in terms of the complex cultural nexus of space, place, and racialization. He offers an analysis of two cultural representations of Pittsburgh's historically Black neighborhood, the Hill District, through Denzel Washington's 2016 film adaptation of August Wilson's award-winning play *Fences* (1983) and popular newspaper representations of gentrification. Sciullo offers a close reading of Pittsburgh to reveal the spatial dynamics of postrace, specifically how the discursive and material intersect in the gentrification of spaces that are racialized.

NOTES

1. Though it was Obama's election that provided the expressed justification for the assertion that the United States had moved beyond race, it is important to note that his campaign, in which he presented himself as a "uniter," not a "divider," was itself based on postracial ideals. He effectively positioned himself as a postracial *candidate* in a postracial *America.* Therefore, postracialism was not merely an assumption projected onto Obama, but was rather one that he himself mobilized as a means of attaining power, thereby further enhancing its rhetorical force.

2. For details, see Civil Rights Division (2015) report.

3. Scholars (Squires, 2014) have addressed the question of taste communities and the consumption of postracial cultural artifacts, but there have been no studies that examine the question of postrace in terms of "high" culture. Our volume seeks to fill this gap in the literature by including several chapters that examine artifacts that can be understood as "highbrow" or "high" culture.

REFERENCES

Aleman, E., Jr., Salazar, T., Rorrer, A., & Parker, L. (2011). Introduction to postracialism in U.S. public school and higher education settings: The politics of education in the age of Obama. *Peabody Journal of Education, 86*(5), 479–487.

Beltran, M. C., & Fojas, C. (2008). *Mixed race Hollywood.* New York University Press.

Benjamin, W. (1969). *Illuminations: Essays and reflections.* Schocken Books.

Boyer, P. (2008, January 27). The color of politics. *New Yorker.* https://www.newyorker.com/magazine/2008/02/04/the-color-of-politics-2

Buonanno, M. (2017). *Television antiheroines: Women behaving badly in crime and prison drama.* University of Chicago Press.

Cho, S. (2009). Post-Racialism. *Iowa Law Review, 94*(5), 1589–1650.

Cineas, F. (2023, June 30). Affirmative action for white college applicants is still here. *Vox.* https://www.vox.com/politics/2023/6/30/23778906/affirmative-action-white-applicants-legacy-athletic-recruitment

Civil Rights Division. (2015, March 4). Investigation of the Ferguson Police Department. United States Department of Justice. https://www.justice.gov/sites/default/files/opa/press-releases/attachments/2015/03/04/ferguson_police_department_report.pdf

Cobb, J. N. (2011). No we can't! Postracialism and the popular appearance of a rhetorical fiction. *Communication Studies, 62*(4), 406–421.

The cooks spoil Obama's broth. (2008, January 26). *The Economist.* https://www.economist.com/united-states/2008/01/24/the-cooks-spoil-obamas-broth

duCille, A. (2018). *Technicolored: Reflections on race in the time of TV.* Duke University Press.

Edgar, A. N., & Johnson, A. E. (2018). *The struggle over Black Lives Matter and all lives matter.* Lexington Books.

Erigha, M. (2019). *The Hollywood Jim Crow: The racial politics of the movie industry*. New York University Press.

Flores, L. A. (2020). *Deportable and disposable: Public rhetoric and the making of the "illegal immigrant."* Pennsylvania State University Press.

Foucault, M. (1984). *The Foucault Reader* (p. Rabinow, Ed.). Pantheon.

Francis, T. S. (2021). *The audacious Josephine Baker: Josephine Baker's cinematic prism*. Indiana University Press.

Freccero, C. (1999). *Popular culture: An introduction*. New York University Press.

Glaude, E. S., Jr. (2014). A requiem for Michael Brown / A praisesong for Ferguson. *Theory & Event*, *17*(3). https://muse.jhu.edu/article/559370

Graham, N. (2010, March 29). Chris Matthews: I forgot Obama was Black for an hour. *Huffington Post*. from https://www.huffpost.com/entry/chris-matthews-i-forgot -o_n_439701

Han, B. M. (2020). *Beyond the Black and white TV: Asian and Latin American spectacle in Cold War America*. Rutgers University Press.

Hartman, S. (2007). *Lose your mother: A journey along the Atlantic slave route*. Farrar, Straus, and Giroux.

Hoerl, K. (2018). *The bad sixties: Hollywood memories of the counterculture, antiwar, and Black Power Movement*. University Press of Mississippi.

Hunt, D., & Ramon, A. C. (2010). *Black Los Angeles: American dreams and racial realities*. New York University Press.

It's been five years since Ferguson: Are racial tensions even worse now? (2019, August 8). *USA Today*. https://www.usatoday.com/story/news/nation/2019/08/08/ferguson -missouri-riots-5-years-since-shooting-race-tensions-worse/1952853001/

Jenkins, H., Peters-Lazaro, G., & Shresthova, S. (2020). *Popular culture and the civic imagination: Case studies of creative social change*. New York University Press.

Johnson, P. E. (2022). Fear of a Black city: Gender and postracial sovereignty in *Death wish* (2018). *Women's Studies in Communication*, *45*(2), 1–22.

Kaplan, M. A. (2010). *Friendship fictions: The rhetoric of citizenship in the liberal imaginary*. University of Alabama Press.

Kennedy, T. M., Middleton, J. I., & Ratcliffe, K. (2017). *Rhetorics of whiteness: Postracial hauntings in popular culture, social media, and education*. Southern Illinois University Press.

Konzett, D. M. C. (2019). *Hollywood at the intersection of race and identity*. Rutgers University Press.

Lacy, M. G., & Ono, K. A. (Eds.). (2011). *Critical rhetorics of race*. New York University Press.

Lopez, L. K. (2020). *Race and media: Critical approaches*. New York University Press.

Maraj, L. (2020). *Black or right: Anti/racist campus rhetorics*. Utah State University Press.

McWhorter, J. (2008, December 30). Racism in America is over. *Forbes*. https://www.forbes .com/2008/12/30/end-of-racism-oped-cx_jm_1230mcwhorter.html#526369cc49f8

Mukherjee, R. (2014). Antiracism limited: A pre-history of post-race. *Cultural Studies*, *30*(1), 47–77. https://doi.org/10.1080/09502386.2014.935455

Mukherjee, R., Banet-Weiser, S., & Gray, H. (Eds.). (2019). *Racism postrace*. Duke University Press.

Noble, S. U., & Roberts, S. T. (2019). Technological elites, the meritocracy, and postracial myths in Silicon Valley. In R. Mukherjee, S. Banet-Weiser, & H. Gray (Eds.), *Racism postrace* (pp. 113–130). Duke University Press.

Omi, M., & Winant, H. (2014). Racial formation. In G. B. Rodman (Ed.), *The race and media reader* (pp. 5–24). Routledge.

Omi, M., & Winant, H. (2015). *Racial formation in the United States* (3rd ed.). Routledge.

Powell, C. M. (2018). The rhetorical allure of post-racial process discourse and the democratic myth. *Utah Law Review, 3*(1), 523–577.

President-Elect Obama: The voters rebuke Republicans for economic failure. (2008, November 5). *Wall Street Journal.* https://www.wsj.com/articles/SB122586244657800863

Sexton, J. (2010). People of colorblindness: Notes on the afterlife of slavery. *Social Text, 28*(2), 31–40.

Sharpe, C. (2016). *In the wake: On Blackness and being.* Duke University Press.

Sisco King, C. (2011). *Washed in Blood: Male sacrifice, trauma, and the cinema.* Rutgers University Press.

Squires, C. R. (2014). *The post-racial mystique: Media and race in the twenty-first century.* New York University Press.

Sugino, C. M. (2019). Multicultural redemption: *Crazy Rich Asians* and the politics of representation. *Lateral, 8*(2). https://doi.org/10.25158/L8.2.6

Taylor, K. Y. (2016). *From #BlackLivesMatter to Black liberation.* Haymarket Books.

Terrill, R. E. (2017). The post-racial and post-ethical discourse of Donald J. Trump. *Rhetoric and Public Affairs, 20*(3), 493–510.

Washington, M. S. (2017). *Blasian invasion: Racial mixing in the celebrity industrial complex.* University Press of Mississippi.

Watts, E. K. (2017). Postracial fantasies, Blackness, and zombies. *Communication and Critical/Cultural Studies, 14*(4), 317–333. https://doi.org/10.1080/14791420.2017.1338742

Willis, S. (2015). *The Poitier effect: Racial melodrama and fantasies of reconciliation.* University of Minnesota Press.

Part 1

Symbolic Violence
and Cultural Appropriation

Chapter 1

BLACKNESS AS SPECTRAL PRESENCE

Postracial Discourses in *Fresh Off the Boat*

PATRICIA G. DAVIS

The television sitcom *Fresh Off the Boat* (2015–2020) was transformative in many ways, particularly in that it represented the first program centered on an Asian American family since Margaret Cho's *All-American Girl* ended its run in 1995 after one season. The show is loosely based on the autobiography of restaurateur and author Eddie Huang and depicts the experiences of a Taiwanese American family after its relocation in the mid-1990s from Washington, DC's Chinatown to a majority-white community in Orlando, Florida, in order to operate a western-themed restaurant. The show initially focused on the oldest child, Eddie, whose character development emphasized his rebelliousness, love of basketball, and immersion in hip-hop culture. However, after cocreator Eddie Huang departed and relinquished much of his creative control, it was retooled in season 2 to focus on the entire family, particularly the parents' business success and their and their children's experiences in trying to assimilate into their suburban community. During the time it aired, the show achieved critical acclaim and popular success and was largely perceived as offering an important refutation of stereotypes of Asian Americans in the mass media.

Nevertheless, the very same factors that seemingly constructed the show as an exemplar of inclusion and innovation rendered it a case study of the circulation of postracial fantasies in contemporary popular culture. Specifically, the series' focus on the Huang family's middle-class entrepreneurial aspirations, respectability, and suburban-style assimilation represents the deployment of the model-minority trope that, when situated within its historical context, advances many of the assumptions implicated in anti-Blackness. These discourses are amplified in the persona of oldest son Eddie, whose appropriation and fetishization of hip-hop culture is presented as inimical to his parents' ambitions while also serving as the primary feature of his ability to navigate the virtually all-white suburban environment in which he finds himself. "Anti-Blackness," in this sense, does not refer to a hatred of Black people, but rather to a set of assumptions that suggest that Blackness operates solely in this referent capacity and is therefore more transactional than substantive. It thus positions its main characters' values and aspirations against an unspoken, unheard, and unseen Blackness.

This dynamic renders Blackness more of a spectral presence than a material one and relies on a form of what I refer to as "racial poaching" wherein selective elements of a marginalized group's cultural expression are symbolically and intentionally "poached" as a means of constructing a set of dominant group identifications. Racial poaching constitutes a form of cultural appropriation and retains many of its core elements particularly in the sense that its objective lies in enabling the dominant culture to absorb the aesthetic innovations of a subordinate culture while rendering the creators invisible under a logic of colorblindness (Hall, 1997). However, racial poaching is distinct in that it is activated through a second nondominant group whose social location situates it in greater proximity to the dominant group and enables it to serve as a mediating body through which the processes of absorption are initiated. In borrowing the cultural products of the more liminal group, the "poachers" are able to enhance their own position on the social hierarchy—thereby reifying it—and, rather than render the originators completely invisible, instead serve as their more "palatable" proxies.

In the case of Asian Americans, as a "white-adjacent" group via the model-minority stereotype, the project of appropriating the symbolic artifacts of hip-hop culture enables the character of Eddie to embody a persona that defies stereotypes of Asian men through the appropriation of the hypermasculine expressions more conventionally assigned to Black men and, in so doing, fit into his majority-white suburban environment. In fact, the show was initially marketed as a hip-hop show, even though African Americans are largely absent as multidimensional characters. At the same time, Eddie's preoccupation constructs a set of tensions with his parents, whose assimilationist values are assumed to be in conflict with hip-hop culture and, by definition, the Blackness for which it serves as signification. As enacted in *Fresh Off the Boat*, racial poaching activates a set of postracial discourses in which the context of celebrating differences gives license to appropriate the cultural products of one marginalized group and shift their most useful features onto another, less "threatening" one. Additionally, the show's celebratory focus on Asian Americans advances the circulation of postracial fantasies by obscuring the realities of the ideologies that inform their core and operate against their primary targets, African Americans. In other words, rather than inhibiting the idea of race altogether—as postracial imaginaries typically do—these discourses embrace racial categories, albeit in a package that is more palatable to predominately white viewers. They are, simply, postracial discourses by another means.

In this chapter, I use *Fresh Off the Boat* as a case to suggest that racial poaching constitutes an essential—yet largely unrecognized—element in the circulation of postracial imaginings in contemporary popular culture. In foregrounding characters of one minority group and co-opting the cultural products of another, less favored group, especially in a way that reinforces dominant values, such representations maintain an illusion that society has moved on from its preoccupation with racial differences while perpetuating the very practices of marginality and invisibility—of displacement—that ensure race continues to shape the popular cultural landscape. During its six-season run, *Fresh Off the Boat* consistently served as an active agent in advancing these postracial imaginings, actuating a program of racial poaching that obscures the anti-Blackness that forms the core of postracialism. I construct this argument in two parts. In the first, I provide relevant historical context for the relationships between Asian Americans and African Americans that renders racial poaching a useful set of actions for the former within contemporary popular culture. In the second, I offer a close textual analysis of episodes from the show, spread out over the course of its six-season run.

BECAUSE WE'RE NOT BLACK: ASIAN AMERICANS AS "MODEL" MINORITIES

In a March 2021 interview coinciding with the release of his film *Boogie* (2021), restauranteur and writer Eddie Huang spoke of the relationships between the Black and Asian American characters, situating them within his oft-stated goal to use popular culture as a vehicle to subvert popular stereotypes of Asian men. In responding to the interviewer's challenge of his comparison between the historic experiences of Asian immigrants and African Americans and his appropriation of Black culture in the film, Huang stated:

> Well, I don't think I'm comparing it. I'm just placing [Asian Americans and African Americans] in the same space. The second one was to also give [the film's protagonist's girlfriend] space to stretch out and lead this conversation about struggle because I do think Black Americans have led the conversation and should lead the conversation and that

Asian Americans have spaces many times because of the work African Americans have done . . . I don't know how to separate myself from the Black culture that's influenced and inspired me. . . . And if one day my work with Black culture offends the Black community and they don't want me to participate in it anymore, I would gladly step away—knock on wood. Like I don't think that day will ever happen because I'm genuine about it, and my experience in America is really—was seen through the Black lens. You know, like, all the culture I was intaking was Black culture. And the friends I connected with—they were either Black or they were also, like me, raised on Black culture because they could not relate to dominant culture. (Chang, 2021)

This was the latest in a series of interviews beginning in 2013, when his autobiography *Fresh Off the Boat* was published, wherein Huang made clear his lifelong desire to contest the model-minority myth and assert an identity more commonly associated with African Americans.

Notably, Huang was able to offer his perspective in a variety of widely distributed media channels because of the presumed uniqueness of an Asian American male performing the mannerisms, vernacular, and worldview perceived to define hip-hop as both a musical genre and a culture. An important element of Huang's embrace of hip-hop involves the adoption of the hypermasculinity long associated with Black men, as he acknowledged in a 2013 interview, in which he declared his memoir to be the "beginning of a movement of big dick Asians" (Ishii, 2013). While dominant social scripts have constructed the "big-dick-energy" trope as equating masculine sexuality to power, Huang's invocation neglects its troubling nature when applied to Black men. Myths connecting phallic size with hypersexuality have been inscribed onto the Black male body both historically and contemporaneously and have underwritten the pathologizing of Black masculinity within and outside of popular culture (Jackson, 2006). Therefore, Huang's positionality as Asian enables him to invoke these myths metaphorically in assertions of perceived hypermasculinity that are commonly read as dangerous when articulated by Black men and used as justification for their containment. Indeed, in her profile of Huang, writer E. Kim (2016) notes that it is Asian Americans' position as the model minority that enables Huang to embrace hip-hop specifically—and Blackness more generally—without facing the same discrimination as African Americans.

These associations inform the show's narrative arc—particularly during the early years of its run—and combine multiple discursive elements characteristic of the historical relationships between Asian Americans and

African Americans that shape the contours of the model-minority stereotype. Additionally, the formations that emerge from Asian Americans' engagement with hip-hop operate interdiscursively with the model-minority stereotype as the culture has long been mobilized as a vehicle for subversion. Hip-hop culture has long been viewed as a type of language that articulates universal themes of understanding and revolution. Nevertheless, in its role as a force for solidarity among marginalized groups, it offers a mode of resistance to the hierarchies that further divide them through the creation of a "model-minority" designation. In *Fresh Off the Boat*, it performs a dual role, highlighting the endurance of the stereotype while serving as the conduit through which Eddie is able to position himself as its antithesis in order to gain entrée into his suburban world.

Media historians (Kawai, 2005; Shim, 1998) note Asian Americans' trajectory from "yellow peril" to "model minority" as American sociopolitical rhetoric shifted away from the socioeconomic dangers presumed to accompany Chinese immigration during the nineteenth century and the World War II–era threats posed by Imperial Japan to the burgeoning domestic threats associated with African American agitation for the dismantling of Jim Crow in the South and nationwide. During the two decades following the war, the erosion of white supremacy as a national doctrine led to the development of a new ideal, one centered on ethnic assimilation. The main assumptions of this paradigm were that cultural differences supplanted biological differences as the primary driver of social outcomes and that Asian Americans, though disadvantaged because of their race, embodied the qualities that enabled them to become successful members of American society (Lee, 1998). This conceptualization not only disregarded differences between the historical experiences of Asian Americans and African Americans but also ignored differences among Asian Americans. At the same time, the doctrine of ethnic assimilation helped advance the nation's Cold War–era needs, as the notion that American society was a *colorblind* one wherein racial minorities enjoyed equal rights and upward mobility became an important defense against the threats of communism. Any group that was unable to achieve equality, so the logic went, should be considered failures at assimilation, not victims of structural racism or of the broader capitalist system that fueled it. Domestically, in negatively comparing vocal African Americans to putatively "quiet" Asian Americans, it sent the message that demands for racial equality would be met with fierce resistance. Indeed, as historian R. Lee (2010) suggests, "the construction of the model minority was based on the political silence of Asian America" (p. 151).

The sociopolitical aims of model-minority discourse were advanced through assigning certain characteristics to Asian Americans and situating them as grounded in notions of American citizenship. These features—always assumed to be inherent to whiteness—were presumed to be beyond the collective reach of African Americans, who were thus constructed as anticitizens: whereas Asian Americans were industrious, upwardly mobile, entrepreneurial, and frugal, African Americans were perceived as shiftless, dependent, and profligate. Additionally, while Asian Americans were viewed as family oriented and seen as placing a high value on educational achievement, African American families were perceived as typified by matriarchal family structures and resistant to the very idea of education. These putative deficiencies, while assumed to be legacies of enslavement as well as continuing discrimination, were nevertheless attributed to fundamental pathologies with respect to Black culture. This view was legitimated with the publication of D. Moynihan's (1965) report, which pointed out the widening gap between African Americans and most other groups and asserted that Black people would never be able to overcome it.

In much the same way that the modifier "model" in model minority operates discursively to emphasize a comparative relationship among groups, this trajectory suggests a relationship between African Americans and Asian Americans in which the assumptions assigned to the latter are reliant on those assigned to the former. Indeed, as J. Lee (1998) points out, in suggesting a comparative relationship among groups in the past and present, the modifier performs rhetorical work that goes well beyond merely categorizing and labeling disempowered groups. It sustains the hierarchies it creates by invoking stereotypes that point to both a microaggression toward Asian Americans and a swipe at African Americans (Singletary, 2021). As C. Sugino (2019) suggests, Asian inclusion must be understood in terms of its relation to anti-Blackness, and as the writer F. Chin (1974; as cited in R. Lee, 2010) expresses it bluntly, "whites love us because we're not Black" (p. 256).

Previous analyses of *Fresh Off the Boat* have examined the show in terms of the model-minority mythologies it reinforces (Phùng et al., 2018). Nevertheless, a more comprehensive examination of the ways in which the show advances the discourse within a more contemporary postracial framework necessitates attention to both the show's and the myth's interdiscursivity with hip-hop culture. As is often the case with essentialized assumptions, the model-minority stereotype has produced resistances, and hip-hop culture has functioned as an influential site for its contestation. Because of its global appeal, hip-hop has long been viewed as an expressive form with resonances that span a wide variety of communities that transcend differences of race, ethnicity, class, and other categories. However, as some scholars suggest, with respect to the relationships between African Americans and

Asian Americans, hip-hop culture represents both opportunities for contact and potential grounds for conflict. For example, O. Wang (2006) traces the history of Asian American hip-hop to argue that its appeal lies in its position as an expression of alterity with which marginalized groups can identify and around which they can unite but nevertheless agrees with G. Lipsitz's (1997; as qtd. in Wang, 2006) point that such "cultural crossings" may not necessarily "advance emancipatory ends" but "rather reinforce existing structures of power and domination" (p. 158).

The role of model-minority mythologies in upholding these structures hinges on two intersecting discourses in *Fresh Off the Boat*. The first involves the constructed dichotomy between Asian and African American masculinities. N. McTaggart and E. O'Brien (2017) suggest that hip-hop is used as a "liberating space" wherein Asian American youth can defy the more traditional expectations of their families and communities and circumvent racial stereotypes, including those connected to gender. The premise of the show—particularly during its first season—involved Eddie's preoccupation with hip-hop and focused on its ability to enable him to assimilate into his new suburban social world, along with some assistance in navigating it. Eleven-year-old Eddie is concerned with fitting in with his peers and attracting girls, tasks made all the more difficult because of feminizing stereotypes of Asian men. His conspicuous embrace of hip-hop (and NBA) culture thus affords him the hypermasculinity typically associated with Black men, which, while creating tensions with his parents, enables him to fit in with his peers. This borrowing of the African American cool aesthetic responds to the second discourse, which involves hip-hop's appeal among white youth and the ways in which white Americans consume Black popular culture and use it to construct identity while simultaneously resisting challenges to the structures of white supremacy. This exploitation of Blackness, which B. Yousman (2003) refers to as Blackophilia/Blackophobia, is essential to the operation of postracial discourses in *Fresh Off the Boat*. Drawing on b. hooks (1992), Yousman argues that white enthrallment with hip-hop culture is based on the need to assuage guilt over Black subjugation, cope with crises of white identity, and attain pleasure from the notion of wading into the "exotic" world of hip-hop, including the misogyny and violence that is part of it. These desires, Yousman suggests, are mediated through the opposing impulses of fascination with and dread of African Americans, a dilemma that *Fresh Off the Boat* resolves through the persona of Eddie as the nonthreatening stand-in for hip-hop's Black creators.

Additionally, the cultural markers of the Huang family's assimilation into stereotypical white-centered Americana—the overwhelmingly white suburb they inhabit, the cowboy-themed restaurant they own, the all-white circle of friends with which they interact—further emphasize the centrality of these dichotomous impulses. Hip-hop provides the veneer of Blackness, but it is a carefully selected version, embodied by a member of a "safe" group. These conditions create an environment in which Black people are largely physically absent, but Blackness itself, particularly its relationship to whiteness, informs the structure of space and life. As if to underscore this dynamic and its constructed contrast between Asian Americans and African Americans, the trailer for the pilot episode introduces its premise by highlighting this assumed disjuncture. The scene opens with a hip-hop-inflected musical score and shows young Eddie showing off his clothing, which is understood to signify the hip-hop aesthetic: gaudy jewelry, sunglasses, a baseball cap turned sideways, and a team-sports jacket, shirt, and shorts. He also uses the lingo and vocal inflections associated with hip-hop. This is then contrasted to his very body—that of a young Asian male, not the Black body we have been primed to associate with these features. The scene then cuts to Eddie in the car with his family traveling to Florida, with Eddie visibly dismayed at the contrast his family presents to the way he sees himself: his parents and brothers are singing along to Ace of Base's "I Saw the Sign." The accompanying voice-over explicitly reveals the show's ethos, that of a family who is moving to Florida in order to pursue the American dream. Eddie's embrace of hip-hop is understood as signifying a rejection of that goal.

Indeed, the Huang family's relocation from Chinatown in the majority-Black urban center of Washington, DC, to the suburbs of Orlando, Florida, may be read as a metaphor for the distinction drawn between the two groups, one that mirrors the evolution of the model-minority stereotype. Given the historical construction of suburbia as a set of white-flight enclaves, suburbs have functioned rhetorically as one of the most visible symbols of the American dream. For immigrant communities, predominately white suburbs index a set of place meanings premised on the assumption of having "made it," as measured by their geographical, material, and symbolic distance from Blackness. While extant academic work has highlighted both the racialization of space, including its enactment via suburbanization (Lipsitz, 2007; Summers, 2019) and the construction of suburbia in film and television (Coon, 2014), M. Schleier's (2021) introduction in their collection of essays—though focused on film—is particularly instructive in terms of how geography functions metonymically in *Fresh Off the Boat*. If, as Schleier argues, Hollywood depictions of suburbia have dismissed its increasing heterogeneities—and the complexities that accompany them—in favor of its more traditional construction as the site of assimilation, alienation, rebellion, and other motivations for (white) youth, what are we to make of its function in the context of postracialism? As A. L. Corbin (2015) points out, when considered within a historical perspective, themes of alienation in mediatized suburbia may also operate as metaphors for displacement, magnifying racial otherness and cultural difference. Eddie's new environment, symbolic of his parents' success and with few people of color, provides ample opportunities for storylines highlighting his cultural alienation, with the hip-hop culture associated with the Blackness left behind serving as a means of addressing it. Eddie thus attempts to leverage the cachet of Blackness in his new environment, one relatively devoid of racial Others yet accessible to him as a member of the model-minority group. The rarefied nature of these environs is emphasized when the family first arrives in their new neighborhood, which features stereotypical markers of white-bread suburbia—a woman pushing a baby in a stroller, a middle-aged man dressed in polos getting mail, and a gaggle of "clueless" housewife types on roller blades, skating menacingly toward Eddie's mother, Jessica. As a means of emphasizing the difference between this new world and the old, younger brother Emery remarks that there are a lot of white people, to which Eddie replies that it's not like DC where the only white people were those who were lost.

Additionally, the Huang family's appropriation of the cowboy motif for the restaurant it owns exploits another trope of stereotypical whiteness—divorced from its multiracial history—while signifying the self-sufficient individualism that presumably defines the family's new life.[1] These cultural codes, as manifested in the show and in contemporary popular culture more broadly, represent a form of cultural translation evocative of the symbolic violence that, in the Bourdieusian sense, naturalizes group distinctions. The model-minority stereotype prompts the misrecognition crucial to the sustenance of the status quo, while postracial discourses serve as its fortification.

Fresh Off the Boat must therefore be situated within a broader discursive field that not only reifies postracial assumptions but also accounts for other media productions airing at the time that functioned to lend credence to the idea that contemporary American society had evolved beyond its racial history. Other television series, including *Black-ish* (2014–2022) and *This Is Us* (2016–2022) feature upwardly mobile Black characters who are presented as confronting occasional "soft" racism but nevertheless thriving in professional and personal environments that are multiracial and relatively free of the structural barriers that continue to constrain the life outcomes of most African Americans. Together, these series are part of a media landscape that advances the neoliberal ethic of Black upper-middle-class aspiration and success that help form the core of the postracial discourses *Fresh Off the Boat* advances more indirectly. At the same time, a number of Asian American pop-cultural figures, including YouTuber Lilly Singh and comedic actress/rapper Awkwafina, have become superstars, who attained visibility through their appropriation of hip-hop culture. This phenomenon, in which Asian American entertainers gain entrée into pop-culture stardom through their appropriation of Blackness while African American representation is itself carefully circumscribed in ways that renders its transgressive potential increasingly ephemeral, comes together in *Fresh Off the Boat*. In the next section, I offer a close reading of specific episodes of the series in order to highlight the features of anti-Blackness that undergird them.

POSTRACIAL IMAGINARIES IN *FRESH OFF THE BOAT*

In order to foster a deeper understanding of the ways in which the strategies of racial poaching enacted in *Fresh Off the Boat* were complicit in promoting postracial assumptions, it is important to note the show's trajectory over the course of its run. Because its marketability was premised on the publicity surrounding its real-life protagonist, its first season focused mostly on Eddie's attempts to adjust to his new suburban environment, particularly his attempts to fit in at his new school. After Huang's departure and as the show gained greater popularity, the later seasons focused more on the entire family, sometimes foregrounding the comedic experiences of various members as they attempted to negotiate the tensions between adhering to their culture of origin and assimilating into their new environment. I therefore offer an analysis of the pilot episode, which was the only season that featured voice-over narration, followed by an episode from its third and sixth—and final—seasons.

The pilot episode begins by focusing viewers' attention on the show's exploitation of hip-hop. As MC Breed's and DFC's "Ain't No Future in Yo Frontin'" plays, eleven-year-old Eddie emerges from a dressing room in a store wearing the clothing associated with hip-hop culture. The camera pans on various parts of his body before showing his face, a framing that highlights the assumed contrast between the music, the clothing, and his Asianness. Throughout the scene, his mother and brother Emery watch his posturing with a mixture of impatience and bemusement. Eddie's vernacular and bodily posture demonstrate a deep identification with the hypermasculinity assigned to Black men. The voice-over narration explains the tensions that define the show's premise: "Mother thought I was trying to cause trouble; she doesn't understand. . . . If you were an outsider, hip-hop is your anthem. I was definitely the black sheep in my family." In the subsequent scene showing the family in their car traveling from DC to Orlando, Eddie's father, Louis, describes to his skeptical family the improvements their new life in Florida will offer to them. When he describes his new restaurant as "big, brown, and beautiful," Eddie replies, "Like Shaq," to which Jessica responds, "Why you like Shaq so much? Why not Pete Sampras?"

While these scenes provide the setup for the ways in which a spectral Blackness mediates Eddie's outsider status within his family and the family's difference from their neighbors, the scenes demonstrating Eddie's attempts to negotiate school life provide the most explicit illustrations of this mediation. In the case of his experiences in school, hip-hop serves as a force for his ability to fit in with his white peers. On the morning of the first day of school, Jessica emphasizes to Eddie that she wants him to be polite and respectful and to not make waves. Eddie is wearing a T-shirt with the Notorious BIG on the front; she asks him why his shirts always have pictures of Black men on them. Eddie remarks that he and BIG are "both dudes with mad dreams just trying to get a little respect in the game." Later, at school, Eddie attempts to blend in with his new classmates. Entering the cafeteria, he first attempts to befriend Walter, the only Black student at the school, and is rebuffed. He is then able to connect with a group of white kids who, noticing his T-shirt (that he claims he stole), claim to like him based on their mutual admiration for BIG. He then faces conflict with the group over his perceived difference, with the group of boys making fun of the Chinese food he brought for lunch. Watching this scene from his own table, Walter observes the irony of "a white dude and an Asian dude bonding over a Black dude. This cafeteria is ridiculous." Later that evening, Eddie convinces Jessica to buy him "white-people food" so that he can better blend in, saying he has to "represent" like (the rapper) Nas. In the car on the way home, he explains that he has three goals: to get a seat at the table, to meet Shaq, and to "change the game . . . possibly, with the help of Shaq." Louis responds by saying, "Damnit, that was beautiful. That dirty, filthy music you listen to turned you into a poet, boy."

In a final coda to Eddie's initially antagonistic relationship with Walter, the two boys engage in physical conflict when Walter pushes Eddie out of the way at the cafeteria microwave. "Get used to it; you're the one at the bottom now," Walter advises Eddie. "It's my turn now, *ch**k*." This interaction spurs him to forge a bond with the white kids who had made fun of him earlier. This is, perhaps, one of the scenes from the show's run that most illustrates the work that racial poaching performs: in emphasizing the paradox inherent in Walter's envy of Eddie's ability to assimilate via hip-hop culture, it further underscores Walter's liminality along with that of hip-hop's Black originators and African Americans more broadly. Though Eddie and Walter eventually become friends, the conflict between the two symbolizes the tensions that arise when racialized groups limit their interrogation of the racial order to the intricacies of their place in it while implicitly accepting its inevitability. It also illustrates pop culture's tendency to exploit the social advantages of adopting hip-hop's aesthetics while maintaining its tendency to construct distance from the group that created them.

By the series' third season, Eddie Huang had left the show and ceded much of his creative control, though he retained some involvement as an executive producer. As a result, storylines no longer centered on his character's experiences and instead focused on those of the entire family. Though hip-hop culture sustained some of its currency via Eddie's interactions with his peers and his family, the nature of the postracial discourses the show promoted took on an additional dimension: the family's adherence to a more neoliberal conception of citizenship wherein belonging is premised on participation in private economic activity and few or no social actions that might disrupt the status quo that supports it. In this conceptualization of cultural citizenship, inclusion becomes the reward granted to those individuals and groups who are willing and able to transform themselves into appropriately mobile, entrepreneurial subjects, whose value as citizens is maximized not only in economic and financial terms but also in their capacities to strengthen a society's understanding of itself as morally upright (Mavelli, 2018). The model-minority discourse enables Asian Americans to embody this commoditized ideal of citizenship in ways that are historically inimical to Blackness, and in *Fresh Off the Boat*, they operate in a subtle manner.

In the fourth episode of the show's third season, "Citizen Jessica," everyone in the family is excited about the upcoming 1996 presidential election between Bill Clinton and Bob Dole, with Louis expressing the importance of voting as a civic responsibility and demonstrating his enthusiasm by dressing in red, white, and blue gear and allowing the restaurant to serve as a polling place. Jessica, in contrast, is apathetic toward a political culture that she regards as boring, particularly in comparison to Taiwan's raucous politics. Later on, Jessica, who has become a realtor, becomes angry at the income-tax increase that the family will incur as a result of the rise in her income from the commission on her first big sale. She later blames Hector, a Hispanic employee at the restaurant, who, earlier that day, had been showing off the accoutrements he'd had added to his car and bragging about how he was able to afford them because he paid no taxes. As Jessica and Louis are watching television that night, Jessica is again angry over the family's potential tax burden and laments the possibility that Hector will be getting services for free, while she has to pay for them. She refers to Hector as an "illegal" immigrant during a conversation with Louis—to which he responds by chiding her about the offensiveness of the term—and blames undocumented immigrants in general for her frustrations with US tax policies, eventually calling in the Immigration and Naturalization Service (INS) to perform a sweep of the restaurant's parking lot. When the INS agents detain Jessica for having failed to renew her green card, she points out to Louis that her precarious status is due to her having made an "understandable" mistake. This plotline is notable in that it depicts Jessica as upset over the financial consequences—in the form of higher taxes—that emerge from her hard work as a realtor. In response, she adopts a conservative political stance in not only blaming Hispanic immigrants for their perceived failure to contribute but also, in responding to her husband's pointing out that she herself is an immigrant, saying that she did it "the right way." In the plotline's resolution, a neoliberal ethic prevails, as Hector promises to teach her how to incorporate as a means of avoiding the higher taxes. This represents the family's integration into the hegemonic conception of Americanness, in which individualism, economic self-interest, and noncooperation with other disenfranchised groups are assumed to be markers of assimilation.

In the meantime, Eddie is lamenting the death of Tupac Shakur and is upset over suggestions that the Notorious BIG was involved and engages his friends in an argument over the matter. At this point, his friendship circle includes Walter, the Black boy with whom he'd clashed in the pilot episode, and several white boys. He methodically lays out his case, revealing his knowledge of the intricacies of the music industry. He eventually concludes that the Notorious BIG could not have been involved and points to what he sees as evidence that Tupac is in fact still alive. It is important to note that throughout the spirited debate among the boys, most of them employ hip-hop-infused vernacular and insults similar to the dozens. His invocation of one of the preeminent icons of Black masculinity, fervent adherence to the mythologies surrounding that icon, and participation in Black vernacular wordplay mobilizes a rebelliousness in the form of Blackness that stands in stark contrast to his parents' displays of hypercitizenship through prescribed civic and capitalistic rituals. This relies on particular cultural codes that situate Blackness, as exemplified by Tupac Shakur and other Black pop-cultural icons, as existing outside of normalized citizenship ideals.

In an episode from the sixth—and final—season titled "S'mothered," Eddie frets over the prospect of introducing his new girlfriend Tina to Jessica. The source of his trepidation is that Tina has a strong personality that, he believes, will cause tension when in proximity to Jessica's tiger mom-like tendency to micromanage his life. Through a series of flashbacks, we see these tendencies in action, and among the demonstrative scenes is one wherein Eddie becomes upset because Jessica altered his NWA shirt reading "Fuck tha Police" to "Respect tha Police." Tina, like all of Eddie's love interests throughout the series' run, is white, a reflection of the virtually all-white world the family inhabits. As she and Eddie walk out of the school one afternoon, she chides him for his reluctance to study and insists that they do so together at his house. Jessica arrives in the family's minivan to pick him up from school and calls out to him, at which point Eddies denies to Tina that Jessica is his mother, telling her that lots of women call his name and that she should get used to it. Noticing Eddie's reluctance to introduce the two, Tina shows up at the Huangs' house unexpectedly and introduces herself to Jessica. Though there is some initial tension between the two, they eventually bond over their shared "no-nonsense" personalities and their abilities to push Eddie to do better in school.

Meanwhile, Louis has decided that he has reached his peak in running his restaurant, determined that he needs to find a new calling, and tries out different possibilities for his next career. With the encouragement of Emery, who is shadowing him for a school assignment, Louis tries out a variety of vocations, including barber and tour guide before eventually deciding to become a motivational speaker. He uses his entrepreneurial success as the basis for his seminars, the first of which features an African American participant, who criticizes him for his lack of motivational skills and walks out. Louis ultimately decides that his attention is better focused on running his restaurant. Here, we see the more implicit operation of the postracialism in which certain features of the model-minority stereotype act as signifiers of idealized citizenship in opposition to an unspoken Blackness. Jessica's demands to Eddie that he respect the police (and this, in 2019, at a time when this exhortation carries significant rhetorical meaning), her tiger-mom-like micromanagement of her sons' educational and love lives, and her love of the singer Amy Grant—a running gag throughout the episode—function in this way, as does Louis's success as an entrepreneur and his desire to move on to the next entrepreneurial success, albeit, in this case, an unfulfilled one. In the final scene, it is revealed that Louis was even given the chance to invest in social media before it exploded, but he declined the opportunity because he thought that the notion of putting photos online was a financial loser. These features, coupled with the virtually all-white suburban world the show foregrounds, constructs a notion of anti-Blackness that, via its subtlety, is perhaps more powerful than it would be if made more explicit.

CONCLUSION

In another 2021 interview promoting his film *Boogie*, Eddie Huang compared the diversity in the film's cast to its lack thereof in *Fresh Off the Boat*. Asserting that the film hewed more closely to his vision for *Fresh Off the Boat* than the series itself had, Huang spoke about the film's hip-hop aesthetic before situating it as a corrective to *Fresh Off the Boat*:

> I finally, for once, feel free of the shadow of that show because I was not proud of it. I felt very disappointed, even though it went on for six seasons and was a commercial success. . . . At the time, a lot of Asians told me "shut up. Let this thing win for us. Let us keep our seat at the table". . . . [An issue] that upset me was it was marketed as a hip-hop show, but where were the Black people? Black people weren't getting paid on that show. They got cameos and things like that. (Watkins, 2021)

This rebuke of the show echoed similar critiques Huang leveled on Twitter in 2015 shortly after the show's debut, in which he criticized the industrial pressures that led to a "whitewashing" of its more transgressive elements and described it as "unrecognizable." Here, during an interview with an African American cultural critic, he spoke briefly—though more directly—about the spectral Blackness that was used to create a narrative premise in which historically feminized Asian American males "borrow" the hypermasculinity historically assigned to Black men. This racial poaching served the dual purpose of enabling a semifictionalized character to fit in at his new school and of drawing viewers to the show that depicted his experiences. It is, perhaps, one of the more interesting ironies that a musical genre that was created as a means of expressing the alienation experienced by one group has now become the means for another group to shed assumptions of perpetual foreignness and assimilate into the dominant culture. Additionally, in addressing the entreaties to keep silent about these racial complexities in the interest of preserving modest goals of representation, Huang also invoked the historical precarity of groups of color, especially the ways in which they are sometimes forced to exploit each other in order to maintain their status. In commenting on these issues, Huang invoked broader issues foregrounding the terms by which media productions centering the experiences of people of color must adhere to in order to attain critical and commercial success. Assimilationist media productions that feature a few people of color operating within arenas of whiteness, particularly when they are marked as signs of progress, can help reinforce dishonest and illusory impressions of racial equality.

Asian American representation, particularly in high-quality media texts, is important. However, the fact that it comes at the expense of African Americans is indicative of society's continuing problems with race in general and remains an influential means of reifying the power of whiteness. *Fresh Off the Boat* thus demonstrates what Sugino (2022) suggests is racism's remarkable capacity to adapt to counterhegemonic forces and co-opt them for its own purposes, by rearticulating anti-Blackness within a seemingly progressive representational focus on Asian Americans. The transformative potential of the show as a purveyor of hip-hop's more subversive themes has been subsumed within the model-minority myth, which, historically, advances an anti-Blackness that the country can't quite seem to overcome and, in the contemporary era, assumes the form of the postracial discourses on which the show relies. President Barack Obama's election in 2008 and reelection in 2012 occasioned a reinvigoration of the colorblind discourses of the past, with "postracial" functioning as updated terminology and popular culture assuming its traditional function of conveying hegemonic assumptions to mass audiences in neat, entertaining packages. Though *Fresh Off the Boat* captures specific moments in time—like all televisual texts do—it represents the culmination of centuries of discourses painting African Americans as existing outside of the bounds of citizenship. That it does so through the subtler means of situating Blackness as a negative referent makes it no less powerful. It is quite telling that, in a contemporary televisual mediascape that is more reflective of the full range of human experiences than it has ever been, anti-Blackness continues to convey a significant degree of currency.

NOTE

1. There have been many academic and popular accounts of the multiracial history of cowboys, including those emphasizing the role of African Americans in cowboy culture. See, e.g., B. A. Glasrud and M. N. Searles (2017), S. K. Gandy (2008), and K. Nodjimbadem (2017).

REFERENCES

Chang, A. (2021, March 11). Writer and director Eddie Huang challenges the model minority myth in *Boogie*. *NPR*. https://www.npr.org/2021/03/11/976166969/writer -and-director-eddie-huang-challenges-the-model-minority-myth-in-boogie

Coon, D. R. (2014). *Look closer: Suburban narratives and American values in film and television*. Rutgers University Press.

Corbin, A. L. (2015). *Cinematic geographies and spectatorship in America*. Palgrave Macmillan.

Gandy, S. K. (2008). Legacy of the American West: Indian cowboys, Black cowboys, and vaqueros. *Social Education, 72*(4), 189–193.

Glasrud, B. A., & Searles, M. N. (2017). *Black cowboys in the American West: On the range, on the stage, behind the badge.* University of Oklahoma Press.

Hall, P. A. (1997). African American music: Dynamics of appropriation and innovation. In B. Ziff & P. Rao (Eds.), *Borrowed Power: Essays on cultural appropriation* (pp. 31–51). Rutgers University Press.

hooks, b. (1992). *Black looks: Race and representation.* South End Press.

Ishii, A. (2013, February 1). Bao wow wow yippee yo yippee yay: Eddie Huang and the rise of the "big dick Asian." *Slate.* https://slate.com/culture/2013/02/eddie-huangs-fresh-off-the-boat-reviewed.html

Jackson, R. (2006). *Scripting the Black masculine body: Identity, discourse, and racial politics in popular media.* State University of New York Press.

Kawai, Y. (2005). Stereotyping Asian Americans: The dialectic of the model minority and the yellow peril. *Howard Journal of Communications, 16*(2), 109–130. doi.org/10.1080/10646170590948974

Kim, E. (2016, December 5). The American imagination: Untangling Eddie Huang, Claudia Rankine, and racial hierarchy. *Brooklyn Uncategorized.* https://www.bkmag.com/2016/12/05/american-imagination-untangling-eddie-huang-claudia-rankine-racial-hierarchy/

Lee, J. (1998). *Dynamics of ethnic identity: Three Asian American communities in Philadelphia.* Garland.

Lee, R. (2010). The Cold War origins of the model minority myth. In J. Y-w. S. Wu & T. C. Chen (Eds.), *Asian American studies now* (pp. 256–271). Rutgers University Press.

Lipsitz, G. (2007). The racialization of space and the spatialization of race: Theorizing the hidden architecture of landscape. *Landscape Journal, 26*(1), 10–23.

Mavelli, L. (2018). Citizenship for sale and the neoliberal political economy of belonging. *International Studies Quarterly, 62*(3), 482–493.

McTaggart, N., & O'Brien, E. (2017). Seeking liberation, facing marginalization: Asian Americans and Pacific Islanders' conditional acceptance in hip-hop culture. *Sociological Inquiry, 87*(4), 634–658.

Moynihan, D. (1965). *The Negro family: The case for national action.* Office of Policy Planning and Research, United States Department of Labor.

Nodjimbadem, K. (2017, February 13). The lesser-known history of African American cowboys. *Smithsonian Magazine.* https://www.smithsonianmag.com/history/lesser-known-history-african-american-cowboys-180962144/

Phùng, T., Hằng, T., & Truong, M. H. (2018). *Fresh off the boat* and the model minority stereotype: A Foucauldian discourse analysis. *VNU Journal of Foreign Studies, 34*(5), 85–101. https://doi.org/10.25073/2525-2445/vnufs.4304

Schleier, M. (2021). Introduction. In M. Schleier (Ed.), *Race and the suburbs in American film* (pp. 1–30). State University of New York Press.

Shim, D. (1998). From yellow peril through model minority to renewed yellow peril. *Journal of Communication Inquiry, 22*(4), 385–409. https://doi.org/10.1177/019685999802004004

Singletary, M. (2021, October 8). Grassley should retire his prejudice about the model minority. *Washington Post*. https://www.washingtonpost.com/business/2021/10/08/grassley-lucy-koh-model-minority/

Sugino, C. M. (2019). Multicultural redemption: *Crazy rich Asians* and the politics of representation. *Lateral, 8*(2). https://doi.org/10.25158/L8.2.6

Sugino, C. M. (2022). Multicultural anti-racism: Anti-Blackness and Asian Americans in *Students for Fair Admission v. Harvard*. *Western Journal of Communication, 86*(4), 423–442. https://doi.org/10.1080/10570314.2022.2087887

Summers, B. (2019). *Black in place: The spatial aesthetics of race in a post-chocolate city*. University of North Carolina Press.

Wang, O. (2006). These are the breaks: Hip-hop and AfroAsian cultural (dis)connections. In H. Raphael-Hernandez & S. Steen (Eds.), *AfroAsian encounters: Culture, history, politics*, (pp. 146–164). New York University Press.

Watkins, D. (2021, March 6). *With basketball drama* Boogie, *Eddie Huang is finally "free of the shadow" of* Fresh off the boat. Salon. https://www.salon.com/2021/03/06/boogie-eddie-huang-salon-taks/

Yousman, B. (2003). Blackophilia and blackophobia: White youth, the consumption of rap music, and white supremacy. *Communication Theory, 13*(4), 366–391.

Chapter 2

A NOTEBOOK FOR *HAMILTON*

OSCAR GINER

At the end of daybreak, the wind of long ago—of betrayed trusts, of
uncertain evasive duty and that other dawn in Europe—arises.
—AIMÉ CÉSAIRE, *NOTEBOOK OF A RETURN TO THE NATIVE LAND*

PROLOGUE

In our mythologically fragmented world, all performances require context.

In the first weeks of 2019, Lin-Manuel Miranda's *Hamilton* played to sold-out houses for three weeks at the Centro de Bellas Artes in Santurce, Puerto Rico. The event was celebrated by the national media and by delighted local audiences. Especially pleased were sympathizers of the statehood option for Puerto Rico, who held demonstrations outside the theater to inquire from an attending delegation of the US Congress whether they were "really living up to the standards of Alexander Hamilton, a disenfranchised immigrant, a poor man from the Caribbean" (Jones, 2019). But in the heart of the Puerto Rican theater community, *Hamilton* shipwrecked against the boulders—the high, rain-forested mountains—of the national identity crisis, which has endured in Puerto Rico at least since the publication of Manuel Alonso's (2007) *El Gíbaro* in 1849. An important, old-time theater producer turned down complimentary tickets to *Hamilton* because (according to him) he dedicated his Saturdays to organizing his office and running household errands. One of the great Puerto Rican playwrights—like an old chieftain rejecting the work of students returning from the Carlisle Indian School—categorically rejected the show: "It is not Puerto Rican." An experimental theater artist of my acquaintance disallowed the production with a bitter query: "Am I supposed to genuflect?" Meanwhile, Miranda waved the Puerto Rican flag at local audiences during standing ovations at curtain calls: "I just love this island so much.... And I want it to be proud of me" (Jones, 2019).

Fig. 2.1. Francisco Oller, *El velorio* (1893).

One wanted to applaud the success of a favorite son, but from another point of view, to legitimize *Hamilton* amounted to a collaboration with the enemy, an ignoble submission to the US empire. *Hamilton* is the kind of play that North Americans—for their own purposes—want Puerto Ricans to write: (1) a story about the "founding fathers"; (2) not in Spanish, but in English; and (3) with enough diversity in the cast to make it palatable to progressives but not too radical for conservative audiences. One wanted to celebrate the show's language, the worthy aspiration for freedom that breathes through the young cast, but the show was in *English*—the language of the colonial oppressor. The modern Puerto Rican theater was born in the 1930s as an instrument to protect, purify, and keep alive Spanish as the defining language of Puerto Rican culture. Playwrights such as Manuel Méndez Ballester, René Marqués, Francisco Arriví, Myrna Casas, and Luis Rafael Sánchez are revered for their philological opposition to the invader.

During the pandemic year, the Disney+ Channel announced that it would carry a film of the original cast of *Hamilton* performing on Broadway. The combination of Miranda's show and Disney intrigued me. *Hamilton*—a hip-hop musical if you will—was deemed appropriate for Disney audiences! I plucked up my courage to view the film on TV and did not care if it spoiled my first impression of the theater version I expected to see in the future. A film cannot substitute for a live performance, but it can serve as a record and may help to prepare us for the live experience.

ISLANDS IN THE STREAM

Alexander Hamilton was born on the British island of Nevis in 1755 and was raised on the island of St. Croix (today, one of the US Virgin Islands). Writing about the Spanish American civilization that developed around the periphery of the Caribbean, J. J. Arrom (1969) has advanced the following:

> One could think that the Caribbean separates those lands, but this is not the case; it unites them culturally. Its waters have been a liquid bridge over the surface of which history has woven a web of imperishable knots. The process was begun by Columbus' ships. It was continued by the heavy galleons filled with treasure which tied the main ports of the region with the strings of their white sails. And also by the slave ships, leaving sad, bloody, painful trails with their infamous loads. (p. 7)

The cultural matrix of those who live on the shores of the sea was created by its waters.

Puerto Rico

Aimé Césaire's (2001) great poem, which established the concept of "negritude," warns us that a return to the native land is fraught with perils, fortuitous occurrences, fortunate encounters, and profound realizations. The island is magical and, like Caliban's island, is full of ghostly sounds, dreams, and ancient voices (Shakespeare, 1955, 3.2.140–148). Boriquén, the Taíno name of Puerto Rico, is a powerful vortex of Antillean mythology. Its original Spanish name was the Island of Saint John the Baptist. There is not a mountain or hidden cave from which the ocean cannot be seen, heard in the distance, or smelt in the evening air. The same divinity that Walt Whitman found in the American landscape was a living presence for Julia de Burgos (1986) in her landscape portrait-poem "Great River of Loíza":

> Coil around my lips and let me drink from you,
> to feel you mine for a brief moment,
> and hide you from the world and hide within you,
> and hear bewildered voices in the mouth of the wind. (p. 64)

The spiritual bastion that is Puerto Rico—much more than its Spanish fortresses—gives to the people courage in the face of adversity.

The political, legal, and economic relations between the island and the United States best resemble the relations between the United States and Native American nations. In practice, the constitution of the Commonwealth establishes Puerto Rico as yet another American Indian reservation. Pro-Commonwealth politicians live under the illusion that Puerto Rico is neither a colony nor a reserve. Proindependence politicians insist that Puerto Rico is too strong a nation to remain a colony (which is true) but deny the fact that the island is too small to become economically viable as a modern democracy (which is a geographical fact).

Jamaica

In 1942, experimental composer John Cage (1942; as qtd. in Sublette, 2004) wrote an article in which he called for an instrument that would reproduce the percussive sounds heard in the "typical Oriental, Cuban and hot jazz ensembles" (p. 474). These technological boxes—and the performative rituals they conjured—began to appear in Jamaica during the "West Kingston sound-system wars" of the 1950s. Dances held by Sir Coxsone Dodd featured a PA system, turntable, receiver, "the most rib-rumbling speakers," up-to-date vinyl discs, a theme song, and top Jamaican DJs (White, 1998, p. 137). The sound systems provided outlets for new Jamaican music—"raw and spacious" tunes that allowed DJs "shouting room"—which was not being played on local radio stations or nightclubs (White, 1998, p. 139). This tradition was brought from Kingston to the Bronx by DJ Kool Herc in the 1970s, who, according to J. Chang (2006), began the "culture" of hip-hop: "Herc . . . stripped down and let go of everything, save the most powerful basic elements—the rhythm, the motion, the voice, the name. . . . He summoned up a spirit that had been there at Congo Square and in Harlem and on Wareika Hill" (p. 85). It was a singular, technological amplification of the drumming rhythms of the African tribes of the Caribbean.

During the 1980s, one crew made a furious statement by adopting a hallowed nomenclature from gangster mythology: Public Enemy. A term once coined by the Chicago press to refer to Al Capone and the title of a classic gangster film by James Cagney, the name was now assumed by a group of Long Island rappers—the children of Black Panthers and of the African American Civil Rights movement. Political in outlook, concerned with the redefinition of Black identity, Public Enemy called for a mythical and aesthetic revolution. Through sober lyrics and evocative visual images exuding an "urgent theatricality," Public Enemy's goal was to "Bumrush the Show" (the title of their first album) and "storm the machines of mythmaking" (Chang, 2006, pp. 249–250):

I'm a Public Enemy but I don't rob banks
I don't shoot bullets and I don't shoot blanks
My style is supreme—number one is my rank
And I got more power than the New York Yanks. (Public Enemy, n.d.)

Language and music, metaphors for the gangster Thompson submachine gun, would be used to cleanse the world. The rebellion of the 1960s had become performance.

CATALOGUE OF OPERAS

Rock/Political

Hamilton exists at the boundary between several genres, and part of its charm is its evocation of each one of them as if the production were a collection of songs and sketches "with an intellectual flavor" of the "lavish spectacular" type, "glorifying song and dance and visual effects" (Latham, 2004, p. 152). Miranda set his work squarely in the tradition of "concept albums," in which songs are woven together by a unity of theme and by the journey of a main character across the songs.[1] Miranda's innovation consists in telling the relatively unknown story of one of the founding fathers in the musical parlance of North American hip-hop: "I'm actually working on a hip-hop album— a concept album—about the life of someone who embodies hip-hop . . . Treasury Secretary Alexander Hamilton" (Miranda & McCarter, 2016, p. 15). Two "concept albums" by Andrew Lloyd Webber and Tim Rice that eventually morphed into live "rock operas" have been specifically acknowledged by Miranda as influences on *Hamilton*: "Structurally, . . . we have a killer telling his story, like Che in *Evita* [1976] and Judas in *Jesus Christ Superstar* [1970]." These works were also "sung throughs": musical works that dispense with dramatic dialogue between songs. Just as the musicals that inspired it, *Hamilton* is composed of arias and recitatives without pause for episodes of spoken words.

Beginning with Bertolt Brecht's *The Threepenny Opera* (1933) as a mother lode, there is an unbroken line of preceding "political" musicals to *Hamilton* (2015), which is a play about politics but is not a political play: from the Broadway run of Brecht and Kurt Weill's "opera for beggars" (Brecht, 1994, p. 89) to the composition of *Cabaret* (1966) to *Hair* (1968), which celebrated the spirit of revolt among young white people against the Vietnam War, to the cartoonish portrayals of the "founding fathers" in *1776* (1969) to the illusion of political commitment in *Evita* (1976) to *Les Mis* (1987), Victor Hugo's tale of nineteenth-century Romantic revolution. The introduction to the lavishly published libretto of *Hamilton* argues that the show represents a "revolution" both political and aesthetic: "There's the American Revolution of the 18th century . . . [and] also the revolution of the show itself: a musical that changes the way that Broadway sounds, that alters who gets to tell the story of our founding, that lets us glimpse the new, more diverse America rushing our way" (Miranda & McCarter, 2016, p. 10). The epilogue of the publication affirms an opposite conclusion: "However innovative Obama's speeches and Lin's show might seem, they are, in fact traditional. They don't reinvent the American character, they *renew* [emphasis original] it" (Miranda & McCarter, 2016, p. 284). This balancing act between a "revolution" that is also "traditional" is one of the signature features of the show and creates a tension that results in both the obfuscation of some of its achievements and the concealment of some of its flaws. *Hamilton* is the genial coagulation, the amiable configuration of certain foundational ingredients of rock/political musicals at the end (not the beginning) of a vital musical tradition. Its politics—like most US politics—are parochial, and its viewpoint on diversity is orthodox.

Classical

A list of the terms under which contemporary American musicals are catalogued would defy the rhetorical powers of Polonius. Their forms vary according to the size and type (comical or tragical) of the spoken-word scenes that appear in-between the music. Their venues include proscenium theaters, concert halls, music halls, lecture halls, gymnasiums, small experimental houses, school auditoriums, churchyards, nightclubs, and cabarets. Miranda's annotations to the *Hamilton* libretto pay homage—through "shout-outs" that often appropriate entire lines—to the following musicals: *South Pacific* (1949), *Beauty and the Beast* (1994), *Pirates of Penzance* (1879–1880 [Broadway and London]), *West Side Story* (1957), *The Sound of Music* (1959), *1776*, and *Merrily We Roll Along* (Sondheim, 1981–1982). He acknowledges the influence of two television shows: *The West Wing* (1999–2006) and *Parks and Recreation* (2009–2015). He also references Akira Kurosawa's *Rashomon* (1950, film), Shakespeare's *Macbeth* (1623, First Folio publication), and the Beatles. This outpour reflects the uncertainty of a devised (in the sense of a collage) production.

In 1943, Richard Rodgers and Oscar Hammerstein's *Oklahoma!* created the model for the classic 1940s and '50s North American musical comedy. Agnes de Mille's original choreography highlighted dance as a vital component of the genre and tilled the ground for the innovations of director-choreographers such as Jerome Robbins (*West Side Story* and *Fiddler on the Roof* [1964]) and Bob Fosse (*Cabaret* [1966] and *Chicago* [1975]). Andy Blankenbuehler's choreography—he also choreographed *In the Heights* (2008) and the recent film of *Cats* (2019)—is one of the highpoints of *Hamilton*. Blankenbuehler does not impose a recognizable personal style on his dancers (like Fosse). His choreography is eclectic—jazz, jitterbug, hip-hop, etc.—weaving an ornate tapestry of continuous, dynamic imagery throughout the show. For a production that describes itself as a "revolution," Blankenbuehler describes his choreography in classic terms: "*Hamilton* ends up being sort of like a ballet in many respects" (Friscia, 2016). In *Hamilton*, the choric Furies of Aeschylus's *Oresteia* (458 BCE, in Athens) become star actors, shapeshifting before our eyes according to the running commentary of Aaron Burr, Alexander Hamilton, George Washington, Thomas Jefferson, et al.

THE MOUSETRAP

There is cultural memory in the theater, dating back to *Hamlet* and Aristotle's theory of catharsis, to uphold the belief that "guilty creatures sitting at a play" can be "struck to the soul" (Shakespeare, 2006, 2.2.524). Such creatures may be moved to proclaim their malefactions or attempt repentance like King Claudius "by the very cunning of the scene" (Shakespeare, 2006, 2.2.525). This explains the deliberate ambush of former Vice President Mike Pence at the Richard Rodgers Theatre by the cast of *Hamilton*.

A few days after the election of 2016, Pence attended a scheduled performance of *Hamilton*. He entered the theater to cheers and boos from the audience and sat through the show without an outward sign of displeasure. He appeared "engaged . . . and applauded after most of its numbers" (Mele & Healy, 2016). There was a standing ovation in the theater after Hamilton spoke the line, "Immigrants, we get the job done!" At the end of the show, as Pence and family members were leaving the theater, Aaron Burr (Brandon Victor Dixon) stepped away from the rest of the cast lined up for the curtain call to read a statement. Pence stood in the hallway outside the auditorium and listened as Dixon read aloud: " We, sir—we—are the diverse America who are alarmed and anxious that your new administration will not protect us, our planet, our children, our parents, or defend us and our inalienable rights" (Mele & Healy, 2016). The statement isolated Pence in the same way that Jean Genet (1960) requested that "a white person, male or female" be highlighted and isolated during performances of his play *The Blacks*. The victim should be dressed in "ceremonial costume" and be led to a seat "in the front row of the orchestra." (Pence was seated in the center orchestra section.) "A spotlight should be focused upon this symbolic white throughout the performance" (p. 4). Victims of alienation, masked horrors witnessing sacrificial violence in a loop of eternal return, Genet's characters are a "form of Incantation," in "what [Antonin] Artaud[2] called 'a metaphysics of spoken language'" (Brustein, 1964, pp. 393–394). Dixon finished his discourse: "We truly hope that this show has inspired you to uphold our American values and to work on behalf of all of us" (Mele & Healy, 2016).

In a country in which Abraham Lincoln was assassinated at Ford's Theater, such a confrontation between performers and a visiting political dignitary may be fraught with tension. But nothing happened. The cunning of the scene did not avail. Pence sat through *Hamilton* pleasantly. Had there been revolution on stage or a repeated *f*-word shouted as an incantation, he would have run out of the theater like Claudius in *Hamlet*, crying for "Light!" The unscripted words aimed at the vice president were not a drumbeat calling for an uprising, but rather a plea for mercy and fair treatment by a slave and immigrant population, which was intimidated by the presence of an overseer.

The next day, Pence declared to Fox News, "I can tell you I wasn't offended.... *Hamilton* is just an incredible production, incredibly talented people. It was a real joy to be there."

AT THE HEARD MUSEUM

The Heard Museum in Phoenix is one of the finest museums of Native American arts, artifacts, and history in the nation. On the topmost floor of the building, there is a permanent exhibit dedicated to the experiences of Native American children in the infamous Bureau of Indian Affairs boarding schools, which flourished across the nation during the past century. The grounds and remaining buildings of the Phoenix Indian School (1891–1990) still stand a few blocks away in Encanto Village. Upon its establishment in 1891, Indian Commissioner Thomas Morgan said, "It's cheaper to educate Indians than to kill them" (Lindauer, 1998).

On the third floor of the Heard, on a small plaque on the wall, there is a photograph of performing-arts activities at an Indian school. Two lines of young indigenous students, male and female, face each other in front of the backdrop of an enormous American flag. The students are dressed in late eighteenth-century European garb: coats and white wigs for the boys, long skirts and white wigs for the girls. Underneath the photo, there is an extended caption:

Assimilation through Performing Arts

Music and pageants were developed as mechanisms to civilize and Americanize Native students. . . .

Christian hymns were sung before meals and at bedtime and became part of the daily routine. School choirs also promoted Christianization and assimilation of the students. Federal policy makers recognized the socialization capacity of school clubs and pageants. Tribal stories were replaced by a new, "American" history and culture. *Students learned new, often-invented stories about George Washington and other American heroes* [emphasis added], and new mythologies like the saga of Hiawatha or the First Thanksgiving.

These new stories were transcribed into plays and vignettes for the students to perform. Insensitive and insulting practices had students playing the roles of both colonized and colonizer in dramatizations of the dispossession and conquest of the Indians [emphasis added].

On reading the caption of the plaque at the Heard, one Puerto Rican actress of my acquaintance commented: "I can't see [*Hamilton*] now except through this."

HIP-HOP OPERA

Predecessors

In the preface to *God's Trombones*, James Weldon Johnson (1990) writes that he wrote his poems "after the manner of the primitive sermons" of African American preachers: "The old-time Negro preacher . . . was above all an orator, and in good measure an actor. He knew the secret of oratory, that at bottom it is a progression of rhythmic words more than it is anything else" (p. 10). It is legitimate to understand sermons in Black churches as precursors of contemporary hip-hop, as artistic expression of a community brought together by the pain and anger of servitude. Johnson subtitled his book of poetry *Seven Negro Sermons in Verse*. A parallel artistic development in two different eras generates the "Ten Crack Commandments" of the Notorious BIG as gospel for our time and Tupac Shakur's *2Pacalypse Now* (1991) as a worthy echo of the old-time sermon, "The Black Diamond Express, running between here and hell, making thirteen stops and arriving in hell ahead of time" (p. 2). The story of Alexander Hamilton is present in Miranda's musical—but not the moral of parables or the poetry of sermons. It is easy to imagine Johnson's reenacted sermons spoken or sung in the voices of Tupac and Biggie. But in which track of the *Hamilton* score can you hear the voices of the classic hip-hop masters?

The *F*-Word

The use of the *f*-word in hip-hop does not preclude an imaginative context. It may be evidence not of a lack of values, but of their undeniable presence. Through sonorous play and deliberate repetition, hip-hop frees language from the constraints of political correctness, from a slavish submission to the manners of polite society, and challenges the notion of what is socially acceptable and artistically tolerable. Savagery and profanity were present in Elizabethan and Jacobean drama, which reflected the fascination with violence and obscenity found in the Greco-Roman theater.

Gangsta rap was born in South Central LA out of the "ashes and ruins of the sixties" (Chang, 2006, pp. 307–309). Not the least threatening aspect of the imaginative world of hip-hoppers is the conviction that our world is a corrupt and decaying Babylon marked by drugs, greed, and power. "Life ain't nothing but bitches and money," rapped NWA (2002). Gangsta rap provided a formal space for the articulation of anger, for the manifestation of wounded affect, and for the affirmation of excluded identities. In the words of C. Gordone (1969), it created an imaginative space for the marginalized, the tortured, and the oppressed who find "no place to be somebody" (as in the title of the play). Gangsta rap's undeniable "misogyny, homophobia and violence" (Chang, 2006, p. 327) were our very own, thrown back at us by a furious Caliban cursing at Prospero, who keeps him chained and subject as a monster (Shakespeare, 1955, 1.2.364–365).

The fire and fury, sex and humor, the Blakean marriage of heaven and hell in hip-hop's poetry are absent from the *Hamilton* film on Disney. You can sense hip-hop's energy in the dancing chorus, but no words are spoken in anger (although, yes, in lamentation), no deep African voices are raised in defiance, no epithets are hurled like daggers. No *f*-words, no *n*-words, no cuss words. At first the lyrics sound sanitized for Disney consumption, but the same relative pulchritude, cleaned-up rhetoric and wholesome quality of the verse is found in the published libretto. Anger, woe, and rebellion are the stuff hip-hop is made on, and although they are constantly called for and conjured by the *Hamilton* cast, they never make an entrance. If *Hamilton*'s verse perished, it would never incite the reaction forecast by Nas (2006) in *Hip-Hop Is Dead*:

> If hip-hop should die before I wake,
> I'll put an extended clip inside of my AK,
> Roll to every station, murder the DJ,
> Roll to every station, murder the DJ.

For all its agile versification, *Hamilton* remains prose-telling in rhyme, accompanied by music.

There is poetry in the sensuous, repetitive hip-hop beat. There is also poetry in the source material: Ron Chernow's magnificent biography of Alexander Hamilton. Just as the spirit of the novel of *Don Quixote* (1605 and 1615) carries *Man of La Mancha* (1965 [Broadway opening]) through to the very end, the mythic voice of Chernow's book crashes occasionally through the conventionalities of *Hamilton*. In an early scene, the Schuyler sisters meet Aaron Burr as they walk through downtown New York. Burr courts the older sister Angelica with a reference to his own patrician lineage: "I'm a trust fund baby, you can trust me!" (Miranda & McCarter, 2016, p. 44). Compare this to the villainous portrait of Burr in Chernow's (2005) book: "Burr, with his customary craft, waited for Hamilton to present his slate [of electors] before revealing his own. When Burr scanned a sheet naming the Federalist candidates, he 'read it over with great gravity, folded it up, put it in his pocket, and . . . said, "Now I have him all hollow,"' said John Adams" (p. 607). Clean lines, swift movements, and deep affect characterize Leslie Odom Jr.'s performance as Aaron Burr. He is the master of ceremonies Archibald Absalom Wellington from Genet's *The Blacks*. Judging by sheer strength of presence and complexity of nature, Odom's Burr is the most delicately crafted performance in the show.

Daveed Diggs's performance as Thomas Jefferson is an exemplar of the comic/critical approach to acting that Bertolt Brecht asked for in his later plays. In the eighteenth century, Denis Diderot (1957) called for a crucial distancing between actor and character in performance. In the scientific age of the twentieth century, Brecht (1964) held that "distance" was the fundamental component of his "alienation" effect (p. 194). Diggs assumes the trickster mask avidly in his portrayal of Jefferson. His distance is created by a comic attitude—"to laugh is to criticize" (p. 101)—that allows him to comment, choose a point of view from which to present character, attaining "coherence . . . by the way in which its individual qualities contradict one another" (p. 196). These scenes plus a coloratura rendition of

"Satisfied" by Renée Elise Goldsberry are the high-performance moments in *Hamilton*.

Actors of African and Native descent have been making fun of white oligarchies —in seasonal rituals and other folkloric expressions—for generations in the Americas. In sacred time, you do not collaborate or compromise. You do not forget that "the master is only the sort of master his servant lets him be" (Brecht, 1964, p. 197). The real threat of hip-hoppers, beyond their language and politics, lies in their passion, their comic intellectual corrective, and their irrepressible exuberance.

THE RIGHT STORY

Is Hamilton an original success, or is it a modern version of a minstrel show? Y. Huang's (2010) incisive book on the figure of Charlie Chan teaches us: "Whether it's a jazzy tune coming from the lips of a Blackface Jew or a yellow lie told by a ventriloquist Swede, the resilient artistic flower has blossomed *in spite of* as well as *because of* [emphases original] racism. This undeniable fact, insulting and sobering, has uniquely defined America" (p. 287). Huang understands that when it comes to acting stereotypes, the key consideration is not the presence of the stereotype, but what the performer does with its *limits* depending on his/her own time and place. Charlie Chan is a "peculiar kind of trickster . . . rooted in the toxic soil of racism." But racism made the image sharper, and the art that invented him "more lethally potent" (p. 287).

The technical proficiency of the performers, the commitment of the production to its vision of diversity, and the skill of the *Hamilton* artists in fusing two conflicting cultural traditions (American history and hip-hop) all belie the categorization of minstrelsy. A uniquely American form of entertainment, minstrel shows grew in the early nineteenth century as an offshoot of the short, comedic song-and-dance routines that were presented between acts of plays. At first, white performers played in blackface. Speaking in absurd dialects, using exaggerated and burnt-cork makeup, and performing the strange antics of caricatures, minstrel shows celebrated "the fun and games of slave life" and portrayed Black people as inferior. After the Civil War, Black performers also toured the country with their own versions of minstrel shows. In 1865–1866, Brooker and Clayton's Georgia Minstrels advertised themselves as "The Only Simon Pure Negro Troupe in the World . . . composed of men who during the war were slaves in Macon, Georgia, who, having spent their former life in Bondage . . . will introduce to their patrons plantation life in all its phases" (Toll, 2019). If the minstrels serenaded from their mythic plantation settings, *Hamilton* sees America as the Promised Land of the ancient Hebrews and is ready to conquer it:

> Foes oppose us, we take an honest stand,
> We roll like Moses, claimin' our promised land. (Miranda & McCarter, 2016, p. 29)

All this occurs in the "greatest city in the world," which is continually encouraged to "rise up!"

The origin of the song "Jumping Jim Crow" tells a cautionary tale against cultural aggrandizement based on commercial success. The song was discovered by Thomas Dartmouth "Daddy" Rice in the hops, dances, and voice of a crippled Black slave who worked with horses. Rice memorized the song, copied the steps and the movements, wrote new verses, and performed his routine on stage. The character "touched a chord in the American heart which had never before vibrated" (Toll, 2019). The act was phenomenally successful, culminating in a performance at the New York Bowery Theater in front of 3,500 people (Tupper, 2018).

Hamilton is a cultural phenomenon; so was Jim Crow. For Jim Crow, the heart of his location is the "Tuckyhoe" plantation in Virginia, and he is partial to the city of New Orleans. The routine did not descend from the heavens of musical comedy; it surfaced from the lower depths of the hell of slavery and its lamentations. What price is riches, fame, and glory if you only tell the wrong story?

REVOLUTIONARY MAXIMS

- *Hamilton* does not tell the full tale of the immigrant experience; it does recount the story of the immigrant experience *in New York*. It is born from the point of view of second- and third-generation immigrants, born in North America from parents born elsewhere. This group looks at poverty and its trappings with nostalgia, having never been poor. It indulges in childhood memories of the "barrio" or "projects" or "ghetto," which their parents feared, hated, and worked hard to leave behind. Having grown up between the Old World and the New, between two (or more) languages and two separate ontologies, these banished children of exiles accept New York City as their country—their *place to be*—and celebrate their life in the city as their defining cultural experience.

- In Chernow's biography, the horrors of the French Revolution were a constant concern for the founders as they built a new society. They feared the revolutionary excesses of the Terror in France. There is no horror of revolutionary excess in *Hamilton* because revolution is contained in the dancing and singing chorus—a modern version of the choric dithyramb of the Greeks. The dialogue is merely an empty medium, referring perfunctory context and background noise for the presentation of historical characters.
- For a true dramatic portrait of revolution, one must go back to Lope de Vega's *Fuente Ovejuna* (1619) and Georg Buchner's *Danton's Death* (1835). For the depiction of an aesthetic revolution, one may revisit Peter Brook's direction of Peter Weiss's *Marat/Sade* (1964) or Samuel Beckett's direction of his own *Krapp's Last Tape* (1958). Even Sherman Edwards's musical *1776* (1969 [first Broadway opening]) acknowledges deep political and social tensions at the signing of the Declaration of Independence in its best song, "Molasses to Rum." The song throws the mournful shadow of slavery over what is an essentially lighthearted spoof.
- In act 1 of *Hamilton*, the charming sequence "Helpless" (sung by Phillipa Soo) begins when Eliza meets Alexander and concludes with their marriage—not easy to achieve when its precedent is the second scene of Shakespeare's *Richard III* (1597), in which Gloucester meets Lady Anne before the corpse of Henry VI. (Gloucester had killed Anne's husband, but by the end of the scene, he wins her in marriage.)
- In his book on the American Revolution, S. Schama (2006) explains the reaction in the South when the British promised to free Black slaves if they joined their war against American rebels: "For the majority of farmers, merchants and townsmen in Virginia, the Carolinas and Georgia (the vast majority of whom owned between one and five negroes), all-out war and separation now turned from an ideological flourish to a social necessity. *Theirs was a revolution, first and foremost, mobilized to protect slavery* [emphasis added]" (p. 67). Wherever you turn with the founding fathers, you inevitably meet the ghost of slavery.
- R. Gilman (1977) outlines a set of defining characteristics of the cabaret "form." *Hamilton* shares one of Gilman's most crucial requisites: "presentations are most often the on-going work of a particular group of talented people with a common esthetic or political view instead of being an ad hoc proposition like most common commercial entertainment." As a historical pageant, a "revue" that prides itself on historical accuracy, *Hamilton*'s natural venue may be the cabaret stage

rather than Broadway. The "active, sometimes aggressive relationship between performers and audience" that is possible in true cabaret would allow political themes—now encumbered by the exuberance of musical comedy—to bloom fully.

- A historical revue should not be confused with the extravaganzas performed under totalitarian regimes to honor the "dear leader" of the nation and his faithful "patriots": Chinese operas that celebrated Mao and the Red Army; Cuban parades in honor of Fidel Castro; patriotic displays during wars such as those in James Cagney's *Yankee Doodle Dandy* (1942). *Hamilton* is more than these, but at its worst, it relies heavily on flag-waving patriotism to hide lapses in dramatic imagination.

Beyond *Hamilton* on the Disney Channel, there is a ray of hope. Young Puerto Rican audiences may sense in the production a parable of freedom for their time. Then Hamilton's example will be honored not by adoring the musical, but by emulating his struggle for the independence of his country from the reigning colonial power of his day. Admiration should give way to the sedulous, revolutionary construction of a new nation and to the righteous demand before the great colonial power of *our day* for independence for Puerto Rico. Independence has been a dream deferred, but now its time has come. Puerto Ricans proud of their heritage and committed to the survival of their cultural identity can take away no less from *Hamilton.*

EPILOGUE

By all North American accounts, *Hamilton* is a crushing success. Some have claimed it to be a political and aesthetic revolution. The production has run continuously in New York for over half a decade. Miranda has become a wealthy man, and the production teams have profited handsomely from the show. The Disney corporation paid $75 million for the worldwide rights of the film with the original cast of the musical—a deal that meant $30 million for Miranda personally. He is touted regularly as a genius and is asked by the mainstream media to comment on all things Puerto Rican. But through the din of the hype—faintly and far away—one hears the voice of the old-time African American preacher:

This is Babylon, Babylon,
That great city of Babylon.

Come on, my friend, and go along with me.
And the young man joined the crowd. ("The Prodigal Son," 1927;
    as qtd. in Johnson, 1990, p. 23)

In the summer of 2019, while touring Spain, Puerto Rican rapper Bad Bunny announced on Instagram: "I'm canceling everything. I'm pausing my career because I don't have the heart or mind to do music. . . . I'm going to Puerto Rico. I'm not going to turn my back on you. We have to continue taking the streets." Pop icon Ricky Martin also posted: "I'm getting on a plane and I'll be [in Puerto Rico] at 7 a.m. [to march]. . . . I want to feel the power of the people. Come demonstrate with us." And Residente, the great rapper idolized by reggaeton enthusiasts, released a track called "Afilando los cuchillos" (Sharpening the Knives), accompanied by Bad Bunny and Puerto Rican singer Ile (all qtd. in Cobo, 2019).

The occasion was the public demonstrations against the administration of Governor Ricardo Rosselló. The Puerto Rican people, led by their civic activists, artists, rappers, and musicians, were in the streets. With their drums and songs, their poetry and their pots and pans, the people created a social and spiritual gale of hurricane proportions. It was one of those times— well-known to Cuban *mambises* and Irish rebels—when poetry jumped from the pages of books and the songs of troubadours. Art became incarnate as the goddess of liberty in the Phrygian cap who was present at the birth of the American Revolution and at the storming of the Bastille by French *citoyens*.

There is a sort of triumph in putting on a Broadway show and making millions of dollars. But the island rappers and musicians, grieved at corruption and offended by arrogance, led the people in toppling their elected, prostatehood government.

Caribbean political leaders understand rebellious poetry. It has been used and misused—by great poets as well as by charlatans and thieves—throughout our wretched history.

We should not misuse our verses. Their power may get lost; their soul may fly away.

NOTES

1. Works such as The Who's *Tommy* (1969), Larry Harlow's Latin opera *Hommy* (1973), and Pink Floyd's *The Wall* (1979) are exemplars of this tradition. *Tommy* and *The Wall* are both "rock albums"; *Hommy* is a "salsa" version of *Tommy*.

2. Antonin Artaud's most influential book on contemporary theater is *The Theater and Its Double* (1958).

REFERENCES

Alonso, M. A. (2007). *El gíbaro* (E. Forastieri-Braschi, Ed.). Editorial Plaza Mayor.

Arrom, J. J. (1969). *Hispanoamérica: Panorama contemporáneo de su cultura*. Harper and Row.

Bradner, E. (2016, November 20). Pence: "I wasnt offended" by message of *Hamilton* cast. *CNN*. https://www.cnn.com/2016/11/20/politics/mike-pence-hamilton-message-trump/index.html

Brecht, B. (1964). A short organum for the theatre. In J. Willett (Ed.), *Brecht on theatre* (pp. 179–205). Methuen.

Brecht, B. (1994). *The threepenny opera* (J. W. Manheim, Ed., & R. M. Willett, Trans.). Arcade Publishing.

Brustein, R. (1964). *The theatre of revolt: An approach to the modern drama*. Little, Brown and Company.

Césaire, A. (2001). *Notebook of a return to the native land* (C. Eshleman & A. Smith, Trans.). Wesleyan University Press. (Original work published 1941).

Chang, J. (2006). *Can't stop, won't stop: A history of the hip-hop generation*. St. Martin's Press.

Chernow, R. (2005). *Alexander Hamilton*. Penguin Books.

Cobo, L. (2019, July 22). Puerto Rican artists Ricky Martin, Residente & Bad Bunny are agents of change calling for governor's resignation. *Billboard*. https://www.billboard.com/articles/columns/latin/8523379/puerto-rican-artists-ricky-martin-residente-bad-bunny-governor-resignation-protests

de Burgos, J. (1986). Rio Grande de Loíza. In M. M. Solá (Ed.), *Yo misma fui mi ruta* (pp. 64–65). Ediciones Huracán.

Diderot, D. (1957). *The paradox of the actor*. Hill and Wang.

Friscia, S. (2016, May 30). Hamilton's Dance Revolution. *Dance Magazine*. https://www.dancemagazine.com/hamilton-dance-revolution-2307024931.html

Genet, J. (1960). *The Blacks: A clown show*. Grove Press.

Gilman, R. (1977, November 6). Historically, cabarets flourish in hard times. *New York Times*. https://www.nytimes.com/1977/11/06/archives/historically-cabarets-flourish-in-hard-times-will-cabaret-catch-on.html

Gordone, C. (1969). *No place to be somebody*. Samuel French.

Huang, Y. (2010). *Charlie Chan: The untold story of the honorable detective and his rendezvous with American history*. W. W. Norton.

Johnson, J. W. (1990). *God's trombones*. Penguin Books.

Jones, C. (2019, January 12). *Hamilton* opens in Puerto Rico. *Chicago Tribune*. https://www.chicagotribune.com/entertainment/theater/ct-ent-hamilton-puerto-rico-0113-story.html

Latham, A. (Ed.). (2004). *Oxford dictionary of musical terms*. Oxford University Press.

Lindauer, O. (1998, March 27). Archaeology of the Phoenix Indian School. *Archaeology.* https://archive.archaeology.org/online/features/phoenix/

Mele, C., & Healy, P. (2016, November 19). *Hamilton* had some unscripted lines for Pence: Trump wasn't happy. *New York Times.* https://www.nytimes.com/2016/11/19/us/mike -pence-hamilton.html

Miranda, L.-M., & McCarter, J. (2016). Hamilton: *The revolution.* Grand Central Publishing.

Nas. (2006). Hip hop is dead [Song]. On *Hip hop is dead.* Def Jam Recordings.

NWA. (2002). Gangsta gangsta [Song]. On *Straight outta Compton.* Priority Records.

Public Enemy. (n.d.). Miuzi weighs a ton [Song]. On *Yo! Bumrush the show.* Def Jam; Columbia.

Schama, S. (2006). *Rough crossings: Britain, the slaves and the American Revolution.* Harper Collins Publishers.

Shakespeare, W. (1955). *The tempest* (D. Horne, Ed.). Yale University Press. (Original work published 1611).

Shakespeare, W. (2006). *Hamlet* (A. Thompson & N. Taylor, Eds.). Bloomsbury. (Original work published 1600–1601).

Shaw, B. (1965). *Bernard Shaw: A prose anthology* (H. Burton, Ed.). Fawcett Publications.

Sublette, N. (2004). *Cuba and its music: From the first drums to the mambo.* Chicago Review Press.

Toll, R. (2019). Blackface: The sad history of minstrel shows. *American Heritage, 64*(1). https://www.americanheritage.com/blackface-sad-history-minstrel-shows#2

Tupper, L. (2018, March 8). Jim Crow: Song, Character, and Symbol. *Music 345: Race, Identity, and Representation in American Music.* https://pages.stolaf.edu/americanmusic /tag/jim-crow/

White, T. (1998). *Catch a fire: The life of Bob Marley.* Henry Holt and Co.

Part 2

The Identity Scripts of Whiteness

Chapter 3

FROM NOOSE TO "NUSE"

Green Book, "Woke" Whiteness, and the Postracial Buddy Film

STEPHEN E. RAHKO AND BYRON B CRAIG

If one were to pick a term to name the condition of American race relations during the year 2020, one could do no worse than "reckoning." "Reckoning" entered America's racial lexicon in June 2020 amidst the historic Black Lives Matter (BLM) protests that swept across the nation denouncing the country's shameful legacy of structural racism and police brutality. The protests prompted an unusual outpouring of pledges from multinational corporations, universities, and the professions to financially support racial-justice initiatives, increase diversity hiring, and to confront the legacy of racism in their institutions, products, and services. Social-media sites, such as Facebook and Twitter (now called X), brimmed with deeply personal testimonials about racism and tips for would-be racial allies. Books about racism quickly climbed the ranks of bestseller lists, and polls indicated popular support among self-identified white Americans for social reform. White celebrities, ranging from YouTube stars such as Logan Paul to Hollywood actresses such as Jane Fonda, confessed to national audiences that their white privilege is a byproduct of American racism ("Jane Fonda," 2020; Schnurr, 2020). Even the disgraced social-media influencer Olivia Jade Giannulli, who became infamous for her involvement in the 2019 Operation Varsity Blues college-admissions-bribery scandal, shared that the episode helped her to discover her own white privilege, which she apparently hadn't recognized until the murder of George Floyd (Cordero, 2020). Yet amidst all the confessionals and pledges for social change and to the chagrin of antiracism activists and Black Twitter, Netflix reported that *The Help* (2011) was the most viewed movie that streamed on its platform during the historic protests (Roberts, 2020).

The conjuncture of nationwide antiracism protests with the popularity of a film about Black servants and their white employers unveils a tension that was at the heart of America's so-called "reckoning" with race: the paradoxical desire of Americans to confront the country's ugly history of racial enmity, violence, and cruelty with uplifting narratives and images of racial redress. As Americans bore witness to the violent spectacle of Derek Chauvin's callous suffocation of George Floyd, they sought comforting stories of racial friendship. The popular desire for comfort and uplift in a moment of such cold indifference to Black life aptly illustrates how taste in popular culture, in this case the consumption of film, operates as a cultural metric for locating and displaying one's proximity to the racial structure of feeling in contemporary American public life.

This tension also marks the extent to which the cultural and affective scripts of whiteness have been transformed since the Ferguson uprisings of 2014 and especially since Donald Trump's ascent to the presidency in 2016. As we map the racial order of things in this precarious political moment, we must acknowledge that whiteness has become symbolically Janus-faced for the rise of white supremacy and Christian nationalism endemic to Trumpism now clashes with a more conscientious brand of "woke" whiteness that explicitly aligns itself with social-justice advocacy.

Since Trump's election in 2016, Hollywood has favored representations of race relations that emphasize white reformation and redemption through interracial friendship. Unlike films that dramatize protagonists as either white saviors or antiracist white heroes, recent films such *The Upside* (2017), *Hidden Figures* (2016), and *The Best of Enemies* (2019) underscore the capacity for whiteness to become woke—that is, to learn and grow from its history of misdeeds against the racial Other. We offer a response to this trend by advancing a critique of the Oscar-winning film *Green Book* (2018). *Green Book* offers a story of how white guilt is cultivated from white hubris and how whiteness becomes woke through its encounter with the racial Other. The film outlines a new stock racial trope that we shall call the "Nuse." We argue that the Nuse (short for Negro muse) is a new figuration of the racial Other that inspires and enlightens whiteness to its misdeeds in order to ultimately teach it how to be more humane.

In this chapter we seek to contribute to the critique of whiteness by focusing on "wokeness" as an emerging site of the rhetorical politics of race. We understand woke whiteness as a specific articulation of the American postracial fantasy that informs the discursive terrain of the politics of representation in American cinema. By dramatizing whiteness as the heroic corrective to its own history of racist sins—at the expense of granting narrative agency to the resilience and defiance of the racial Other to overcome systems of oppression—we argue that films such as *Green Book* only serve to perpetuate the ideological legacy of American structural racism since they recenter rather than decenter whiteness under the aegis of a moral awakening of its own making and on its own terms. Recent buddy films such as *Green Book* can be understood as aspirationally postracial rather than antiracist since they propose interracial friendship as the means to transcend race as a structuring condition of sociality, opportunity, and possibility in both politics and everyday American life. Our chapter proceeds by first providing historical context for woke whiteness, which we claim emerged as an identity script because of the failure of progressive neoliberalism. Next, we map how the buddy film came to be informed by the rise of woke whiteness and its deeper postracial aspirations through the figure of the Nuse. Finally, we examine different variations of the Nuse in buddy films released after 2016, focusing especially on *Green Book*.

WOKE WHITENESS AND THE FAILED POSTRACIAL PROJECT OF PROGRESSIVE NEOLIBERALISM

Over the past decade, but especially in the immediate aftermath of the Trump administration, wokeness has emerged as a flashpoint in American politics that has become a popular subject for innumerable opinion editorials, internet diatribes and manifestos, as well as all varieties of political grandstanding. The concept of "staying woke" or "waking up" to the realities of racism has long been a staple of Black political struggles since the early twentieth century, but the term developed into a popular watchword for Black Lives Matter during the Ferguson protests of 2014.

After Ferguson, "woke" quickly evolved into a catch-all summation for progressive and leftist political ideology that became a common expression among self-identified whites to announce their views on matters of race and identity politics (Romano, 2020). The popular adoption of the term by white progressives and liberals, however, helped to transform the rhetorical signification of the word as it became more widespread on social media and in mainstream American political culture. Like critical race theory and the *New York Times'* 1619 Project, the term has been strategically repurposed and weaponized by conservatives into an empty signifier meant to spawn and stroke a moral panic among Americans who oppose more racially inclusive cultural norms and egalitarian public-policy proposals. Political conservatives, and many centrists, now frequently evoke the term "woke" to announce their opposition to so-called "cancel culture" and what they consider to be cultural denunciations of whiteness (e.g., "white privilege," the renaming or removal of memorials celebrating violent white historical figures), with many even claiming that wokeness threatens free speech and the political project of Western liberalism (Goldberg, 2021; "The Woke Future," 2021). The hysteria surrounding wokeness has made it a preferred political epithet in the latest front of America's seemingly never-ending culture wars that ambitious politicians and pundits invoke ad nauseam to build an audience and political brand (Hind et al., 2023; Serwer, 2023). The political Right's weaponization of the term, moreover, has become a dangerous pretext for not only maintaining and justifying systemic racial inequality but also silencing critical discourse on the topic of race itself. To be sure, since 2022, a growing number of conservative state legislatures and governors with presidential aspirations, led by Ron DeSantis of Florida, have leveraged woke hysteria to enact authoritarian laws that critics, educators, and school librarians claim censor their ability to teach matters of history and identity, especially regarding topics of race and gender (Mier, 2023).

While the term "woke" indubitably conjures explicit attitudes on matters of racial inequity across the ideological spectrum, our chapter focuses on white liberals and progressives. Media studies scholars have long documented the disproportionate cultural and economic importance of affluent and socially left-leaning white audiences to the culture industries. Indeed, white liberal and progressive audiences have historically been imagined as a highly desirable and "quality" demographic market, making them a key consumer that is heavily sought after by the culture industries (Nygaard & Lagerwey, 2020).

We argue that the ardent adoption of the term "woke" by self-identified "white" bourgeois liberals and progressives is in fact an outgrowth of postracial discourses since 2008 and a deeper expression of their desire to move beyond race once and for all. The postracial claim—that America has reached a moment in its history in which racial equality necessitates neither the law nor state policy—first emerged after the 1960s only to become an iteration of the concept of "colorblindness"—that is, the notion that Americans should pretend to not see race. However, the idea that America had become "postracial" became a dominant point of social and ideological consensus with the election of Barack Obama as president in 2008. For proponents of this claim, Obama's triumph went beyond the notion that we should be "blind" to matters of race since his election proved that, in America, race no longer matters. Indeed, for them, Obama's election meant that we were now beyond race rather than merely "blind" to it.

The postracial consensus posits that racial discrimination can no longer be declared systemic in a way that warrants the state to intervene and promotes the idea that race be disregarded as a category for government policy. Hence, criticisms regarding the racial disparities in healthcare, criminal justice, housing, wealth, access to education, and even voting are, in the parlance of our postracial times, disingenuous expressions of "political correctness" or "playing the race card." Accordingly, policies seeking to correct the historical legacy of racial discrimination are said to perpetuate the race problem by creating a new class of victims through purported "reverse racism" (Craig & Rahko, 2021, pp. 262–263).

Numerous critics have argued that Obama's presidency not only signified postracialism through his rhetorical evasion of race but also substantively promoted it through neoliberal public policy (Dawson & Francis, 2016; Reed, 2018). Obama's presidency embodied what N. Fraser (2019) calls "progressive neoliberalism"—that is, the dominant hegemonic bloc of American politics since 1992 that strategically combines the political economy of neoliberalism with a progressive identity politics of recognition (p. 13). As an alliance of the new social movements (feminism, antiracism, multiculturalism, environmentalism, and LGBTQ+ rights) with Wall Street, Silicon Valley, and Hollywood, progressive neoliberalism embraced financial globalization and deregulation with a superficial commitment to social equality and emancipation. Reducing equality to meritocracy, the "progressive-neoliberal program for a just status order," she notes, "did not aim to abolish social hierarchy but to 'diversify' it" (p. 13).

Progressive neoliberalism hegemonically harmonized with the ideology of postrace for the priority of each involves affirming minority difference and promoting so-called "'deserving' individuals from 'underrepresented groups'" without recourse to egalitarian redistributive public policy measures (Fraser, 2019, pp. 13–14). Within the parameters of these linked discursive formations, "diversity," notes R. T. Halualani (2011), comes to be "de-raced" and emptied of its substantive content (p. 248). As she explains, the postracial articulation of "diversity" is rhetorically idealized and abstracted such that racial and ethnic cultural groups are drained "of any particular histories, social structures, or structural inequalities" and instead flattened to be deemed "the *same* and *equal* precisely because they are all equally *different*" (p. 248). This abstract and raceless articulation of "diversity" achieves the postracial ambition of recuperating the state as a "race-less arbiter of society" (p. 248) while simultaneously encoding the dominant position of whiteness "since the interests of a hegemonic white-centered racial state are promoted, advanced, and strengthened" (p. 259).

Over the course of the Obama presidency, however, the postracial project of progressive neoliberalism fell into crisis. The project was disrupted during his second term by the spectacle of numerous high-profile killings of unarmed Black citizens—first Trayvon Martin, then Michael Brown, Sandra Bland, Tamir Rice, and countless others at the hands of police—and the subsequent BLM protests in Ferguson during the summer and fall of 2014. But the election of Trump in 2016, notes Fraser (2019), dealt progressive neoliberalism a fatal blow that engendered a hegemonic legitimacy crisis that America is still navigating with uncertainty (pp. 9–13). In the wake of such uncertainty and disruption and with the moral ethos and self-image of whiteness now in disrepair, white progressives and liberals have found themselves in the awkward position of having to reconcile their own hegemonic position of social power with the mounting evidence that, in fact, race still matters in America and that it still determines social outcomes in matters of prosperity and penury as well as matters of life and death.

The election of Trump proved to be a catalyst for woke whiteness and specifically one of its most potent underlying affective dispositions: white guilt. While a vast body of scholarship responding to the rise of Trumpism has rightly focused on the racial attitudes of white conservatives on matters of immigration and racial resentment against the changing demographics of America, a clear countervailing trend emerged among white progressives and liberals (Dionne et al., 2017; Hochschild, 2018; Metzl, 2019). Survey and polling data collected after 2016 shows a sharp shift in white liberal attitudes on race in the decade since the Ferguson uprisings. In 2010, for example, 40 percent of white liberals agreed that Black Americans who can't get ahead are mostly responsible for their own plight. By 2019, that number plunged to 24 percent. Concomitantly, in 2014, 40 percent of white liberals agreed that discrimination was the main reason Black Americans couldn't get ahead, but by 2019, that figure had increased to over 70 percent (Herndon, 2019; McElwee, 2018).

This shift in racial attitude was accompanied by the rise of a new performance of whiteness that critics have named "performative wokeness" (Díaz, 2020). Motivated by white guilt and shame, white liberals and progressives began to describe their whiteness explicitly and ritualistically as if it were an original sin foundational to their very being. Though secular in nature, performative wokeness has a stunning similarity to Catholicism. Drawing on the work of Peggy McIntosh, workshops on racial awareness, for instance, frequently encourage participants to openly "confess" their "white privilege"— that is, unearned advantages bestowed on them for their accidental whiteness (Jackson, 2019; Lensmire et al., 2013, pp. 410–416). Rituals of confession, moreover, have been accompanied by public performances of competitive virtue signaling—during which woke people of privilege express outrage to other people of privilege about social injustices—and privilege checking—during which woke people of privilege shame other people about their unearned privileges—for the purpose of strategically elevating their symbolic standing (Saltman, 2018, pp. 403–404). Such public performances are rooted in white guilt for they are acts of redress meant to actively atone for white privilege.

In a strange reversal, whiteness, over the past decade, has gone from an unstated, yet omnipresent and ubiquitous, reference point in American culture to an increasingly essentialized identity marked at once by hypervisible displays of violent racial animus *and* a series of gaudy public performances of white guilt. Indeed, performative wokeness can be understood as a cultural expression of what we elsewhere call "bourgeois sentimentality" (Craig & Rahko, 2016, p. 293). We draw our understanding of the politics of sentimentality from J. Baldwin's critique of the concept in his well-known excoriation of Harriet Beecher Stowe's *Uncle Tom's Cabin*. In "Everybody's Protest Novel," Baldwin (1984) identifies "sentimentality [as] the ostentatious parading of excessive and spurious emotion" and "inability to feel" that is at once a "mark of dishonesty" and a perilously utopian "devotion to a Cause" (pp. 14–15). "The wet eyes of the sentimentalist," Baldwin continues, "betray his aversion to experience, his fear of life," (p. 14) for "in overlooking, denying, [and] evading his complexity—which is nothing more than the disquieting complexity of ourselves—we are diminished and we perish" (p. 15). Sentimentality, he concludes, "is always, therefore, the signal of secret and violent inhumanity, the mask of cruelty" (p. 14).

The safety pin—which emerged as a symbol popular on social media after Trump's election to publicly display woke allyship with vulnerable minority communities—is a quintessential example of Baldwin's concerns. While it perhaps temporarily marked a form of public solidarity against hate crimes, it also served as a public and apologetic performance of the woke to shame other white Americans for voting for Trump at the expense of a deeper commitment to dismantle institutions of structural racism that woke whites themselves typically benefit from. Like other kitsch that strive to "raise awareness," the safety pin was ultimately a form of symbolic currency that reduced the complexities, time burden, and labors of political judgement and action—such as grassroots organizing, canvasing, and meeting with legislators—to affective transactions meant to build cultural capital and elevate one's social status among woke members of what E. Currid-Halkett (2017) calls the "aspirational class" (pp. 46–77).

The superficiality underlying woke whiteness is also revealed by surveys among whites taken during and after the George Floyd protests of 2020.

Whereas polls taken during the 2020 protests found that support for BLM skyrocketed among white Americans, by 2021, attitudes had plummeted, with white support of the movement dropping below pre-2020 levels. Support for remedial policies such as the defunding and demilitarization of policing, reparations, or other race-specific restorative-justice measures also remain low, which suggests that most white Americans prefer performative political gestures to compensate for their unwillingness to materially renounce their own tangible systematic social advantages, wealth, and political power made possible by policies such as exclusionary zoning, inheritance laws, and legacy college admissions, not to mention other forms of what R. V. Reeves (2017) calls "opportunity hoarding" (pp. 95–122; see also Chudy & Jefferson, 2021; Ore, 2021; Williams, 2021).

There can be no doubt that whiteness is a distinctive ontological and phenomenological experience of the world, but it is also an identity strategy of symbolic self-presentation. To be sure, scholars have long recognized whiteness to be a strategic rhetoric (Buerkle, 2019; Nakayama & Krizek, 1995). So, contrary to its conservative and centrist detractors, wokeness is not a strategy for disavowing whiteness, white American heritage, or so-called "Western" values so much as it is a strategy for *recentering* whiteness at a time when its cultural authority is in crisis. Seeking to redraw the hegemonic boundaries of racial politics, woke whiteness consciously displays its own self-awareness of the racial order of things, yet, in its conspicuous public displays of agony over race, aspires for a postracial condition where race no longer matters. It performatively congratulates itself for its own self-sanctimonious racial catharsis yet yearns for a bland "diversity" and raceless multiculturalism in which it maintains its hegemonic position as it always has: an unnamed and unspoken dominant symbolic reference in matters of culture, language, social mores, the law, and, of course, material wealth and property. In short, wokeness can be understood as whiteness's hegemonic adaptation to maintain itself as a structure of power in a new racial landscape marked by its own impending demographic eclipse, legitimacy crisis, and violent radicalization under Trumpism.

"BI" BECOMES "POST": THE POSTRACIAL BUDDY
FILM IN THE ERA OF WOKE WHITENESS

The rise of woke whiteness has noticeably altered the landscape of American media and popular culture. For our purposes, we will narrow our analysis of these changes to focus on one specific genre of cultural representation: the American buddy film. If, as we have argued thus far, woke whiteness as an identity strategy is affectively invested in the ostentatious pageantry of racial awareness to audiences who care deeply about white privilege and social injustices, then one's public display of taste in popular culture becomes a crucial site for public performances of wokeness. Indeed, as C. R. Squires (2014) argues, the consumption of popular culture in our postracial times becomes a public posture for "doing" race (p. 167).

The buddy film has long been a mainstay of American popular culture that stretches back to the early decades of classical Hollywood cinema. The genre centers around two characters, often of the same gender, whose diegetic pairing drives the narrative through their shared experience, be it an adventure or quest, road trip, or social dilemma. The two characters usually feature sharp personality contrasts that shape the development of their onscreen relationship. Often, though not always, their personality contrasts serve comic ends, which has made the buddy film a profitable narrative formula capable of attracting a broad demographic audience. Moreover, the genre is marked by the narrative device of friendship that forms between the paired characters, which has made it a site for negotiating a vast range of political problems, including race.

Politically inflected buddy films about American race relations have appeared in Hollywood cinema since at least *The Defiant Ones* (1958) and *In the Heat of the Night* (1967), but scholars have often expressed doubt over the genre's capacity to seriously address the complexities of race. This is especially the case with biracial buddy films, which have been a profitable staple of the genre since the 1980s. E. Guerrero (1993), for example, argues that interracial buddy films have served the ideological purpose of containing Black stars to the pleasures of a dominant-white consuming audience. Others, such as M. Kaplan (2010), argue that popular films about interracial friendship serve as "compensatory devices" that employ "the liberal figure of private citizenship to resolve imaginatively an otherwise intractable structural contradiction" (p. 153). In *The Trouble with Friendship*, B. DeMott (1998) notes that popular cinematic depictions of interracial friendship minimize, if not completely ignore, the depth of divergent sociopolitical experiences between Black and white citizens. Such narratives privilege the affective commonalities that underlie the shared bond of friendship that binds the characters of biracial buddy films, which serves to shift the responsibility for structural racial inequities from the acrimonious field of popular politics to the private domain of individual conscience and choice. Biracial buddy films, accordingly, function to reassure audiences about their own moral fitness and competence rather than to challenge their racial prejudices and sensibilities, much less the political legitimacy underlying the structures of American liberal democracy (pp. 7–23).

If the biracial buddy film contains Blackness and serves to ideologically reassure white audiences, its techniques for doing so have shifted to accommodate the affective political sensibilities of its woke white audiences. Since Trump's election in 2016, Hollywood has favored representations of race relations that emphasize white reformation and redemption through interracial friendship. Unlike films that dramatize protagonists as either white saviors or antiracist white heroes, recent films such *Hidden Figures, The Upside,* and *The Best of Enemies* underscore the capacity for whiteness to become woke—that is, to learn and grow from its history of misdeeds against the racial Other (Lacy, 2010; Madison, 1999).

The growing importance of wokeness as an underlying theme in the buddy film represents an important pivot in postracial popular culture that scholars of the topic should take note of. To this point, scholarship on postracial popular culture in the United States has focused on dramatizations of whiteness and specifically on the role of white protagonists (Bineham, 2015; Griffin, 2015; Murphy & Harris, 2018). However, to understand the shift taking place since 2016, we argue that scholars should shift their focus to the way the racial Other, and specifically Blackness, is represented and dramatized in films about interracial relationships. Indeed, in this chapter, we seek to inaugurate this reframing in order to demonstrate how the redemption of whiteness in these emerging postracial narratives depends on a specific figuration of Blackness that makes white racists woke. We call this new racial stock trope the "Nuse."

The Nuse (short for Negro muse) is a new figuration of Blackness that enlightens and inspires whiteness to be more humane. Like other historical stereotypes of Blackness, the figure restricts Black agency in the service of whiteness, but it accomplishes this task by new means of narrative technique. Unlike other recurring stereotyped representations of Blackness—such as coons, mulattoes, mammies, magical Negroes, or bucks—the Nuse is not a fiction that intends to dramatize Blackness as inferior or even subhuman. It does not seek to justify the death or even political disenfranchisement of Blackness. Rather, the Nuse is a figure that justifies white forgiveness and absolution through the narrative device of friendship. It absorbs racial animus and forgives whiteness for its hatred, clumsiness, and ignorance. It is patient in the face of white racism and generously teaches whiteness the steps of its own redemption. Through the Nuse, the terms of the onscreen relationship between white and Black characters in buddy films has shifted to respond to a more woke and racially aware audience.

It is not surprising that the Nuse has emerged in an era when American (neo)liberalism has come to recognize and seek symbolic atonement for its failed promises to citizens of color who have endured its history of violence and political disenfranchisement. To be sure, like woke whiteness, films featuring the Nuse seek to ideologically recenter the postracial fantasy of moving beyond race in American life. Marketed primarily to a white racially aware audience that is anxious, agonized, and ashamed of its privilege yet unwilling to abdicate it through substantive social and political change, these films offer them reassurance through cinematic catharsis.

Accordingly, these films mark an important ideological redrawing of the rhetorical politics of race in an era of white guilt and violent white grievance. Unlike white savior films, such as *The Help* or *The Blind Side* (2009), white protagonists become heroic because they are capable of being saved by the racial Other from the racism that stems from their original sin of whiteness. Like other genres of postracial films, postracial buddy films also downplay the significance of race and promote narratives of individual initiative but do so by showing how white racists can be redeemed through their encounter with the Nuse. Unlike films such as *Mississippi Burning* (1988), however, the emerging postracial buddy film does not necessarily subscribe to the myth of white innocence and does not pretend that there has always been an ample supply of good white people, or even white heroes, to compensate for white racists (Squires, 2014, p. 201). Instead, these films emphasize the transformational possibilities of bad white racists to become redeemable and woke. The transformational and redemptive potentialities of whiteness, in turn, become the basis in these narratives for renewing an ideological commitment to the postracial project after the failed hegemony of progressive neoliberalism.

For the remainder of this chapter, we offer an analysis of recent films that feature the Nuse coupled with a close reading of the Oscar-winning film *Green Book*, a film that Steven Spielberg has called the best buddy comedy since 1969's *Butch Cassidy and the Sundance Kid* (Stolworthy, 2019). *Green Book* offers a story of how white guilt is cultivated from white hubris and how whiteness becomes woke through its encounter with the racial Other. We argue that *Green Book* represents a quintessential example of the Nuse as a new postracial narrative device.

GREEN BOOK AS EXEMPLAR OF THE POSTRACIAL BUDDY FILM IN THE ERA OF WOKE WHITENESS

The Nuse is a complex and multifaceted racial trope that can take many shapes and appear in many varieties of narrative form. While our critique of this figuration focuses primarily on biracial buddy films, it is important to state up front that the Nuse is not strictly a buddy film figure. Films featuring the Nuse often revolve around interracial friendship, but not all follow the classic "buddy" formula. *Hidden Figures* is not a buddy film per se but does orbit around Taraji P. Henson's working relationship with her soft racist and misogynistic NASA supervisors, played by Kevin Costner and Jim Parsons, with whom she develops an affectionate bond. The film dramatizes her relationship with them, and by the end of the film, Costner and Parsons clearly embrace her as part of the NASA family.

The Nuse can appear as a range of potential characters. Sometimes the Nuse is a brilliant and underappreciated mathematician, such as Henson's character, Katherine Johnson, in *Hidden Figures*. Sometimes the Nuse can take the form of a struggling and delinquent Black male, such as Kevin Hart in *The Upside*, or a civil rights activist, such as Ann Atwater (also played by Henson) in *The Best of Enemies*. White characters transformed by the Nuse can range as well. White characters in these films can come from the working class (*Green Book*, *The Best of Enemies*), the upper-middle-class professions (*Hidden Figures*), or the 1 percent (*The Upside*). Sometimes the white character can be a Klan member (*The Best of Enemies*), a tolerant progressive (*The Upside*), or an upper-middle- and working-class white person who either harbors segregationist sympathies or hostile phobias of the racial Other (*Hidden Figures*, *Green Book*).

Set in 1962, *Green Book* follows the friendship forged between African American classical pianist and composer Don Shirley (played by Mahershala Ali) and white nightclub bouncer Tony Lip (played by Viggo Mortensen). From the outset, the film clearly establishes that the narrative will center around the character arc of Lip. An Italian American hailing from the Bronx, Lip is an Archie Bunkeresque caricature of working-class exuberance: he is tough, garrulous, boorish, and vulgar yet charmingly likable and sincere. We first meet him roughing up boisterous patrons at his nightclub, and throughout the film, he voluminously smokes and eats. He is a proud family man, but he has a Bunkeresque character flaw that is revealed early in the film: he harbors racist feelings for the racial Other and specifically African Americans. We learn this when Lip throws away glassware because his wife let two African American repairmen drink from it. We learn the pervasiveness of these racist attitudes when he, his Italian American family, and his mob associates refer to Shirley and other African Americans as "eggplants" and "coal." As an Italian American, Lip surely would have experienced plenty of discrimination himself, but the film only thinly insinuates it, thus setting up a white-Black binary (Bernstein, 2017; Staples, 2019).

From here, *Green Book* clearly establishes that the film will center around a story of white redemption. Lip's precarious working conditions, we soon learn, lead to a provisional layoff when his nightclub closes for three months for remodeling and repairs. Desperate for work, he leverages his (possibly mob-affiliated) contacts to find a temporary gig working with Shirley's record company as his factotum chauffer and de facto bodyguard.

The character contrast between Shirley and Lip is temperamentally quite sharp. A doctorly trained musician, who also happens to be a refined and homosexual aesthete with little patience for sloppiness, Shirley (or "Doc" as Lip calls him) is highly educated and accomplished. In some ways, Shirley represents a continuation of the magical Negro, but he's also quite different. The magical Negro is often a figure with supernatural powers (e.g., Whoopi Goldberg in 1990's *Ghost*) or a figure that is committed to white subservience (e.g., Morgan Freeman in 1989's *Driving Miss Daisy*); Ali is neither. Instead, Ali's character offers a narratological apology for whiteness by absorbing its worst impulses, forgiving it, and ultimately showing it how to reform itself.

The Nuse is marked by three characteristics that are required for it to realize its figural role in fulfilling white redemption, and Shirley displays all of them: he cultivates white guilt and sympathy for Black suffering, immerses whiteness in Black spaces, and imparts lessons to whiteness. The combination of these characteristics sets up whiteness to assume a new and revised heroic role marked not by its violent domination of the Black body through the noose (e.g., lynching), but rather by its transformation through racial awareness (e.g., wokeness).

CULTIVATING WHITE GUILT: SYMPATHY FOR BLACK SUFFERING

The defining feature that threads woke-era buddy films together lies in the way the figure of Blackness, the Nuse, foregrounds a narrative of white redemption. Black characters in these films must overcome obstacles placed by whiteness but, in absorbing the pain and humiliation of these obstacles, teaches whiteness how to become racially aware and thus more sympathetic and humane. The Nuse's struggles reveal the misdeeds of whiteness, which sets the terms for the white character arc to follow. This usually involves white characters observing and realizing the racial hypocrisies of whiteness. White characters, for example, learn to identify with the Black experience by directly observing the pain and humiliation of segregation or the fear of violent death that haunts Black encounters with the police (*The Upside, Green Book*) or the Klan (*The Best of Enemies*).

Fig. 3.1. Kevin Costner desegregates a NASA ladies room to make room for racial meritocracy in *Hidden Figures*.

Upon this revelation, white characters commence their diegetic racial awakening as they soon discover how whiteness ideologically blinds white people as they commit their racialized misdeeds. The Nuse's struggles emotionally move white characters to sympathize with the racial Other, which cultivates white guilt as a crucial part of the white character's diegetic development. White characters eventually act on their guilt by either advocating or acting on behalf of the racial Other. This can take a range of forms depending on the plot, including advocating for racial integration and the elimination of racial barriers to meritocracy (*Hidden Figures, Green Book, The Best of Enemies*) or acts of kindness that are completely dependent upon white wealth and social capital (*The Upside*).

There are countless examples of this white character arc across these films, but we will limit our focus to two examples. In *Hidden Figures*, the Nuse (Taraji P. Henson) teaches her white colleagues the pains caused by segregation as she absorbs the humiliation of walking across the NASA campus to use the bathroom for "colored" in the rain. This emotionally moves Kevin Costner, her NASA supervisor, to in effect desegregate NASA bathrooms when he destroys the "Colored ladies room" hallway sign. In *Green Book*, we see Lip's transformation as he observes Shirley get beat up in a segregated bar in Louisville and when he is denied services at a suit shop in Macon and bathroom services at a concert in Raleigh. From there, a series of events unfold where Lip becomes able to express his capacity to grow his tolerance for cultural difference, the most (in)famous of which involves him bribing police officers after Shirley is found soliciting gay sex at a YMCA in Macon. Through these struggles, the Nuse serves the narrative development of whiteness by teaching it sympathetic tolerance and how to embrace the cultural differences of the racial Other.

IMMERSING WHITENESS IN BLACK SPACES

If the biracial buddy films of the 1980s and 1990s were marked by the dislocation of Black characters from Black spaces, as Guerrero (1993) observes, then woke-era biracial buddy films do the reverse. Instead, we frequently see white characters enter Black spaces. We see this in *The Best of Enemies* when Sam Rockwell tours Black schools, and we see this in *The Upside* when Bryan Cranston accompanies Kevin Hart to the poorer and racially darker neighborhoods and public-housing projects of New York City. Such racial tourism serves a crucial diegetic purpose, for by exploring Black spaces, it becomes possible for white characters to learn what the racial Other experiences and what it's like to be Black. It is also through this racial tourism that white characters become aware of the inherent value of racial diversity.

This is also evident in *Green Book* when Lip accompanies Shirley to Black motels and a Black bar on their final stop touring the Deep South, but the film approaches this matter in a more controversial and perverse manner than the others. As critics, including Shirley's real-life family, note, the film depicts Lip's financial struggles as well as his cultural tastes in food and music to be more aligned with Blackness than Shirley, who is often portrayed as culturally distanced and detached from his own community (Harris, 2019). Nonetheless, like the other films, we can see Lip change as he immerses in Black spaces and learns more about the Black experience through his travels below the Mason-Dixon line.

FROM NOOSE TO NUSE: FROM LYNCHING THE BLACK BODY TO LEARNING FROM ITS WISDOM

The final characteristic of the Nuse is that it imparts lessons to whiteness. The Black body becomes an oracle for white misdeeds, incompetence, and incapacity. Whiteness in these films consults the Nuse to deepen its own understanding and humanity and to compensate for its moral and spiritual deficits. The woke, postracial buddy film is ultimately about the journey the white buddy takes toward his or her own awakening about race relations, and the job of the racial Other is to be his or her guide toward self-realization. The lessons the Nuse imparts to whiteness in these films varies. Sometimes the Nuse teaches whiteness what authentic patriotism and devotion to the nation looks like (*Hidden Figures*); other times, the Nuse teaches whiteness the art of romantic courtship (*The Upside, Green Book*) or what authentic acts of kindness look like (*The Best of Enemies*). The Nuse even imparts lessons for

Fig. 3.2. The "Nuse" (Don Shirley) teaches Tony Lip the art of writing a love letter in *Green Book*.

commercial success, such as when former Klan leader E. P. Ellis (Sam Rockwell) discovers that his service station can economically thrive by selling to Black customers in *The Best of Enemies*.

In *Green Book*, we continually witness Shirley impart lessons to Lip that refine his tastes, diction, temperament, ethics, and etiquette. The most memorable of these episodes comes in a scene during which Shirley teaches Lip the art of writing a love letter to his wife. On a spiritual level, however, Shirley teaches Lip what it means to have courage and dignity in the face of violent Jim Crow hostility and dehumanizing discrimination. This motif unfolds throughout the entire film but is most evident during their final tour stop when Shirley refuses to play after he is denied dining services.

It's difficult to overstate the radical historical reversal the Nuse fulfills. Instead of whiteness "civilizing" the racial Other, as R. Kipling's myth of the "white man's burden" advised, the figure of the Nuse in fact inverts Kipling's myth, for it is the racial Other that performs the labor of civilizing whiteness. Through the help of the Nuse, Lip's character arc becomes evidence of a whiteness authentically in touch with its inner truth and humaneness that it once fell astray from. Ideologically, the Nuse enables whiteness to maintain its place as hegemonic center under the aegis of the agency of the meritocratic racial Other.

CONCLUSION: FULFILLING WHITENESS'S POSTRACIAL FANTASY BY MEANS OF THE RACIAL OTHER

In the wake of the failures of progressive neoliberalism and the legitimacy crisis of whiteness, the Nuse has emerged as a new postracial figuration of

Blackness meant to fulfill the affective and ideological needs of woke white audiences. The recent buddy films we have critiqued in this chapter can be understood as aspirationally postracial rather than antiracist since each proposes interracial friendship as the means to transcend race as a structuring condition of sociality, opportunity, and possibility in both politics and everyday American life. Indeed, beyond absorbing, absolving, and forgiving the misdeeds of whiteness, the Nuse is a multifaceted trope that also fulfills a variety of popular postracial narratives, particularly the postracial myths of meritocracy (*Hidden Figures, Green Book*) and the triumph of individual initiative over racially structured economic inequity (*The Upside*; see also Noble & Roberts, 2019). The point of Don Shirley's tour in *Green Book,* for instance, is to expose the Jim Crow South to the musical genius of a Black man and thus encourage racial assimilation based on the "worthy ones."

Yet the emergent woke, postracial buddy film also aesthetically represents the same sentimentalist dangers that repulsed Baldwin. Since these films revolve around how the white buddy has his heart transformed through his interaction with the racial Other, these films ultimately suggest that the crisis of American race relations is best solved through the spiritual awakening and renewal of whiteness rather than structural reforms of a historically white-dominated, capitalist social order. By fetishizing the problem of race sentimentally in terms of the feelings one purportedly holds in one's heart, films such as *Green Book* minimize and invalidate the complexities of both the Black experience and American racism in the name of creating diegetic and narrative space for white characters such as Lip to fully blossom from racist to woke. But does Lip's wokeness in fact abstain and absolve him from his anti-Blackness earlier in the film? Does the racial awakening that motivates his character arc in fact change the structural antagonism between white and Black that underlies American capitalism? These questions are intentionally never posed to the audience for the film was intended for the edification of white audiences seeking a cathartic experience about whiteness reformed.

The rhetorical dynamics of *Green Book* force us to interrogate the form and content of the stories of race we need in an era punctuated by white nationalism and racialized violence. In the aftermath of Charlottesville and Trump's failed coup on January 6, 2021, we suggest that we need to see more cinematic stories that reveal the raw violence of whiteness rather than make apologies for white redemption. The film *The Green Room,* for example, reveals such a representation of whiteness through its disturbing story of white-nationalist terrorism. HBO's series *Watchmen*—which evokes the memory of the 1921 Tulsa Race Massacre and imagines an America in which the minority becomes the majority, chronically threatened by white terrorism—offers another story. Indeed, Hollywood would be better served telling stories that honestly dramatize the history of white violence rather than make apologies for it.

REFERENCES

Baldwin, J. (1984). *Notes of a native son.* Beacon Press.

Bernstein, D. (2017, March 22). Sorry, but the Irish were always "white" (and so were Italians, Jews and so on). *Washington Post.* https://www.washingtonpost.com/news/volokh-conspiracy/wp/2017/03/22/sorry-but-the-irish-were-always-white-and-so-were-the-italians-jews-and-so-on/

Bineham, J. (2015). How *The blind side* blinds us: Postracism and the American dream. *Southern Communication Journal, 80*(3), 230–245. https://doi.org/10.1080/10417 94X.2015.1030084

Buerkle, C. W. (2019). Adam mansplains everything: White-hipster masculinity as covert hegemony. *Southern Communication Journal, 84*(3), 170–182. https://doi.org/10.1080/10 41794X.2019.1575898

Chudy, J., & Jefferson, H. (2021, May 22). Support for Black Lives Matter surged last year: Did it last? *New York Times.* https://www.nytimes.com/2021/05/22/opinion/blm-movement-protests-support.html

Cordero, R. (2020, December 8). Lori Loughlin's daughter Olivia Jade breaks silence on college admissions scandal: "We messed up." *Entertainment Weekly.* https://ew.com/tv/lori-loughlin-daughter-olivia-jade-breaks-silence-college-admissions-scandal/

Craig, B. B., & Rahko, S. E. (2016). Visual profiling as biopolitics: Or, notes on policing in post-racial #AmeriKKKa. *Cultural Studies ↔ Critical Methodologies, 16*(3), 287–295. https://doi.org/10.1177/1532708616634775

Craig, B. B., & Rahko, S. E. (2021). From "Say my name" to "Texas bamma": Transgressive *topoi*, oppositional optics, and sonic subversion in Beyoncé's "Formation." In C. Baade & and K. McGee (Eds.), *Beyoncé in the world: Making meaning with Queen Bey in troubled times* (pp. 260–284). Wesleyan University Press.

Currid-Halkett, E. (2017). *The sum of small things: A theory of the aspirational class.* Princeton University Press.

Dawson, M. C., & Francis, M. M. (2016). Black politics and the neoliberal racial order. *Public Culture 28*(1), 23–62. https://doi.org/10.1215/08992363-325004

DeMott, B. (1998). *The trouble with friendship: Why Americans can't think straight about race.* Yale University Press.

Díaz, V. (2020). Performative wokeness / white victimhood: The hypocrisy of celebrity villainization of paparazzi. *Women's Studies in Communication, 43*(4), 363–368. https://doi.org/10.1080/07491409.2020.1833635

Dionne, E. J., Jr., Ornstein, N. J., & Mann, T. E. (2017). *One nation after Trump: A guide for the perplexed, the disillusioned, the desperate, and the not-yet deported.* St. Martin's Press.

Fraser, N. (2019). *The old is dying and the new cannot be born: From progressive neoliberalism to Trump and beyond.* Verso.

Goldberg, M. (2021, February 26). The campaign to cancel wokeness. *New York Times.* https://www.nytimes.com/2021/02/26/opinion/speech-racism-academia.html

Griffin, R. A. (2015). Problematic representations of strategic whiteness and "post-racial" pedagogy: A critical intercultural reading of *The help. Journal of International and Intercultural Communication, 8*(2), 147–166. https://doi.org/10.1080/17513057.2015 .1025330

Guerrero, E. (1993). The Black image in protective custody: Hollywood's biracial buddy films of the eighties. In M. Diawara (Ed.), *Black American Cinema* (pp. 237–246). Routledge.

Halualani, R. T. (2011). Abstracting and de-racializing diversity: The articulation of diversity in the post-racial era in Zwick's *Blood diamond.* In M. G. Lacy & K. A. Ono (Eds.), *Critical rhetorics of race* (pp. 247–264). New York University Press.

Harris, H. R. (2019, February 27). Don Shirley's family dismayed by *Green book* Oscar wins, calls portrait of pianist false. *USA Today.* https://www.usatoday.com/story/life /movies/academy-awards/2019/02/25/don-shirleys-family-green-book/2979734002/

Herndon, A. W. (2019, October 14). How 'white guilt' in the age of Trump shapes the Democratic Party. *New York Times.* https://www.nytimes.com/2019/10/13/us/politics /democratic-candidates-racism.html

Hind, H., Sadowski, A., & Lee, J. (2023, June 8). *200+ things that Fox News has labeled "woke."* Media Matters for America. https://www.mediamatters.org/fox-news/200-things-fox -news-has-labeled-woke

Hochschild, A. R. (2018). *Strangers in their own land: Anger and mourning on the American right.* New Press.

Jackson, L. M. (2019, September 4). What's missing from "white fragility." *Slate.* https:// slate.com/human-interest/2019/09/white-fragility-robin-diangelo-workshop.html

Jane Fonda says even "the poorest" of white people have privilege: "We need to recognize that." (2020, June 2). *People.* https://people.com/movies/jane-fonda-speaks-out-on -white-privilege-in-wake-of-george-floyds-death/

Kaplan, M. A. (2010). *Friendship fictions: The rhetoric of citizenship in the liberal imaginary.* University of Alabama Press.

Lacy, M. (2010). White innocence heroes: Recovery, reversals, paternalism, and David Duke. *Journal of International and Intercultural Communication, 3*(3), 206–227. https:// doi.org/10.1080/17513057.2010.487221

Lensmire, T. J., McManimon, S. K., Tierney, J. D., Lee-Nichols, M. E., Casey, Z. A., Lensmire, A., & Davis, B. M. (2013). McIntosh as synecdoche: How teacher education's focus on white privilege undermines antiracism. *Harvard Educational Review, 83*(3), 410–431. https://doi.org/10.17763/haer.83.3.35054h14l8230574

Madison, K. J. (1999). Legitimation crisis and containment: The "anti-racist-white-hero" film. *Critical Studies in Mass Communication, 16*(4), 399–416. https://doi.org/10.1080 /15295039909367108

McElwee, S. (2018, May 23). The rising racial liberalism of democratic voters. *New York Times.* https://www.nytimes.com/2018/05/23/opinion/democrats-race.html

Metzl, J. M. (2019). *Dying of whiteness: How the politics of racial resentment is killing America's heartland*. Basic Books.

Mier, T. (2023, February 24). Florida bill would allow DeSantis to ban CRT and gender studies from state schools. *Rolling Stone*. https://www.rollingstone.com/politics /politics-news/florida-bill-desantis-ban-crt-gender-studies-1234686704/

Murphy, M. K., & Harris, T. M. (2018). White innocence and Black subservience: The rhetoric of white heroism in *The help*. *Howard Journal of Communications, 29*(1), 49–62. https://doi.org/10.1080/10646175.2017.1327378

Nakayama, T. K., & Krizek, R. L. (1995). Whiteness: A strategic rhetoric. *Quarterly Journal of Speech, 81*(3), 291–309. https://doi.org/10.1080/00335639509384117

Noble, S. U., & Roberts, S. T. (2019). Technological elites, the meritocracy, and postracial myths in Silicon Valley. In R. Mukherjee, S. Banet-Weiser, & H. Gray (Eds.), *Racism postrace* (pp. 113–134). Duke University Press.

Nygaard, T., & Lagerwey, J. (2020). *Horrible white people: Gender, genre, and television's precarious whiteness*. New York University Press.

Ore, E. J. (2021). Conspiring against white pleasures. *Quarterly Journal of Speech, 107*(2), 250–253. https://doi.org/10.1080/00335630.2021.1915458

Reed, T. F. (2018). Between Obama and Coates. *Catalyst, 1*(4). https://catalyst-journal .com/2018/03/between-obama-and-coates

Reeves, R. (2017). Dream hoarders: How the American upper middle class is leaving everyone else in the dust, why that is a problem, and what to do about it. Brookings Institution Press.

Roberts, R. (2020, June 6). *The help* tops Netflix during protests, and Twitter is shaking its head. *Los Angeles Times*. https://www.latimes.com/entertainment-arts/movies/story /2020-06-06/the-help-netflix-twitter-protests

Romano, A. (2020, October 9). A history of "wokeness." *Vox*. https://www.vox.com/culture /21437879/stay-woke-wokeness-history-origin-evolution-controversy

Saltman, K. J. (2018). "Privilege-checking," "virtue-signaling," and "safe spaces": What happens when cultural politics is privatized and the body replaces argument. *Symploke, 26*(1–2), 403–409.

Schnurr, S. (2020, June 3). Logan Paul acknowledges his "white privilege" in passionate speech on racism in America. *Entertainment News*. https://www.eonline.com/news /1158236/logan-paul-acknowledges-his-white-privilege-in-passionate-speech-on -racism-in-america

Serwer, A. (2023, March 21). "Woke" is just another word for liberal. *The Atlantic*. https:// www.theatlantic.com/ideas/archive/2023/03/bethany-mandel-woke-interview -definition/673454/

Squires, C. R. (2014). *The post-racial mystique: Media and race in the twenty-first century*. New York University Press.

Staples, B. (2019, October 12). How Italians became 'white.' *New York Times*. https://www .nytimes.com/interactive/2019/10/12/opinion/columbus-day-italian-american-racism .html

Stolworthy, J. (2019, February 15). Steven Spielberg thinks *Green book* is "best buddy comedy" since *Butch Cassidy and the Sundance Kid*. *Independent*. https://www

.independent.co.uk/arts-entertainment/films/news/steven-spielberg-green-book-butch
-cassidy-sundance-kid-buddy-movie-oscars-2019-a8780511.html

Williams, J. P. (2021, May 25). A year after George Floyd's killing, white allyship fades. *US News and World Report*. https://www.usnews.com/news/national-news/articles/2021
-05-25/a-year-after-george-floyds-killing-white-support-for-black-lives-matter-fades

The Woke Future. (2021, January 6). *Persuasion*. https://www.persuasion.community/p
/the-woke-future

Chapter 4

"THE SONGS THAT UNITE [US]"

White Liberalism and Postracial Promises
in NPR's *American Anthem*

JACLYN S. OLSON

On the Fourth of July, 2018, NPR Music launched a correspondingly patriotic series titled *American Anthem*. Beginning with "Battle Hymn of the Republic" and ending with Frank Sinatra's "My Way," this yearlong series comprised of fifty songs, nominated by listeners, staff, and panelists, that reflect various aspects of American identity. According to executive producer Ellen Silva, this series is both a response and a corrective to contemporary unrest: "During a time of heightened cultural turbulence and conversation, *American Anthem* will explore historical and modern songs that unite, challenge, and celebrate the American people" ("NPR Launches," para. 2). Each song is accompanied by a written feature to delve deeper into its cultural footprint, but by their inclusion in the series, the fifty songs, most of which are notably unpatriotic, are rendered signifiers of American identity. Taken together, the range of songs, artists, and attitudes about America recasts patriotism and national identity across a more complex musical terrain. Thus, in this series, "Dixie," "The Star-Spangled Banner," and "Battle Hymn of the Republic" exist alongside Lady Gaga's "Born This Way," Blink-182's "Adam's Song," Public Enemy's "Fight the Power," Duke Ellington's "Black, Brown, & Beige," and Kendrick Lamar's "Alright." By supplementing, not replacing, the traditional register of American patriotic music with "new" anthems that "unite, challenge, and celebrate the American people," the series offers a bricolage of "American anthems" to mirror the multicultural bricolage of the nation. Though NPR's audience demographic is largely educated, left leaning, affluent, and white, the songs and stories featured in *American Anthem* are mobilized to reflect a nation marked by difference—of race, gender, sexuality, class, and so on (Cwynar, 2016). What unites "the songs that unite us," then, is what S. Ahmed (2004) calls "the promise of cohesion within multiculturalism" (p. 135).

In its attempt to offer a revised, more democratic, and diverse set of national "anthems" NPR Music entered a discursive struggle over the relationship between the United States' national anthem and American identity. In 2017, San Francisco 49ers quarterback Colin Kaepernick drew attention (and ire) for kneeling during the pregame national anthem to protest brutality and systemic racism in the United States. The National Football League's disavowal of Kaepernick during this time stands in stark contrast to the league's decision to play "Lift Ev'ry Voice and Sing" before week-one games during the 2020–2021 season to show solidarity with the Black Lives Matter movement. In response to reports that the Dallas Mavericks had not played the national anthem before any pre- or regular-season games "because many feel the anthem doesn't represent them," the National Basketball Association recently mandated this pregame ritual (Coleman, 2021, para. 8). Most jarring, perhaps, is the video footage from the January 6, 2021, insurrection at the Capitol shows white nationalists and pro-Trump rioters violently gaining access to the building, their "U-S-A" chant mutating into a spirited rendition of "The Star-Spangled Banner." These examples, though disparate and indicative of a range of political commitments, spotlight the anthem as a contested and affectively resonant terrain across which struggles over nation, identity, and power take place.

For this reason, the way *American Anthem* mobilizes the affective economy of the anthem is inextricable from the racialized politics of the national anthem and its relationship to notions of belonging, justice, and equality. I argue that *American Anthem*'s curated collection of songs that uplift and celebrate difference as a harbinger of national unity is a permutation of what C. R. Squires (2014) terms "the postracial mystique": the circulation of media texts that articulate a vision of an "already-achieved multicultural nation," obfuscating inequalities while accentuating (racial) difference as "evidence" of progress (p. 6). *American Anthem*, which launched at the height of Donald Trump's presidential term, "a time of heightened cultural turbulence and conversation," offers an array of songs and stories selected to "unite, challenge, and celebrate" the nation and its citizens as though these songs could facilitate communication across difference in ways that language alone cannot ("NPR Launches," para. 2). Series curator E. Blair (2018) cites S. L. Redmond's work on Black anthems in the African diaspora to spotlight the communicative work of anthems: "Anthems demand something of their listeners" and "stir a certain type of belief in their listeners or their performers" (para. 4). Yet herein lies the obvious postracial problem: by transmuting Black anthems like "Lift Ev'ry Voice and Sing" and "We Shall Overcome"—or other songs that represent racial, cultural, sexual, class, or geographic difference—into an homage to America, *American Anthem* repeats tactics of racial absorption, necessitating the obvious signifiers of Blackness and Otherness to fulfill its own postracial fantasy. Though *American Anthem* appears to produce a revised aesthetic model of an inclusive American identity, its fidelity to tropes of the postracial and/or multicultural nation exceeds appropriation, instead signaling a form of symbolic violence akin to predatory inclusion under neoliberal racial capitalism (McMillan Cottom, 2020). Put differently, this logic assigns value to the aesthetics of difference to revitalize the white nation-state that marginalizes and hierarchizes that very difference in order to retain dominance.

For this reason, I use *American Anthem* to explore the racial logics that reiterate the "anthem" as a signifier of the white neoliberal American nation-state, even in its attempt to embrace and accentuate racial difference as evidence of the overcoming of that division. In what follows, I provide a brief overview of the communicative and aesthetic significance of the anthem in the popular, cultural, and national imaginary in order to provide context for *American Anthem*. Then, I explore how the concept of "postrace" operates rhetorically and affectively within the white American imaginary. Attending to the postracial logics that animate *American Anthem* highlights the racial politics that underlie the diverse soundscape of the multicultural nation offered by *American Anthem*. I conclude by reflecting on the capacities and limitations of the anthem, as an aesthetic form, to offer a substantive critique of the American nation-state. From this, I point toward the inability of the liberal nation to purge itself of the violent regimes of dominance and subordination that sustain it.[1]

NATIONAL SONGS AND THE RHETORICAL
PRODUCTION OF NATIONAL IDENTITY

A national anthem is one of the focal elements of a nation's symbolic imaginary. As discrete rhetorical texts, national songs are resources for the creation, maintenance, and contestation of national identity, accruing meaning through circulation in everyday and often-ritualized performances (Branham, 1996, 1999; Branham & Hartnett, 2002; Koons, 2015). When the national anthem is played in the United States, audiences are often instructed to stand, remove their hats, and sing along in order to performatively enact and actualize the bonds of national love. Yet, as Redmond (2013) writes, the demands of an anthem are more than a prescribed set of physical responses and gestures. Performing or listening to an anthem, unlike other songs, also entails "subscription to a system of beliefs that stir and organize the receivers of the music" (p. 2). Given the ubiquity of patriotic anthems at civic and military ceremonies and sporting events, these songs reaffirm the sovereignty and singularity of the nation, inviting citizens to respond by their performance (Redmond, 2013). In this way, then, national songs are embedded in what L. G. Berlant (1991) terms the "national symbolic," a set of discursive and cultural materials that forge an intimate attachment between citizen and nation (p. 21). The national symbolic habituates individuals to "value certain abstract signs and stories as part of their intrinsic relation to themselves, to all citizens, and to the national terrain" (p. 21). Understood in this way, though national songs are often played in select political, cultural, and ceremonial contexts, their rhetorical and discursive effects also permeate the latent cultural and social imaginary by informing understandings of citizenship, belonging, and national identity.

This configuration of national songs in the United States allows for the line between the nation—an abstracted set of ideals and scripts for belonging to a collectivity—and the state—the formalized mechanisms of institutional power that designate (non)citizenship—to blur, if not dissolve (Butler & Spivak, 2007). Particularly in the United States, national songs are both expressions of patriotism by singers and audiences and rhetorical tools to construct a sense of national identity among citizens. For this reason, national songs, like "America (My Country 'Tis of Thee)," were often used in the civic training and "Americanizing" of children, immigrants, Indigenous people, and so on (Branham, 1999). In addition, particularly in moments of perceived national crises, national songs serve as important mechanisms for unification and self-definition by facilitating the patriotic performances required to produce a sense of stability in the nation (Branham, 1996, 1999). Uplifting the importance of a shared national identity to invigorate a shared national love, the institutionalization and popularization of national songs serve to obscure differences among citizens by "subsuming the many into one" (Branham, 1999, p. 24).

Of course, for those who are *not* invited to partake in the affordances of (white, masculine, heteronormative, legal) citizenship, the homogenizing work performed by anthems is necessarily an act of erasure, if not violence. E. K. Watts (2001) explores the rhetorical limits of participating in sonic affirmations of citizenship, especially for those long denied the affordances of this citizenship. In his revisions to "My Country 'Tis of Thee," W. E. B. Du Bois occasioned rhetorical voice by writing into the song's lyrics the truth of institutional racism, the afterlives of slavery, and the falsity of America's promises for Black Americans; rather than celebrating the idealized nation, these revisions force a public encounter with and acknowledgement of the failures of the nation to live up to its own promises. Yet, in considering subversive Spanish-language performances of the national anthem, J. Butler and G. Spivak (2007) ask, "Is it still an anthem to the nation and can it actually help undo nationalism?" (p. 69). For this reason, efforts to challenge the nation through the promises that inhere in national music alone ought to be closely scrutinized. Describing the racialized violence that inheres in nation-building projects, M. Franz and K. Silva (2020) argue that ethnoracism and nationalism are inseparable ideological structures: "National imaginaries come into being and are enlivened *through* [emphasis original] their imbrication in racializing assemblages. Even if these assemblages change over time (i.e., who is considered white in the United States), they form part of the discursive and institutional fabric that stitches together the national imaginary" (p. 9). Thus, by their investment in the nation-state, patriotic songs are necessarily harnessed to a racializing assemblage comprised of contingent relations of power, subjugation, and biopolitical designations of who belongs to the national body and who does not.

POSTRACE ANTHEMS IN THE SONIC EPISTEME

By looking "beyond obvious patriotic songs" to instead "shine a light on specific communities and subcultures," the implicit assumption that drives *American Anthem* is that more traditional register of patriotic songs—"The Star-Spangled Banner," "My Country 'Tis of Thee," and so on—is inadequate, having become stained by the virulent white nationalism and heated divisions of the Trump era ("NPR Launches," para. 3). In response, *American Anthem* recommends a new look at what constitutes an eponymous American anthem in order to acknowledge the nation's shortcomings, remember that which makes America worth celebrating, and to unite as Americans accordingly. By the editors' own definition, an anthem is "a rousing or uplifting song identified with a particular group, body, or cause"; this intentionally general definition is a marked attempt to play with the formal and aesthetic character of what would normally be considered an anthem in order to wrench it away from overtly patriotic associations (Blair, 2018, para. 2). Thus American anthems need not be *about* America or explicitly praise or take pride in the nation. Instead, these songs ought to "unite us, inspire us, or say something about what it means to be an American" (Blair et al., 2019, para. 1).

Out of this formulation, these "anthems" subvert the obvious signifiers of American patriotism while still drawing on a national anthem's affective resonance to provide a new script for American identity and pride—one that emphasizes the sonic, cultural, and thematic dissonance between these songs, resulting in a list comprised of "songs as traditional as Woody Guthrie's 'This Land Is Your Land,' or as defiant as Public Enemy's 'Fight the Power'" (Blair et al., 2019, para. 1).

On the surface, this "new" assortment of anthems represents and celebrates the American nation based on its complex histories and (racial, sexual, gendered, geographical) differences, challenging the white, masculine patriotism latent in the call to "Make America Great Again." Tapping into anthems' rhetorical and performative energies, as well as specific feelings of unity and pride anthems conjure, *American Anthem* harnesses these affects and redirects them toward songs that instead reflect diversity, protest, celebration, and struggle; perhaps if we listen to these songs as evidence of the nation's rich history, we can remember what makes America *already* great or even begin the work of *truly* making America great again. Even songs like "Dixie" and "God Bless the USA," songs that are rife with varying degrees of racist, reactionary, right-wing connotations, are included and framed as opportunities to explore their complex circulatory movements and contend with the "uglier" side of the nation's history. What results, then, is a collection of fifty songs that trace the aural history of the nation and its citizens; though each song has a unique cultural footprint and various political orientations, taken together, these distinctions dissolve and are subsumed into the series' formulation of "the songs that unite us." "Us," here, refers to *all* Americans.

The transformation of this diverse array of nonpatriotic songs *into* American anthems reflects an investment in the transcendent capacities of music to accomplish that which discourse or legislation cannot: to rehabilitate a divided nation. Yet since "discourses of nation and people are saturated with racial connotation," the racial politics at work in the series, even under the guise of inclusion, requires further scrutiny (Gilroy, 2002, pp. 60–61). For this reason, I situate *American Anthem* in the context of what R. James (2019) calls the "sonic episteme." The sonic episteme, for James, is a framework of assumptions and practices that uphold an idealized version of sound. Operating in the sonic episteme means thinking and theorizing with sound to capture ineffable, affective, and embodied experiences; shed the constraints of the visual or verbal; and liberate us and our work from identity-based hierarchies. Reflecting the commitments of the sonic episteme, *American Anthem* is driven by this idealized concept of sound in its attempt to evade the hierarchized exclusions built into the ideological scaffolding of the nation and create a new sonic register that amplifies multiculturalism. However, as James asserts, the sonic episteme not only fails to subvert regimes of domination and subordination, but actually provides a more flexible, neoliberal vocabulary to enable these regimes through less obvious (and, of course, aural) means. In this way, the sonic episteme mobilizes sound "to pass off reinvestments in dominant institutions (the academy, white supremacy, etc.) as revolutions that overcome them" (p. 17). Thus, while intended as a corrective to exclusions and erasures that inhere in the traditional register of patriotic songs, *American Anthem*'s celebration of inclusion, difference, and recognition instead repeats the rhetorical tropes of the postracial in sonic form.

As Squires (2014) and others[2] write, the election of former President Barack Obama seemed to signal, for many, a postracial era, celebrating the "demise" of race as a barrier to success, if not as a social reality. Of course, the believability of a postracial nation quickly dissolves when held against the rates of poverty and incarceration for Black and Latinx folks, Indigenous genocide, and violent regimes of police brutality and racial profiling that have killed countless unarmed Black men and women (Squires, 2014). Yet these brutal facts are not enough to dissipate faith in the postracial once and for all; neoliberal logics allow these disparities to be dismissed as exceptional, leaving the postracial fantasy intact. Thus attending to the various cultural and discursive forms the postracial may take highlights its serviceability as a distinct racial formation. Put differently, to celebrate the postracial as the achievement of a liberal nation or, conversely, to deny the postracial as a fantastic myth misses the rhetorical and affective work of the postracial in the white American imaginary. According to Watts (2018), "The [postracial] . . . registers a repetitive convulsion in the social body triggered by ruptures or fractures in what Berlant calls the 'sovereign sensorium' of a society, felt as threats to the imaginary and symbolic status of masculine whiteness" (p. 443).

Far from a synonym for racial equality, postracial discourses are more insidiously underwritten by the anxiety of an impending loss of whiteness's significance as a marker of social power. After all, as Watts (2018) writes, "a postracial America is also a post-white America" (p. 443). This threat against whiteness—its devaluation as a signifier of status and sovereignty, its claim to the nation—is what paradoxically invigorates the postracial fantasy as what Watts describes as a site of enjoyment; this discursive trick continues to identify and (violently) manage Black bodies in order to resecure the legitimacy of white masculine sovereignty. In this way, the impossibility of postracial discourses to fully eliminate race and racism from the civic body is, essentially, failure by design. Postracial discourses simultaneously provide the vocabulary to announce (and celebrate) the "end" of race while requiring the repetition of racialized tropes to leverage threats to whiteness.

For this reason, the anti-Black violence that has persisted in spite of the Obama presidency's postracial promise, culminating in and continuing well past the Ferguson uprisings and the election of Donald Trump, poses a different but related threat to the white American imagination. These pivotal and spectacular moments of state-sanctioned violence, white-supremacist rhetoric, and unanswered calls for justice continue to directly threaten the *viability* of the postracial as a coherent mode of discourse that sustains the white neoliberal national imaginary. As a "public" radio institution, imagining an "educated and affluent, White, middle-class baby-boomer core audience" whose "cultural tastes. . . . reflect a cosmopolitan-omnivorous disposition," NPR Music's *American Anthem* series is well positioned to intervene in this national-identity crisis (Cwynar, 2016, p. 6). Refiguring the abstract liberal guarantees of equality, justice, and inclusion for all, the neoliberal nation-state's investment in the postracial enlivens the affective economy of these ideals while the structures that exert control and violence over nonnormative bodies go untouched. When the optics of a fundamentally good, tolerant, and liberal nation start to flicker, enjoyment of the postracial can be "a way to set things right (again)" (Watts, 2017, p. 9). In the section that follows, I posit that the *American Anthem* mitigates "the anxieties of the post-white society," relying on a celebratory multiculturalism to reupholster the fabric of the nation-state according to tropes of inclusion and diversity (Watts, 2017, p. 9).

"UNITING, CHALLENGING, AND CELEBRATING" THE WHITE LIBERAL NATION-STATE

Taking seriously Watts's (2017) claim that the postracial registers affective ruptures in the white social body, then, I argue that *American Anthem* serves as a response to a specific form of white anxiety centered on the fracturing myths of the white liberal nation-state. This anxiety often takes the form of the habitual assurance by political leaders in moments of duress that "this is not who we are": a claim that is feeble at best, ignorant and ahistorical at worst. At the time of this series' launch, the narratives of social and racial progress that white liberal America tells about itself were becoming increasingly unsustainable as a result of intensifying racist violence and a wildly popular, white-nationalist president. By marshaling the rousing affective resonance of the anthem to rehabilitate these narratives, *American Anthem*'s effort to "democratize" national songs performs the classic neoliberal move

of incorporating and valuing identity-based difference as a means of pro-
claiming equality, without attending to the structural and systemic obstacles
that preclude that equality for so many. The idea that music and sound can
transcend the limitations of public discourse and uniquely respond to the
emergency of contemporary racialized political divisions by "uniting, challenging, and celebrating" the American people diverts attention away from
the material effects of institutionalized violence. A mere aesthetic adjustment,
such as a diversified set of national anthems, is enough to remind us who we
are: a nation worth loving, comprised of "universal, liberated (multicultural)
subject(s)" (p. 6).

Thus the logic undergirding *American Anthem* reflects an investment in
the fundamental goodness of the (white) liberal nation-state that requires
that each song is stripped of their specific sociohistorical and political resonance to index multicultural idealism as proof that the nation is worthy of
love; after all, for Ahmed (2004), "love is crucial to the promise of cohesion
within multiculturalism" (p. 135). Multiculturalism sustains the "good" image
the nation has of itself—a nation worth loving—but only insofar as visible
differences can be diluted and incorporated into the nation. The bodies of
immigrants and nonwhite citizens attest to "what the nation can give to others" but only on the condition "that they give up visible signs of their 'difference,'" such as headscarves or native languages (p. 132). Those who fail to fully
assimilate threaten the coherence of the national body and are thus blamed
for the nation's failures to fulfill its promises of the "good life." Moreover, any
form of resistance or outcry by marginalized communities can be dismissed
as a lack of gratitude toward the "good" nation; the nation's love for Others
is merely the liberal nation's love for itself in disguise. For Redmond (2013),
Black anthems—such as "We Shall Overcome," "Lift Ev'ry Voice and Sing," "To
Be Young, Gifted, and Black," and "Fight the Power"—have been so resonant
among Black diasporic political movements because their circulation was
untethered to state or governmental regimes; instead, these songs became
"a sphere of influence to define new culture-political communities in direct
defiance of the regimes erected to contain them" (p. 7). Though they stand in
opposition to the white American nation-state, these songs are evacuated of
their political specificity by their inclusion in this series in order to serve as
a tribute to America: a gesture that not only reifies the multicultural liberal
nation-state but repeats the erasure it purports to ameliorate.

American Anthem's appropriation of Black anthems not only affirms the
inadequacy of recognition as a liberal corrective to histories of marginalization and exclusion but also showcases the ease with which the anthem as
an aesthetic object lends themselves to the maintenance of the postracial

fantasy. Relying on Black anthems to unite *all* Americans and speak to the experiences of *all* Americans neutralizes the song's revolutionary function for the communities about and by whom they were written. Moreover, projecting Americanness onto these songs guarantees that *all* Americans have a claim to identification with them despite their particularity and historical location in Black political formations, "demonstrating that identification has become the politics of the postracial" (Redmond, 2016, p. 38). Sonic histories of racial identity formation and resistance, which would otherwise destabilize the optics of liberal progress, are here offered as evidence of the nation's multicultural character and postracial achievements. While postracialism often relies on the visual signifiers of Blackness—or an emphasis that "we do not see race any more"—*American Anthem* provides a way to recuperate the postracial narrative through aural, sonic, and affective means (Cobb, 2011). Further, as J. K. Puar (2017) notes, white liberalism is "not a conservative, racist formation bent on extermination, but an insidious liberal one proffering an innocuous inclusion into life" (p. 31). Thus what appears to be a corrective to histories of exclusion actually functions as symbolic violence that uproots and appropriates Black histories in order to frame the nation as a liberal space of diversity and inclusion. This maneuver soothes the injury to the postracial "progress" narrative such that the nation-state can sonically and musically reinvest in the enjoyment of the postracial without calling into question the white supremacy on which the nation was built.

A case study of *American Anthem* sheds light on how the idea of the anthem is routinely deployed to announce and secure the neoliberal American nation-state—a security that requires multicultural and racial difference in order to perform tolerance and evade meaningful structural change. Here, the rhetoric of postrace does not signal a raceless society or one free from the constraints of racism. Instead, postracial fantasies ensure the durability of the white social body by enacting the liberal narratives of equality and progress while leaving intact racist regimes of dominance and subjugation. James (2019) writes, "a society already organized by centuries of systemic domination doesn't fix that domination; it updates and intensifies it" (p. 27). If the patriotism of old has become gauche or too closely aligned with right-wing conservativism, a postracial patriotism must aesthetically reinvent itself to celebrate multiculturalism in a way that preserves whiteness; following Watts (2017), Blackness must be made "to appear and disappear over and over again" and be stripped of its power in order for the postracial fantasy to thrive (p. 11). The anthem, as an aesthetic form, allows these logics to remain hidden; the sonic episteme enacts the same neoliberal structure of relation, only shifted from the realm of the visual to the aural and sonic (James, 2019). The national anthem's capacity to stimulate the affective economies of nation and identity makes it appear to be a promising way to bridge divides and make progress sound and *feel* immediate while necessarily foreclosing the radical possibilities it purports to offer. Celebrating the nation's alleged postracial, multicultural achievement not only intensifies violence and erasure against nonwhite bodies but *serves to bolster white patriarchal investments in the American nation-state*, ensuring its continuance. Though aimed at inclusion and restoring complexity to what comprises a national anthem, *American Anthem* fundamentally disables the question of whether or not the American nation-state itself is able to be remediated.

CONCLUSION

In light of recent struggles over national self-definition and calls for unity, liberals and conservatives alike have invoked the anthem as a metonym for the American people and its values; *American Anthem* is one instance of many. Unlike right-wing state and cultural actors that regard national songs as a metonym for more virulent forms of patriotism, this series evinces a discursive trend in the United States for those on the left to invoke the anthem as a corrective to what's ambiguously termed "division." For example, the climactic moment in President Joseph Biden's inaugural address was his recitation of a verse from Gene Scheer's "American Anthem," a song characterized by, according to Scheer, "a sense of yearning to be a part of not just our own personal stories, but the American Story" (Kaufman, 2021, para. 6). This moment resonated with Jennifer Lopez's performance of "This Land Is Your Land" and "America, the Beautiful," interpolated with Spanish-spoken lines from the Pledge of Allegiance and her 1999 hit "Let's Get Loud," a performance which reflected the more tolerant, equitable, and just America implicitly promised by the incoming Biden-Harris administration. Even Garth Brooks's performance of "Amazing Grace" concluded with a request for viewers across the nation to join him in singing the last verse as "one nation, united." These invocations of unity through sound and music serve an explicitly rehabilitative function; amidst the political discontent following a hotly contested election and the January 6 insurrection, these reminders of our shared national identity seem to be designed to dissipate that which divides us and soothe a wounded nation. This political spectacle showcases the serviceability of music and song to negotiate and refigure the contours of American identity, particularly in the context of racial and political unrest.

The critique I offer here extends beyond one NPR Music series and toward the uncritical use of the anthem as a nationalizing aesthetic object. Anthems are dense rhetorical signifiers of the nation that call listeners to action, to perform and enact a system of shared values and political commitments. In many ways, progressive interventions into national identity that occur at the level of the anthem is an attempt to move beyond the nation as we know it and imagine one anew. Yet, I argue, what makes the anthem such an appealing terrain for staging a reconfiguration of national identity is precisely what makes it so fraught. In her critique of posthumanism, T. L. King (2017) reminds readers that the category of the human subject in Western philosophical traditions is premised on violence; white subjects can only actualize *as* human subjects through Black and Native subjugation. Rather than "successfully offering a way around and beyond the entrapments of liberal humanism," to decenter the human subject only serves to obscure the "bloody trail of white/human-self-actualization" that liberal humanism leaves in its wake (p. 178). King's (2017) critique here serves as a reminder that, while anthems appear to be a powerful tool for the (re)organization of national identity, the racialized dynamics of nation building and US white supremacy are hardly elided by nominal liberal correctives like *American Anthem*, only given a minor aesthetic adjustment.

In this way, *American Anthem* necessarily falls short of its progressive aims. Following King's argument, there would be no properly *American* anthem that extends the promises of the liberal nation to those previously excluded because the ideological foundation of the nation as we know it is premised on the exclusion and subjugation of Black and brown citizens. By merely reminding us that we are all Americans, *American Anthem* retells the narratives of liberalism that "take liberties with the histories and present of power and manifest themselves not as solidarities but as violent displacements" (Redmond, 2016, p. 19). Thus the songs that unite "us" do so by erasing and displacing those already subjected to institutionalized racist state violence. Without challenging the systems of power that structure liberal citizenship or interrupting the anthem as a nationalizing aesthetic form, the anthem continues to uplift and sing the white nation-state—an old patriotism in a new key—in perpetuity.

NOTES

1. Here, I follow L. Lowe's (2015) approach to modern liberalism as "political emancipation through citizenship in the state, the promise of economic freedom in the

development of wage labor and exchange markets, and the conferring of civilization to human persons educated in aesthetic and national culture," all of which serve to unify "particularity, difference, or locality through universal concepts of reason and community" (p. 4).

2. See Squires et al. (2010); Watts (2017); J. N. Cobb (2011); R. Mukherjee et al. (2019).

REFERENCES

Ahmed, S. (2004). *The cultural politics of emotion*. Routledge.

Berlant, L. G. (1991). *The anatomy of national fantasy: Hawthorne, utopia, and everyday life*. University of Chicago Press.

Blair, E. (2018, May 28). What's your American anthem? *NPR*. https://www.npr.org/2018 /05/28/614114943/whats-your-american-anthem

Blair, E., Cole, T., Boilen, B., & Hilton, R. (2019, 2 July). The songs that define us, from NPR's *American anthem* series. *NPR*. https://www.npr.org/sections/allsongs/2019 /07/02/737639126/the-songs-that-define-us-from-nprs-american-anthem-series

Branham, R. J. (1996). "Of thee I sing": Contesting "America." *American Quarterly*, 48(4), 623–652.

Branham, R. J. (1999). "God save the _____!" American national songs and national identities, 1760–1798. *Quarterly Journal of Speech*, 85(1), 17–37. https://doi.org/10.1080 /00335639909384239

Branham, R. J., & Hartnett, S. J. (2002). *Sweet freedom's song: "My country 'tis of thee" and democracy in America*. Oxford University Press.

Butler, J., & Spivak, G. C. (2007). *Who sings the nation-state? Language, politics, belonging*. Seagull Books.

Cobb, J. N. (2011). No We Can't! Postracialism and the Popular Appearance of a Rhetorical Fiction. *Communication Studies*, 62(4), 406–421. https://doi.org/10.1080/10510974 .2011.588075

Coleman, M. (2021, February 10). NBA says all teams will play the national anthem at games. *Sports Illustrated*. https://www.si.com/nba/2021/02/10/nba-national-anthem-policy -all-teams-must-play-song-mavericks

Cwynar, C. (2016). NPR Music: Remediation, curation, and National Public Radio in the digital convergence era. *Media, Culture & Society*, 1–17. Retrieved December 5, 2023, from https://www.academia.edu/29646090/NPR_Music_Remediation_curation_and _National_Public_Radio_in_the_digital_convergence_era

Franz, M., & Silva, K. (2020). Introduction: Theorizing belonging against and beyond imagined communities. In M. Franz & K. Silva (Eds.), *Migration, identity, and belonging: Defining borders and boundaries of the homeland* (pp. 1–27). Routledge.

Gilroy, P. (2002). "There ain't no black in the union jack": The cultural politics of race and nation. Routledge Classics.

James, R. (2019). *The sonic episteme: Acoustic resonance, neoliberalism, and biopolitics*. Duke University Press.

Kaufman, G. (2021, January 20). President Joe Biden quotes stirring song "American anthem" during inauguration address. *Billboard*. https://www.billboard.com/articles /news/politics/9513788/joe-biden-quotes-american-anthem-song-inauguration -address/

King, T. L. (2017). Humans involved: Lurking in the lines of posthumanist flight. *Critical Ethnic Studies, 3*(1), 162–185. https://doi.org/10.5749/jcritethnstud.3.1.0162

Koons, C. C. (2015). The rhetorical legacy of "The battle hymn of the republic." *Southern Communication Journal, 80*(3), 211–229. https://doi.org/10.1080/1041794X.2015.1030085

Lowe, L. (2015). *The intimacies of four continents*. Duke University Press.

McMillan Cottom, T. (2020). Where platform capitalism and racial capitalism meet: The sociology of race and racism in the digital society. *Sociology of Race and Ethnicity, 6*(4), 441–449. https://doi.org/10.1177/2332649220949473

Mukherjee, R., Banet-Weiser, S., & Gray, H. (Eds.). (2019). *Racism postrace*. Duke University Press.

NPR launches *American anthem* series. (2018, July 4). *NPR*. https://www.npr.org/about -npr/625782846/npr-launches-american-anthem-series

Puar, J. K. (2017). *Terrorist assemblages: Homonationalism in queer times* (2nd ed.). Duke University Press.

Redmond, S. L. (2013). *Anthem: Social movements and the sound of solidarity in the African diaspora*. New York University Press.

Redmond, S. L. (2016). "As though it were our own": Against a politics of identification. In N. Elia, D. M. Hernández, J. Kim, S. L. Redmond, D. Rodríguez, & S. E. See (Eds.), *Critical ethnic studies* (pp. 19–42). Duke University Press. https://doi.org/10.1215 /9780822374367-002

Squires, C. R. (2014). *The post-racial mystique: Media and race in the twenty-first century*. New York University Press.

Squires, C., Watts, E. K., Vavrus, M. D., Ono, K. A., Feyh, K., Calafell, B. M., & Brouwer, D. C. (2010). What is this "post-" in postracial, postfeminist . . . (fill in the blank)? *Journal of Communication Inquiry, 34*(3), 210–253. https://doi.org/10.1177/0196859910371375

Watts, E. K. (2001). "Voice" and "voicelessness" in rhetorical studies. *Quarterly Journal of Speech, 87*(2), 179–196. https://doi.org/10.1080/00335630109384328

Watts, E. K. (2017). Postracial fantasies, Blackness, and zombies [Electronic version]. *Communication and Critical/Cultural Studies, 14*(4), 17 pp. https://doi.org/10.1080/1479142 0.2017.1338742

Watts, E. K. (2018). "Zombies are real": Fantasies, conspiracies, and the post-truth wars. *Philosophy & Rhetoric, 51*(4), 441–470. https://muse.jhu.edu/article/711673

Chapter 5

EXCAVATING THE RUINS OF TULSA'S GREENWOOD DISTRICT

Lovecraft Country and the Epistemic Violence of Postracial Trauma

BYRON B CRAIG, STEPHEN E. RAHKO, AND J. SCOTT JORDAN

On June 10, 2020, amidst the COVID-19 pandemic and historic protests for racial justice following the murder of George Floyd, President Donald Trump announced that he would restart his 2020 campaign rallies on Juneteenth in Tulsa, Oklahoma. The announcement, which came merely days after Trump had urged governors to "dominate the streets" and threatened to deploy the military to quell nationwide Black Lives Matter (BLM) protests, was immediately received with derision (Conant, 2020). Critics pointed out that the president—who courted the alt-right, praised "both sides" after Charlottesville, and directed law enforcement to use tear gas and riot-control tactics to clear peaceful BLM protestors from Washington, DC's Lafayette Square for a photo op at St. Johns Church—was using Juneteenth and the violent legacy of the Red Summer as a dog whistle to gin up enthusiasm among his mostly white electoral base (Karni et al., 2020).

Trump's controversial Tulsa rally became a flash point during the summer of 2020, a summer that reignited a deeper and more uncomfortable question: What does America owe to its victims of racial violence? The question has been posed for decades by Black scholars and activists, perhaps best typified by R. Robinson's (2000) *The Debt*, but it forcefully reentered American public discourse with the publication of T.-N. Coates's "The Case for Reparations" (2014), which appeared only two months before the Ferguson uprisings in August 2014. During the Trump administration, the renewal of debates around reparations and the legacy of racial violence condensed around the Tulsa Race Massacre of 1921. Indeed, Human Rights Watch issued a report calling for reparations for the victims of the massacre just weeks before Trump's Tulsa rally (Brown, 2020). The Tulsa Race Massacre of 1921 is emblematic of the violent racial history of American capitalism, an event in which white mobs destroyed Black capital when they pillaged Tulsa's Greenwood District, a thriving center of Black wealth and economic development popularly described as "Black Wall Street."

The massacre's legacy of political trauma has been the subject of numerous references in recent American popular culture, namely HBO's popular television series *Watchmen* (2019) and *Lovecraft Country* (2020), each of which made the massacre a seminal part of its plot and helped spur public momentum for reparations. To be sure, in September 2020, the three living survivors of the massacre filed a lawsuit against the city of Tulsa and Tulsa County seeking reparations, but a judge dismissed the case in July 2023 (Romero, 2023). Despite this setback, HR 40, a bill that would create a commission to study reparations from 1619 to the present, was voted out of the House Judiciary Committee in April 2021 for the first time since the legislation was first introduced by the late John Conyers in 1989. Even in the absence of reparations for survivors of the Tulsa Race Massacre, much less a federal plan for reparations, several states and municipalities have convened their own commissions (Moore, 2023). The fate of HR 40 remains uncertain, and it is unclear if its passage would even begin to meaningfully redress the debt America owes to the victims of anti-Black racial violence. Yet the growing public and congressional support for reparations is a unique development in our current post-Ferguson period since it marks the enduring legacy of racial violence as an organizing symbolic force capable of constituting fugitive counterpublics in an era that seeks to claim race no longer matters. Indeed, as we will seek to demonstrate below, claims to trauma are never neutral.

In this chapter, we advance an analysis of HBO's *Lovecraft Country* to map its popular dramatization of the cultural trauma of racialized violence. We argue that the series' depiction of the Tulsa Race Massacre represents a discursive response to the phrase "All Lives Matter," a slogan that has been circulating as a conservative counterpoint to BLM since 2014. As we outline below, we understand the phrase "All Lives Matter" to be emblematic of what we shall call a "postracial discourse of trauma," a popular rhetoric of race that strategically seeks to undermine race-specific claims to historical and systemic injustices. We begin by first reviewing recent work about race trauma from within the interdisciplinary field of trauma studies. We then critique "All Lives Matter" as a "postracial discourse of trauma." Finally, we advance an analysis of *Lovecraft Country* to demonstrate how it disrupts America's postracial political condition.

"ALL LIVES MATTER," AGGRIEVED WHITENESS,
AND THE RHETORIC OF POSTRACIAL TRAUMA

Once the province of the psychological sciences, "trauma" has become an important keyword in the theoretical humanities and a rigorous site of inter-disciplinary inquiry and critique. In the past decade, scholars from across the humanities have invigorated cultural and philosophical reflections on the topic, particularly regarding matters of race. "Trauma" refers to forms of psychic wounding or damage incurred by the subject that take affective, cor-poreal, and temporal dimensions. Trauma can be experienced both psycho-logically—that is, an event of significant emotional anguish that overwhelms and fragments the ego's capacity to maintain a sense of minimal safety and psychic cohesion—and culturally, which involves a symbolic breach in col-lectively and socially shared forms of identity and meaning (Caruth, 1996; Cooper, 1986; Eyerman, 2002).

On the question of "race trauma," theories of cultural trauma offer a par-ticularly robust conceptual site of interdisciplinary convergence for rhetori-cal critics, psychologists, social theorists, and philosophers committed to a critical project of racial critique (Flores, 2016; Lacy & Ono, 2011; Salter & Adams, 2013). Racialized trauma, we posit, is a cultural form of trauma that is symbolically mediated through the sociality of language. "To conceptualize trauma within the context of a shared *symbolic world* [emphasis original]" (p. 143), notes G. Yancy (2018), is to presuppose a "reality of being embodied with others" and a "reality of being exposed," where "bodies have no edges" and where "the body does not terminate at some fictive corporeal edge" (p. 142). The materiality of trauma "begins within the socio-historical space of the precarious, a condition in which all of us are exposed to vulnerability" (p. 143). Yet in a socio-symbolic order marked by racialized difference and enmity, particularly anti-Blackness, "one experiences both the precarious and a racialized precarity" that "denotes forms of racialized instability with deep implications for one's social and existential welfare" (p. 144). Racial-ized trauma is predicated relationally through our shared coexistence with others, but such trauma, as R. Eyerman (2002) argues, "need not necessarily be felt by everyone in a community or experienced directly by any or all" (p. 2). "While it may be necessary to establish some event as the significant 'cause,'" he notes, "its traumatic meaning must be established and accepted, a process which requires time, as well as mediation and representation" (p. 2).

Scholars from across the humanities have produced an impressive range of studies that have theorized and documented the complexities of race trauma across a variety of cultural contexts and registers. This includes the traumatic impact of the white gaze (Yancy, 2018) and representations of trauma in popular film (Sisco King, 2011), as well as the meaning and mediation of trauma through public memorials and performances, art, and cultural practices (Owen & Ehrenhaus, 2014; Sturken, 2007; Wieskamp & Smith, 2020). Moreover, thanks to the powerful public advocacy for racial justice from Indigenous peoples, Black Lives Matter, and the immigrant-rights movement over the past decade, race trauma has become a popular topic in both American politics and public discourse. The social and racial turbulence of 2020 that stemmed from the COVID-19 pandemic and the lynchings of George Floyd and Breonna Taylor surely supplies more than enough evidence in this regard.[1]

Since the Great Recession (2007–2009), however, the public and political discourse of race trauma has also been noticeably informed and reframed by whiteness. A discursive shift in the rhetoric of race trauma began when researchers and journalists started to discover and emphasize the scale and severity of *white* precarity in the United States amidst a slow economic recovery. To be sure, since the 1980s, the Left in the United States—by which we mean labor, immigrant-rights, and anti-war activists, democratic socialists, Marxists, anarchists, and radical environmentalists, feminists, and queer activists—has made the social trauma associated with the intense precarity and inequality made possible by neoliberal statecraft a focal point of political critique. The zenith of leftist opposition came with the abrupt cancelation of the WTO Ministerial Conference of 1999—which came to be called thereafter the "Battle of Seattle"—when leftist activists, protestors, and scholars successfully organized what at the time was the largest antiglobalization protest in the history of late capitalism. Despite years of protests and academic studies, the leftist critique of neoliberal precarity was ignored and often derisively mocked by the mainstream media and other institutional agents of the political culture in the United States.

Sadly, it took the misery of the Great Recession among *white* households for mainstream American media, think tanks, and other influential cultural actors to begin to seriously pay attention to the social crises crushing the American working class and downwardly mobile members of the middle class left behind by deindustrialization, downsizing, automation, and the rapid expansion of the platform-based gig economy (Rahko & Craig, 2021). The trauma of white precarity has come to be summarized by the trendy nomenclature "deaths of despair," a phrase first coined in 2015 by Princeton economists A. Case and A. Deaton (2015) to describe the sharp rise in deaths by suicide, drugs and alcohol, poisoning, and chronic liver disease among middle-aged whites without a college degree.

At first, white "deaths of despair" were often rhetorically explained through narratives of cultural dysfunction. Between 2012 and 2016, for example, influential conservative-thought leaders, such as Charles Murray and J. D. Vance, liberal-thought leaders, such as Robert Putnam and the popular conservative weekly *National Review*, began turning to long-standing cultural and biological explanations once reserved for Black, Hispanic, and Indigenous poverty to explain the growing downward mobility of impoverished whites (Hosang & Lowndes, 2019, pp. 58–64). Vance's (2016) best-selling memoir, *Hillbilly Elegy: A Memoir of Family and Culture in Crisis*, which blamed white precarity on social pathologies stemming from welfare dependency, was particularly forceful in popularizing the narrative of white cultural dysfunction in mainstream American culture. Cultural explanations for downwardly mobile whites serve to discursively indemnify the role neoliberal statecraft has played in structuring sociopolitical arrangements that drive inequality. Issues such as the loss of collective bargaining, austerity-driven assaults on the social safety net, the financialization of the US economy, and the plethora of forms of financial predation and plunder that underwrote the 2008 financial crisis were summarily dismissed and ignored by this ideologically potent narrative (Rahko, 2011).

By 2016, the trauma of white precarity had become a salient topic in American public life and found a new expression in the populist presidential candidacies of Senator Bernie Sanders and reality television star Donald Trump. Dismissed early on as an illegitimate spoiler for Hillary Clinton's historic presidential bid, Sanders campaigned on a populist, progressive agenda that sought to build a durable multiracial and multigenerational coalition across communities whose livelihoods had been destroyed by neoliberal statecraft and the Great Recession. Trump, in contrast, took a much darker approach. If much of mainstream political culture prior to 2016 had largely dismissed the victims of white precarity as a new pathological genetic subset of whiteness proper, Trump offered status-anxious white Americans a powerful narrative of victimization and grievance that sought to stroke, justify, and channel their frustrations and anger toward the racial Other, be it nonwhite immigrants, Mexicans, Muslims, or Black people (Mutz, 2018).

In *Apocalypse Man: The Death Drive and the Rhetoric of White Masculine Victimhood*, C. R. Kelly (2020) brilliantly outlines how Trump's rhetoric seized on tropes of white victimization and marginalization to articulate suffering as a precondition for political subjectivity. His popular 2016 campaign slogan, "Make America Great Again," illustrates the extent to which aggrieved whiteness, particularly white masculinity, has become symbolically organized around melancholic investments in an imagined past marked by preeminence and domination or what Trump colloquially calls "winning." Trump's rhetoric summons an American subject who understands themselves in opposition to cultural pluralism and racial equality and implores them to define their identity in terms of suffering and persecution. "Trump's subject," Kelly observes, "is owed something that was taken from them by racial Others: jobs, respect, prosperity, safety, freedom, and community without the threat of difference" (p. 133).

It was within this cultural milieu that the phrase "All Lives Matter" emerged and gathered popular resonance, especially among white conservatives. First appearing in the wake of the 2014 Ferguson uprisings, the phrase quickly circulated as a conservative rejoinder to "Black Lives Matter." Trump, who has frequently accused the Black Lives Matter movement of being a symbol of hate, first began using the phrase in early 2016 (Swan, 2016). The phrase has since become a mainstay of conservative opposition to public claims of racial suffering, appearing on signs, in chants, and throughout the conservative mediascape during the Trump years and especially during the George Floyd protests of 2020. But, to paraphrase H. Gray (2019), what makes the phrase "All Lives Matter" possible, and what does the phrase itself make possible (p. 24)?

We understand the phrase "All Lives Matter" to be emblematic of what we shall call a "postracial discourse of trauma," a popular rhetoric of (white) race trauma that strategically seeks to undermine race-specific claims to historical and systemic injustices. Like other universal formulations, "All Lives Matter" establishes an exclusionary norm of postracial solidarity that rules out in advance the possibility of race-specific claims to suffering and trauma, which disrupt the borders of the "postracial" itself. The phrase, in effect, offers a response to the specificity of race trauma—be it Black trauma or otherwise—by proposing that we universalize trauma and suffering while negating the specificity of racial grieving.

The formulation signifies a conservative white identity that imagines itself as uniquely traumatized and under siege in the face of a new multicultural reality marked by the decentering of so-called "Western" values and the impending demographic eclipse of whiteness itself. The phrase "All Lives Matter" reflects C. A. Young's (2019) observation that "postraciality is supposed to signify the end of race-thinking, [but] in practice it means the rise of an explicitly white racial consciousness" (p. 87). According to this worldview, Young continues, "it is actually white people who are most disadvantaged precisely because they allegedly do not make identity-based claims on the state in the way that racial and ethnic minorities do" (p. 87).

Indeed, "All Lives Matter" is a raceless abstraction for talking about race trauma that is ironically racialized by whiteness and where the rhetorical labor of the "postracial" serves to frame white-grievance politics. Leveraging metonym as its master trope, the phrase, as B. Biesecker (2017) describes it, is a "cunning rhetoric of democratic indifference" (p. 420) that advocates "on behalf of a respectability politics" (p. 412), which renders "vital *but otherwise unqualified* [emphasis original] human life" (p. 418) unworthy of grieving and public mourning. The public performance of grieving and mourning is instead reserved for the victims of traumatic developments considered worthy of recognition by the white conservative narrative of grievance, including Black and undocumented immigrant criminality (i.e., looting, gang violence), Muslim terrorism, the rural opioid crisis, or so-called "cancel culture" and "political correctness."

"All Lives Matter" reveals how whiteness strategically adopts its own hermeneutics of *racial* suspicion vis-à-vis other races to protect its privileged gaze. Surely, the cultural status of whiteness relies on claims to biological and moral supremacy relative to other races or peoples on matters of intelligence, art, or taste, but this is not all for it must also maintain its cultural position by negating or denying the legitimacy of claims to sympathy, suffering, and trauma by the racial Other as well. Whiteness balances its supreme identity position by simultaneously dramatizing itself as both heroic and tragic, as both superior and most worthy of sympathy. It must monopolize sympathy and empathy for itself while declaring that similar claims by the racial Other are made in bad faith.

Accordingly, the phrase "All Lives Matter" diverts one's attention away from the very real toil, struggle, suffering, and trauma entailed in the cultural infrastructure that generates a perch for privilege in the first place, while simultaneously bestowing reverence, benevolence, and moral stature to those who participate in this collective, hegemonic act of ignoring. The discursive practice of directing one's privileged gaze "elsewhere" in ways that simultaneously imbue one with a sense of moral righteousness illustrates how "All Lives Matter" performs the psychological labor of identity saving for whiteness in an era when its legitimacy and longevity is under threat. The phrase illustrates how whiteness's reconstitution through a Trumpian rhetoric of grievance opens performative space for the privileging of its own vulnerability over that of others and where whiteness refuses to recognize the vulnerability and structural precarity of the victims of its own history of racialized violence. In this way, "All Lives Matter" also enacts a form of epistemic violence that directly challenges claims to race trauma by the racial Other in ways that allow the hegemonic adherent to experience the act of negation as moral. It negates what psychologists, particularly those working from the phenomenological tradition, have called the "ruins" of racial trauma (Trigg, 2009).

Representation, however, offers a site for negotiating the memory of America's history of racial violence and racial trauma. Following A. S. Owen and P. Ehrenhaus (2014), we ask: How do popular representations open possibilities for engaging the legacies of racial violence that are foreclosed by other discursive and social practices (p. 72)? In what follows, we shall argue that the HBO series *Lovecraft Country* (2020) confronts the hubris of "All Lives Matter" by allegorically situating the violence of the Trump era as a direct lineage from Jim Crow white-on-Black violence. *Lovecraft Country* offers a timely representation of the history of the racial trauma of Blackness in the United States. It embodies a form of counter storytelling that responds to the epistemic violence of postracial universalisms, such as "All Lives Matter" (Salter & Adams, 2013). The series offers a rhetorically compelling representation of the ruins of Blackness in a country culturally and politically constituted by a history of anti-Black racial violence.[2] To be sure, the traumatic violence depicted in this series allegorically illustrates, by the generic means of Gothic horror, the various material and rhetorical performances that form what E. J. Ore (2019) astutely calls the "constitutive relationship between democracy and antiblack violence" (p. 26).

REPRESENTING THE RUINS OF BLACKNESS: *LOVECRAFT COUNTRY*, RACIAL VIOLENCE, AND THE HISTORICAL ECHOES OF WHITE SUPREMACY IN THE UNITED STATES

Lovecraft Country (2020) is a Gothic horror series developed by Misha Green for HBO that is based on Matt Ruff's 2016 novel of the same name. The series follows Korean War veteran Atticus "Tic" Freeman, his childhood friend Letitia "Leti" Lewis, his loving Uncle George, and his father, Montrose, as they travel across 1950s Jim Crow America. Over the course of their journey, they encounter not only the horrors of supernatural monsters but, more pointedly, the horrors of whiteness and American capitalism. Airing during the final months of the Trump administration, the series can be understood allegorically as a commentary on the historical lineage from Trump's racial politics to Jim Crow and the legacy of slavery in a way that disrupts (white) America's affective investment in the fantasy that race either never mattered or no longer structures everyday life.

In the pilot episode, "Sundown," for example, the protagonists travel to Ardham, Massachusetts, and find themselves attacked by white mobs. They eventually escape to find themselves at the lodge-sized home of Samuel Braithwaite, a descendant of Titus Braithwaite, who made his fortune in the shipping industry during the slave trade. Samuel is the leader of an occult order of white men known as the Sons of Adam who plan to sacrifice Tic during a ritual devised to take them to the Garden of Eden and grant them eternal life. They need Tic's blood for the ritual because he, too, is a descendent of Titus Braithwaite through the bloodline of Tic's runaway slave ancestor, Hannah. During the ritual, Samuel is able to open an interdimensional portal, but something goes wrong, and he and all the other Sons of Adam are incinerated. The Braithwaite family's slave-based wealth, narratively coupled with Samuel's aspiration to sacrifice Tic's Black blood for his own immortality, allegorically reflects how historically dependent the sustenance of whiteness and America's continental capitalist system has been on violence against Black bodies.

Throughout its ten episodes, *Lovecraft Country* depicts a panoply of racial horrors that comprise the historical Black experience in America, including mob violence, torture, kidnappings, Tuskegee-inspired medical experiments, and Klan-inspired cross burnings. As the Black protagonists encounter these violent events, the series offers an all-too-rare example of narrative empathy for the victims of racialized violence and thus reveals the very real fears and trauma African Americans have historically experienced. *Lovecraft Country*, with its focus on the trauma of *actual* historical racial violence, offers a response to and reprieve from the ambience of speculative and ahistorical trauma captured by the postracial universal "All Lives Matter." Indeed, *Lovecraft Country*'s depiction of racial violence and trauma does not aesthetically fetishize it; instead, the series allows its audience to contextualize the complex manifestations of structural racial inequality and the lived traumatic pain of anti-Blackness generated by it, which the phrase "All Lives Matter" seeks to negate and obfuscate. The best example of this comes in episode 9, "Rewind, 1921," which visually and dramatically depicts the Tulsa Race Massacre of 1921.

The Tulsa Race Massacre was one of many violent episodes of white-supremacist terrorism that pillaged Black communities across the United States between 1919 and 1921. During the Jim Crow era, African Americans were not allowed to purchase commodities or services in predominantly white areas, which forced Black communities to adopt a posture of self-sufficiency and self-reliance to survive. In 1906, O. W. Gurley, a wealthy Black landowner from Arkansas, purchased forty parcels of land he planned to divide into lots to sell exclusively to Black buyers. His forty parcels became the basis for the Greenwood District. Covering thirty-five city blocks, the Greenwood District became prosperous and economically self-sufficient and home to Black professionals, entrepreneurs, and upscale hospitality, eventually earning the nickname "Black Wall Street." In 1921, however, the Greenwood District was burned to the ground by white violence, leaving hundreds of Black citizens murdered and countless homeless (Johnson, 1998).

Lovecraft Country weaves the Tulsa Race Massacre into its narrative through a key plotline around *The Book of Names*. In the HBO series, this is a book of spells that involve the creation and transformation of life. It was found by Titus Braithwhite and used in a ritual meant to grant him immortality. As was the case for his descendent Samuel Braithwhite, the ritual failed and left everyone present dead except Tic's ancestor Hannah, who, pregnant with Titus's child, escapes the burning building carrying *The Book of Names*. Since *The Book of Names* is about lived life, it serves as ongoing testimony to the hopes and trauma of Tic's ancestors.

In "Rewind, 1921," the protagonists, with the help of their friend Hippolyta, use an interdimensional time machine to travel back to Tulsa, Oklahoma, on May 31, 1921—the beginning day of the Tulsa Race Massacre—to retrieve *The Book of Names* from Tic's maternal great-grandmother Hattie in order to save Tic's niece Diana ("Dee") from an evil spell. It is clear from the moment the characters conceive of traveling back to Tulsa that the massacre diegetically represents a distinctively dark incident of horror within the series. To be sure, the writers of the episode place Tic, Leti, and Montrose in the Stradford Hotel, the site that set off the massacre after an African American elevator operator was accused of making improper physical and sexual advances toward a young white woman, an allegation that was never proven. Montrose, who survived the Tulsa Race Massacre and clearly suffers from posttraumatic stress stemming from it, is reluctant to travel back in time to experience it a second time and has painful flashbacks throughout the episode that clearly illustrate, in dramatic terms, the legacy of violence on the Black psyche. Indeed, we see Montrose frequently remind us of the impact the massacre has had on his life.

Throughout the episode, the protagonists both witness and flee violent white mobs attacking Black citizens and firebombing the Greenwood District. Two scenes stand out as exemplary representations of the ruins of Blackness at the hands of white violence. In one scene, we witness Montrose and Tic making their way through Tulsa when they happen upon the younger version of Montrose from 1921, who is having a conversation with his boyhood love, Thomas. Later in the episode, we see Thomas murdered by a white mob, which Tic witnesses for the first time and Montrose traumatically reexperiences once more.

By creating a scene in which present, older Montrose is with his son, Tic, as they both witness a truly traumatizing event in Montrose's early life, *Lovecraft Country* challenges the hubris of contemporary claims to postracial trauma stemming from Trumpian-motivated white grievance. The testimony to the legacy of racial violence provided by this scene defies description in linear time. *Lovecraft Country* imbues in the viewer a feeling of unbridgeable void between the viewer's absolute "here" and "now," Montrose's and Tic's "here" and "now" and the "then" and "there" of Montrose's suffering. The experience, the phenomenology of the trauma, spans across times and generations and creates a space that affords Montrose and Tic, as well as the viewer, a means of experiencing the traumas of the past in terms of the tumultuous racial politics of the Trump era, especially the turbulence experienced during 2020 in which the episode aired. Yet in representing violence in this way, *Lovecraft Country* simultaneously invites the audience to make the history of American racial violence productive, to take the so-called "reckoning" America experienced during 2020 seriously, and to imagine the possibility of a new future that aspires for a more just racial politics rather than a disavowal of race itself. Representing the ruins of Blackness in this way ruptures the observer's "here" and "now" and creates an experiential void between the present and the "there" and "then" of slavery and Jim Crow culture that challenges the audience to take responsibility for violence committed in the name of the shared imaginary we collectively call "America."

The second scene involves Leti's retrieval of *The Book of Names* from Hattie. As the white mobs begin setting Black neighborhoods on fire, we witness Hattie saying the Lord's Prayer as she is engulfed in flames. As we watch Hattie burn to death, the image of her incineration is accompanied by a voice-over of poet and legendary social activist Sonia Sanchez (1995) reading her poem "Catch the Fire":

> Where is your fire?
> You got to find it and pass it on. . . .
> Where is your fire? I say where is your fire?
> Can't you smell it coming out of your past? (pp. 15–17)

Sanchez's tone is defiant, and when accompanied by the image of Leti crying as Hattie perishes, the voice of Sanchez captures the paradoxical nature of Blackness in the United States: it finds resiliency even as it suffers cruel and violent revilement. As she burns, Hattie remains steadfast, intensely staring

Fig. 5.1. Hattie passes on *The Book of Names* before succumbing to the flames of white violence in *Lovecraft Country*.

into the eyes of Leti as she holds the precious *The Book of Names*. *The Book of Names*, which in the series symbolizes the intergenerational struggle of Blackness in modernity, is being passed to a new holder, who must learn to persevere in the face of the violence of anti-Blackness. This point is punctuated by Sanchez's words when she proclaims, "you got to find it and pass it on."

Hattie's incineration at the hands of white mobs offers a dramatic rebuke to the way Trump and conservative media figures fetishized looting and property damage during the turbulence of the 2020 presidential campaign. Trump—who eagerly sought to stroke racial unrest to gin up his electoral base through racist tweets, such as "When the looting starts, the shooting starts"—and his attorney general William Barr, for example, promptly blamed the vandalism of the George Floyd protests on leftists while summarily ignoring the fact that the Minneapolis Police identified white supremacists immersing themselves among protestors and intentionally vandalizing buildings to spur media spectacles of violence to benefit Trump's "law-and-order" campaign rhetoric (Burns, 2020; MacFarquhar, 2020). The scene offers a stark reminder of the dark historical lineage of white-supremacist violence connecting the past and the present. *Lovecraft Country* provides symbolic resources for reminding its audience that the very violence of white supremacy that destroyed Black life and property with firebombing and vandalism in 1921 Tulsa shares the same sinister roots that support Trumpian protofascism, be it the strategic vandalization of American cities to support fascistic media narratives or outright failed coup attempts, as in the insurrection on January 6, 2021. The symbolic lineage represented in this scene reminds the audience of the violent ways race has structured America's past and continues to echo in the present and thus reveals the vacuousness of slogans such as "All Lives Matter" or the claim that race no longer matters in the United States.

Indeed, the scene puts to shame the hollowness and hubris of whiteness's tragic Trumpian turn. Hattie's bravery in the face of her own death illustrates the disgrace of Trumpism, especially its affective investment in its own perceived racial "suffering," which, in the end, should be best understood as merely a performative facade enabled by and based in a series of ritualized cultural practices of narcissistic patronization of the racial Other meant to indulge a fragile identity grounded in grievance and ahistorical claims to being a "victim" of "oppression" in the most abstract and absurd possible meanings of both words. Our choice of the word "absurd" may seem harsh, but we find it a fitting description of a politicized identity that, long ago, sowed the seeds of its own precarious plight when it decided to embrace neoliberalism's destruction of poor communities of color in the 1980s only to become swallowed whole by the same policies decades later. As it licks its wounds from neoliberalism's wrath, which are very deep and real, however, this strand of whiteness nonetheless continues down the path of self-destructive madness and embarrassment as it seeks to find historical redemption in the nostalgic celebration of its violent past of segregation and slaveholding. Rather than finding common cause and solidarity with the penury of the racial Other, it instead accuses these potential political allies of "playing the race card" at their expense in a zero-sum competition of the races while it sides with a political class that only seeks to monetize their grievances and paranoia, be it building a wall on the Mexican border or finding alternatives to the COVID-19 vaccine (Frenkel, 2021; McGhee, 2021; Schwartz, 2020; Shamsian, 2021).

Having retrieved *The Book of Names*, the episode ends with Leti, Tic, and Montrose escaping the massacre through the interdimensional portal that carries them back to their present in the 1950s. As they jump through the temporal portal, the camera focuses on Montrose as he turns and looks upon the burning streets of the Greenwood District. Behind him, the interdimensional portal pulsates with different realities as if promising Montrose and the viewer that the future can be different. Standing in an almost reverent pose with tear-filled eyes, Montrose looks out over Tulsa, allowing the traumas of the scene to move through him. This juxtaposition of the traumatized past and pulsating, potential futures provides yet another bridge across the

Fig. 5.2. Montrose looks upon the Greenwood District engulfed in flames in *Lovecraft Country*.

experiential void created by Montrose's witnessing of the ruins of Tulsa. Suddenly, Montrose begins to recite the names of persons murdered in Tulsa during the massacre: "Peg Leg Taylor's last stand on Standpipe Hill. Oh, that was something. Still, they burned down Byar's Tailor Shop. Dr. Jackson, 'best Negro surgeon in all America.' . . . Shot in the face. Mrs. Rodgers lost her invalid daughter. White Phelps took in Negroes, hid 'em in the basement. Commodore Knox. They did him in the worst. And Thomas?" The scene offers a penetrating counterargument to the epistemic violence entailed in postracial universals such as "All Lives Matter." If the postracial fantasy's reinscription during the Trump era and its unsettling aftermath depends on the negation of race-specific claims to suffering and mourning from the history of white-supremacist violence and the structural racism of capitalism—as evidenced by the recent moral panic over critical race theory—then Montrose's remembrance of the Black lives who perished at Tulsa symbolically summarizes, for the audience, a painful truth of the Black experience that Yancy (2018) eloquently captures when he reminds us that "it is my fate to *make peace with a traumatized experience* [emphasis original], a life of mourning" (p. 149). Indeed, chants such as "Black Lives Matter" would have never been needed had there been evidence of sincere transracial empathy for the precarity and dispossession that constitutes the racial divides of the history of American capitalism. But in the absence of such empathy, there was and will always be an urgency to publicly display acts of mourning for those whose racial existence has been so dehumanized and deemed so disposable so as to go unnoticed. *Lovecraft Country* reminds us that the race problem of American democracy that W. E. B. Du Bois (1897) diagnosed over a century ago is regrettably alive and well, especially in our purportedly "postracial" times.

CONCLUSION

In this chapter, we have sought to contribute to and enrich both trauma studies and the cultural critique of the postracial by identifying and advancing the concept of postracial discourses of trauma. We have argued that the rise of postracial trauma, which is best exemplified by postracial universals such as "All Lives Matter," has accompanied the way Trumpism has reshaped whiteness as an identity category of American public and political culture. Moreover, we have proposed an analysis of *Lovecraft Country*, which aired during the months leading up to Trump's 2020 reelection bid, as a popular text that offers a dramatic response to the hubris of the white-grievance politics that Trumpism has unleashed.

Shows such as *Lovecraft Country* matter because they offer a counter story to an emerging rhetoric of whiteness that reifies suffering as a precondition for political subjectivity. If, following G. Yancy and J. Butler (2015), we understand whiteness as a "claim to dominance" that is "fortified through daily acts which may not seem racist at all precisely because they are considered 'normal,'" then, as a culture, we need to tell stories that dramatically reenact the history of violence and heroic resistance against it that constitute the American experience. Failure to do otherwise will only normalize the epistemic violence of postracial universals such as "All Lives Matter" that underlie the identity politics of whiteness. Historically informed dramas, such as *Lovecraft Country* or Barry Jenkins's *Underground Railroad* (2021), or films that address the racial violence of our contemporary era, such as *Fruitvale Station* (2013) and *Monsters and Men* (2018), are not trauma porn that fetishize violence for its own sake since they tell an uncomfortable truth about the trauma that constitutes the American experiment itself. In an era when the teaching of Black history is now threatened by censorship from conservative state legislatures and governors, such historically informed dramas are crucial (Mier, 2023). As Yancy (2018) eloquently elaborates:

> Yet these stories much be told. For it is in the telling that we gain a sense of coherence if only in the moment of the telling. Remembrance can be painful, it has the potential to re-traumatize. However, to narrate the truth about one's life under white supremacy, to begin to see

that one is *not* insane, that one's story is vital, is honest, that one's pain is real has the power to *re-member*, to put the shattered pieces back together yet again. Telling such narratives is linked to countering epistemic violence. (p. 159)

Indeed, in our purportedly postracial times, we must tell stories of America that simply, as J. Baldwin (1965) pleads, "accept our history" and the complex ways our history shapes the political crises that currently threaten America's struggle to build a democracy that does not depend on violent racial subjugation and economic subordination.

NOTES

1. Following E. J. Ore (2019), we understand the killings of Floyd, Taylor, and countless other unarmed Black citizens at the hands of police as lynchings. Ore defines a lynching "as a violent rhetorical performance that enacts the color-line logic of the racial contract" (p. 17) so as to demarcate and maintain a white racial order. The racialized violence of *Lovecraft Country* offers its audience a horrifying symbolic vocabulary for Ore's claim.

2. D. Trigg's (2009) phenomenological examination of what it's like to experience a ruin provides an informed means of understanding how one uses media and imagery to reveal what is being ignored in identity-sustaining epistemic violence. As regards the phenomenology of ruins, Trigg states, "the ruin's capacity to haunt the viewer effectively undercuts a claim of temporal continuity and, instead, offers a counter-narrative in which testimony becomes guided by voids rather than points of presence" (p. 89).

REFERENCES

Baldwin, J. (1965, March 7). The American dream and the American Negro. *New York Times*. https://archive.nytimes.com/www.nytimes.com/books/98/03/29/specials/baldwin-dream.html?_r=1

Biesecker, B. A. (2017). From general history to philosophy: Black Lives Matter, late neoliberal molecular biopolitics, and rhetoric. *Philosophy & Rhetoric, 50*(4), 409–430. https://doi.org/10.5325/philrhet.50.4.0409

Brown, D. L. (2020, May 29). Human Rights Watch calls for Tulsa Race Massacre reparations a century after violence. *Washington Post*. https://www.washingtonpost.com/history/2020/05/29/human-rights-watch-calls-tulsa-race-massacre-reparations-century-after-violence/

Burns, K. (2020, May 29). The racist history of Trump's "when the looting starts, the shooting starts" tweet. *Vox*. https://www.vox.com/identities/2020/5/29/21274754/racist-history-trump-when-the-looting-starts-the-shooting-starts

Caruth, C. (1996). *Unclaimed experience: Trauma, narrative, and history*. Johns Hopkins University Press.

Case, A., & Deaton, A. (2015). Rising morbidity and mortality in midlife among white non-Hispanic Americans in the 21st century. *Proceedings of the National Academy of Sciences of the United States of America, 112*(49), 15078–15083. https://doi.org/10.1073/pnas.1518393112

Coates, T.-N. (2014, June 15). The case for reparations. *The Atlantic*. https://www.theatlantic.com/magazine/archive/2014/06/the-case-for-reparations/361631/

Conant, C. (2020, June 1). 2020 daily trail markers: Trump declares 'we will dominate the streets.' *CBS News*. https://www.cbsnews.com/news/2020-daily-trail-markers-trump-declares-we-will-dominate-the-streets/

Cooper, A. M. (1986). Toward a limited definition of psychic trauma. In A. Rothstein (Ed.), *The reconstruction of trauma: Its significance in clinical work* (pp. 41–56). International Universities Press.

Du Bois, W. E. B. (1897). Strivings of the Negro people. *The Atlantic*. https://www.theatlantic.com/magazine/archive/1897/08/strivings-of-the-negro-people/305446/

Eyerman, R. (2002). *Cultural trauma: Slavery and the formation of African American identity*. Cambridge University Press.

Flores, L. A. (2016). Between abundance and marginalization: The imperative of racial rhetorical criticism. *Review of Communication, 16*(1), 4–24. https://doi.org/10.1080/15358593.2016.1183871

Frenkel, S. (2021, July 24). The most influential spreader of coronavirus misinformation online. *New York Times*. https://www.nytimes.com/2021/07/24/technology/joseph-mercola-coronavirus-misinformation-online.html

Gray, H. (2019). Race after race. In R. Mukherjee, S. Banet-Weiser, & H. Gray (Eds.), *Racism postrace* (pp. 23–36). Duke University Press.

Hosang D. M., & Lowndes, J. E. (2019). *Producers, parasites, patriots: Race and the new right-wing politics of precarity*. University of Minnesota Press.

Johnson, H. B. (1998). *Black Wall Street: From riot to renaissance in Tulsa's historic Greenwood District*. Eakin Press.

Karni, A., Haberman, M., & Epstein, J. (2020, June 19). How the Trump campaign's plans for a triumphant rally went awry. *New York Times*. https://www.nytimes.com/2020/06/18/us/politics/trump-rally-tulsa-juneteenth.html

Kelly, C. R. (2020). *Apocalypse man: The death drive and the rhetoric of white masculine victimhood*. Ohio State University Press.

Lacy, M. G., & Ono, K. A. (Eds.). (2011). *Critical rhetorics of race*. New York University Press.

MacFarquhar, N. (2020, July 28). Minneapolis police link "umbrella man" to white supremacy group. *New York Times*. https://www.nytimes.com/2020/07/28/us/umbrella-man-identified-minneapolis.html

McGhee, H. (2021). *The sum of us: What racism costs everyone and how we can prosper together*. One World.

Mier, T. (2023, February 24). Florida bill would allow DeSantis to ban CRT and gender studies from state schools. *Rolling Stone*. https://www.rollingstone.com/politics/politics-news/florida-bill-desantis-ban-crt-gender-studies-1234686704/

Moore, K. K. (2023, February 15). Five principles for making state and local reparations plans reparative. *Working Economics Blog, Economic Policy Institute.* https://www.epi.org/blog/five-principles-for-making-state-and-local-reparations-plans-reparative/

Mutz, D. (2018). Status threat, not economic hardship, explains the 2016 presidential vote. *Proceedings of the National Academy of Sciences, 115*(19), E4330–E4339.

Ore, E. J. (2019). *Lynching: Violence, rhetoric, and American identity.* University Press of Mississippi.

Owen, S. A., & Ehrenhaus, P. (2014). The Moore's Ford lynching reenactment: Affective memory and race trauma. *Text and Performance Quarterly, 34*(1), 72–90. https://doi.org/10.1080/10462937.2013.856461

Rahko, S. E. (2011). Negotiating economic judgment in late-modernity: Knowledge, action, and the global financial crisis. *Electronic Journal of Communication, 21*(3–4). https://www.cios.org/www/ejcmain.htm

Rahko, S. E., & Craig, B. B. (2021). Uprooting Uber: From "data fracking" to data commons. In B. Dolber, C. Kumanyika, M. Rodino-colocino, & T. Wolfson (Eds.), *The gig economy: Workers and media in the age of convergence* (pp. 190–204). Routledge.

Robinson, R. (2000). *The debt: What America owes to Blacks.* Plume.

Romero, D. (2023, July 8). Lawsuit seeking reparations for Tulsa Race Massacre is dismissed. *NBC News.* https://www.nbcnews.com/news/us-news/lawsuit-seeking-reparations-tulsa-race-massacre-dismissed-rcna93257

Salter, P., & Adams, A. (2013). Toward a critical race psychology. *Social and Personality Psychology Compass, 7*(11), 781–793.

Sanchez, S. (1995). *Wounded in the house of a friend.* Beacon Press.

Schwartz, M. S. (2020). Missouri sues televangelist Jim Bakker for selling fake coronavirus cure. *NPR.* https://www.npr.org/2020/03/11/814550474/missouri-sues-televangelist-jim-bakker-for-selling-fake-coronavirus-cure

Shamsian, J. (2021, May 25). A judge reminded everyone that Steve Bannon was accused of taking $1 million from a border wall fundraising scheme while approving Trump's pardon. *Business Insider.* https://www.businessinsider.com/steve-bannon-indictment-border-wall-fundraising-scheme-dismissed-trump-pardon-2021-5

Sisco King, C. (2011). *Washed in blood: Male sacrifice, trauma, and the cinema.* Rutgers University Press.

Sturken, M. (2007). *Tourists of history: Memory, kitsch, and consumerism from Oklahoma City to Ground Zero.* Duke University Press.

Swan, J. (2016, February 29). Trump to protesters: All lives matter. *The Hill.* https://thehill.com/blogs/ballot-box/presidential-races/271159-trump-to-protesters-all-lives-matter

Trigg, D. (2009). The place of trauma: Memory, hauntings, and the temporality of ruins. *Memory Studies, 2*(1), 87–101.

Vance, J. D. (2016). *Hillbilly elegy: A memoir of a family and culture in crisis.* Harper Press.

Wieskamp, V. N., & Smith, C. (2020). "What to do when you're raped": Indigenous women critiquing and coping through a rhetoric of survivance. *Quarterly Journal of Speech, 106*(1), 72–94. https://doi.org/10.1080/00335630.2019.1706189

Yancy, G. (2018). Black embodied wounds and the traumatic impact of the white imagi-
    nary. In E. Boynton & P. Capretto (Eds.), *Trauma and transcendence: Suffering and the
    limits of theory* (pp. 142–162). Fordham University Press.

Yancy, G., & Butler, J. (2015, January 12). What's wrong with 'all lives matter'? *New York
    Times.* https://archive.nytimes.com/opinionator.blogs.nytimes.com/2015/01/12/whats
    -wrong-with-all-lives-matter/?_r=3&referrer

Young, C. A. (2019). Becked up: Glenn Beck, white supremacy, and the hijacking of the
    civil rights legacy. In R. Mukherjee, S. Banet-Weiser, & H. Gray (Eds.), *Racism postrace*
    (pp. 86–112). Duke University Press.

Part 3

Postrace Rereleased

Chapter 6

MAKING AMERICA *BAMBOOZLED* AGAIN

CHRISTOPHER GILBERT

> It appeared that in addition to reacting to whatever ignorant, hare-
> brained notion had set him off in the first place, the Negro was apt to
> double up with a second gale of laughter, triggered, apparently, by his
> own mental image of himself laughing at himself laughing upside down.
> It was, all whites agreed, another of the many Negro mysteries with
> which it was their lot to contend, but *whatever* [emphasis original] its
> true cause, it was most disturbing to a white observer.
> —RALPH ELLISON, "AN EXTRAVAGANCE OF LAUGHTER,"
> IN *THE COLLECTED ESSAYS OF RALPH ELLISON*

From whence comes the term "a barrel of laughs"? The story goes that, throughout the peculiar institution, Black slaves were prohibited from laughing in plain view. It was believed that nothing in the daily experience could or should inspire laughter. Moreover, white masters grasped the rhetorical force in acts of laughing *at*, laughing *off*, and (perhaps most critically) laughing *with*. When Black slaves would laugh, they stuck their heads into barrels. Their laughter would burst out, resounding in a large cask. And there you have it: a barrel of laughs.

Laughter is at once a perilous and a necessary risk. This is something of a punch line to a peculiarly American joke (Parvulescu, 2010, pp. 74–75). Accounts of *Homo ridens* (laughing human), *Homo risens* or *Homo risibilis* (risible or laughable creature), *Homo rhetoricus* (playful *rhētōr*), and *Zoion gelastikon* (laughing animal) substantiate a sense of humor as the crucial mark of humanity. It is what enables us to look upon our situations and our scrapes for the follies that provoke them. It is likewise what provides the possibility "to put suffering to shame, if only for a fleeting instant" and then again to win a victory "over the blackness of life"—or, better, "its whiteness"

(Eckardt, 2017, p. 77). It made good comic sense for Black slaves to conceal their "desire to laugh" (Dundes, 1973, p. xv). After all, no true Black person was fully human in the dark hereditament of American chattel slavery. Black laughter, as R. Ellison (1986) describes it, entails the need to secure "a means of protecting the sensibilities of whites" (p. 188). The dictum "keep 'em laughing" resonates with this need, and it can be traced from the antebellum period to the blackface minstrelsy.

The blackface minstrelsy is a vital source of both Black and white laughter (Mahar, 1999). Just as laughing barrels were established to "control Negro laughter" (Ellison, 1986, p. 192), blackface repackaged racism as entertainment that could be used to stage Blackness and sustain the rhetorical invention of supremacy in the white imagination (Lott, 1993, p. 4). The blackface minstrelsy, which came to prominence in the early nineteenth century and grew in popularity during the formative years of the Jim Crow era, let laughter out of the barrel. Yet it did so as "an index of popular white racial feeling" (Lott, 1993, p. 5). It kept "darky entertainers" in their place (Hyman, 1973, p. 47). According to M. Watkins (2012), these "comic minstrel caricatures" (p. xv) showed forth a "niggling truth" (p. xiv), though, about the influence of a nagging bad faith in racial representation *de profundis comici* or from the depths of comicality. Take the "Minstrel Man" of Langston Hughes's (1925) unsettling poem:

> Because my mouth
> Is wide with laughter
> And my throat
> Is deep with song,
> You do not think
> I suffer after
> I have held my pain
> so long.
>
> Because my mouth
> is wide with laughter,
> You do not hear
> My inner cry,
> Because my feet
> Are gay with dancing,
> You do not know
> I die. (p. 144)

The comic minstrel caricature inspires laughter and tears in the same instance.

Fig. 6.1. Actors perform *Mantan: The New Millennium Minstrel Show* in *Bamboozled* (New Line Cinema, 2000), directed by Spike Lee.

Blackface is remarkable because it captures racial oppression in the crucible of comic expression. More specifically, it codifies Blackness as an indication of something less than human: lazy, ignorant, lustful, craven, thievish, *laughable*. The minstrelsy, writes Toni Morrison (2020), "had virtually nothing to do with the way black people really were; it was a purely white construction" (p. 37; see also Toll, 1977). So when Spike Lee brought it back to life in his tendentious and purportedly satirical film *Bamboozled* (2000), many critics and commentators unsurprisingly labeled it a flawed attempt to uproot Black caricatures so inveterate as to be impervious to satire (Ebert, 2000). The film tells the story of Peerless Dothan, better known as Pierre Delacroix (played by Damon Wayans), an educated Black writer for a corporate television network, CNS, who creates a minstrel show for the screen age. The show, like *Bamboozled*, is supposed to satirize how racism persists in networks that only really care about representations of Blackness that are built on racialized buffoonery. It backfires, of course. Set in an Alabama watermelon patch and fronted by the Black duo of street performer turned headliner, Manray (played by Savion Glover, whose character is renamed after vaudeville comedian Mantan Moreland), and his promoter turned comic companion, Womack, a.k.a. Sleep 'n Eat (played by Tommy Davidson), *Mantan: The New Millennium Minstrel Show* becomes a wild success (figure 6.1). White audiences love it. Many Black audiences do too. The white male television executive who signs off on it eventually takes to blackening up before the filming of each episode. Put simply, Lee's film mocks the trenchantly (un)funny Otherness that pervades "conventional ways of looking at blackness" (hooks, 2015, p. 4). The ostensive problem is that *Bamboozled* reflects the satirical minstrelsy at the center of its storyline by betraying the failed notion that people can be made better if only a comic spirit can prevail over crudeness, prejudice, and cruelty (Busack, 2000). However, there is a bigger problem, and it is reinforced by the rerelease of *Bamboozled* in 2020 as part of the Criterion Collection—an honor that seems to belie the fact that what many now dub a "masterpiece" was a box office disappointment. The film actually grounds postracialism in what Ellison (1973) designates as the "black-faced figure of white fun" (p. 59). White fun is to Black caricatures as postracialism is to minstrel comicality.

Bamboozled posits a white-culture industry that traffics in fantasies of whiteness and Blackness by consigning racialism to the rhetorical spaces of entertainment, festivity, and amusement. Lee's newfangled blackface minstrelsy puts a satirical spin on turn-of-the-twentieth-century racism. Coincidentally, the film's twentieth anniversary truly makes hindsight twenty-twenty. *Bamboozled* lampoons the false promises of postracialism. In the years between the film's initial release and its addition to the Criterion Collection, we saw the election of America's first Black president only to see Barack Obama succeeded by the first white president (Coates, 2017). The presidency of Donald J. Trump was a byproduct of what T.-N. Coates (2017) calls "the bloody heirloom," or a hand-me-down of white supremacy, the basis for which is a *comic* idea that "ensures the last laugh" of whiteness as an affirmation of its dark racial inheritance.

Here, then, is the hook of this chapter: *Bamboozled* is more a forecast than a look back, exemplifying satire as the fountainhead for *what might come* of racism as the means to keep people laughing. Postracialism is a myth (Kendi, 2021). The era of Trumpism has fomented not just an ideology of "making America great again" by instantiating whiteness as the standard for official politicking and doing cultural politics but also a rhetorical platform for making America bamboozled again by espousing white-supremacist perspectives in plain view through comic cruelty and festive enjoyment. The laughter of Trumpism is a yoke that celebrates a shared amusement in sanctimony, truculence, and the suffering of nonwhite Others (Serwer, 2009). White supremacy is a comic foil for the follies of racial caricature. The cruel laughter that peals from it urges a constituency to laugh at "de blacks" as they sit upon the nests of hornets and dance upon their heads. Trumpism illustrates the "glowing amulet" of white supremacy and its "eldritch energies" (Coates, 2017), which *Bamboozled* altogether summons up and predicts. The deep-*seeded* racism that *Bamboozled* reaps is so telling of postracialism because of what is destined to resurface so long as laughter (and satire besides) can be turned back on itself, grievance can be converted into gratification, and prejudice can be profitable. Minstrel legacies underwrite the joke of postracial whiteness. Trumpism stokes the motivation to make Black representations into blackface caricatures again through what J. Baldwin (1985) characterized as the false choice for people of color to either act "just like a n****r" or act out against racial difference (p. 275). This chapter unpacks how white culture is bamboozled by the temptation to contain Blackness in comicality so as to leave racist imagery behind by throwing it in our faces.

THE JOKE OF POSTRACIAL WHITENESS

In the dark history of minstrel shows, jokes on Blackness did the most damage when they provoked white tears of laughter.

A brief detour into some definitions and explanations is merited here. First, with regard to Trump, there is a troubling basis for approaching Blackness as a performance insofar as the forty-fifth president portrayed himself as the "least racist person" despite an extensive history (to be sure, a record of written and spoken words) of anti-Blackness. For instance, when he made his self-proclamation, Trump was responding to a gaggle of reporters about accusations of his racial insensitivity. It just so happens that this response was issued while Trump was on his way from the White House to deliver a speech in Jamestown and, with it, to thread a needle between the four hundredth anniversary of the first Africans being enslaved in the United States and the historic establishment of American self-government (R. Wright, 2019). Here, he was a figment of presidential fidelity. Elsewhere and above all on social media and on the stump, Trump was the white face of anti-Black fun. Second is the matter of Blackness as a performance. Trump does not perform as one identifiable with Blackness. He *does* activate a notion of Blackness as a categorical placement of people according to perceived, or pronounced, racial identities. Expressed another way, Blackness itself is posed as a push and pull of avowals and disavowals, expansions and delimitations of images or ideas, and constructions and deconstructions of what makes up Black life. As E. P. Johnson (2003) attests, Blackness is an embodied phenomenon and a discourse, meaning that it is not only in the flesh that it is appropriated, substantiated—performed (pp. 42, 160). Blackness is therefore about more than identity politics, more than a struggle over racial borders and boundaries. It is about what passes for "authentic" and what pays or not in the culture industries of race.

The thing about this is that, with a backdrop of so-called postracialism, there is a framework for not only revealing racism but also reveling in it. To make fun of racism and racists early in the twenty-first century is to risk the activation of white tears (Kunzru, 2017; see also Liebow & Glazer, 2019). So if Blackness is a performance, then whiteness is a postracial imaginary in esse. It is reproduced, "tearfully," when Blackness is cast as a threat to white supremacy. Blackness (never mind whiteness) is funny when it comes from the postracial humor of something like *Dear White People*. It is perilous, if not terrifying, when it spirals out of the rage, victimhood, and hostility of something like Trumpism. The pop-cultural, politics-as-entertainment aura that animates widespread appeal of Trumpism galvanizes a "self-conscious form of white-identity politics" that is "vulgar, aggressive, boastful, selfish, promiscuous, [and] consumerist" (Williamson, 2017). Some have grown wary of white ressentiment (Anderson, 2016; see also Grossberg, 2018; Kelly, 2020a; McVeigh & Estep, 2019; Ott & Dickinson, 2019). Just as concerning is a *white* minstrelsy that fortifies supremacist attitudes and refuses to put all jokes aside.

The "white minstrelsy," or the exaggerated performance of whiteness that amounts to a caricature of its roots in rebel attitudes and Jim Crow realpolitik, had its master of ceremonies in candidate Trump as the "hostile-jaunty guy in the big flappy suit, with the vaudeville hair, the pursed lips, and the glare," who joked and jibed his way to the presidency on a platform of pushing buttons about race, misogyny, scandal, corruption, and minoritarianism (Nussbaum, 2017). Trump hates to be made fun of, hates being laughed at, and cannot bear a joke against him. His call "to Make America Great Again was a plea to go back in time, to when people knew how to take a joke" (Nussbaum, 2017), when the strange admixture of comicality, sentimentality, and absurdity made sense in the racial fantasies at the core of white supremacy (Lott, 1993, p. 101), when the blackface minstrelsy was popular . . .

Cut to the scene from *Bamboozled* that captures Delacroix's pitch for an authentic show about Blackness and thus sets forward the impetus for *Mantan*. Delacroix sits across from CNS executive Thomas Dunwitty (played by Michael Rappaport). "The material you've been creating," says Dunwitty— who is the epitome of a racist *imposteur* disguised as a man of the Black community—"is too white bread. White people with black faces." Dunwitty is stirred up. Delacroix speaks softly as Dunwitty looks on with frustration from behind his desk. Delacroix makes the case for a dramatic take on the "Negro middle class"—a Black family in white suburbia, a Black family in a small southern town, still governed by the KKK, Black women raising sons, etc. "It's too clean, too antiseptic," says Dunwitty. "Too white?" Delacroix asks. Dunwitty clarifies. "The reason why these shows didn't get picked up is because nobody, no-motherfuckin'-body, n****rs and crackers alike, want to see that junk." Dunwitty then rambles about how he is blacker than Delacroix before prodding him to entertain viewers, not enlighten them. Interestingly, a line from the original screenplay but not in the final version of the film has Delacroix rejoin with mock incredulity. "What is it you want from me? Some plantation follies? Some sitcom that takes place on a watermelon patch?" "Yes! Yes! Yes!" Dunwitty exclaims (Lee, n.d.). In jokes, racist heirlooms and racial heritages can make unpopular, offensive images and ideas more palatable to a general populace (S. Clark, 2020). The New Right that grew out of Trumpism exploits the very orientation that Dunwitty describes. In and through it, a new minstrelsy is the comic resource for a way of political being. Trumpism normalizes racial difference as *the* fact of American life.

Repetition matters as much as difference here, especially when it comes to a comic way. Postracialism in particular is a carefully crafted narrative about how racialism is endemic to representational politics. The "white minstrelsy" of Trumpism showcases supremacist motivations as "ordinary and ubiquitous yet jarring and spectacular, just like blackface" (Benjamin, 2018). Some say the infamous red "Make America Great Again" (MAGA) hat is an emblem of racial hatred (J. Wright, 2019; Omari, 2019). Some peg Trumpism as a species of "Jim Crow nostalgia" (Boyd, 2008; see also Kelly, 2020b). Early twentieth-century white supremacy, much like that which is satirized in *Bamboozled*, is entertaining. It harnesses logics of "slaveability" that situate Blackness as something to be bought and sold (Smith, 2012, p. 68). A joke of postracial representation is that color lines resist oppression when the problem of who *owns* the power to oppress is left unsolved. A joke of postracial rhetoric is that we might move beyond Blackness when the real problem is moving beyond *whiteness*. Postracial allyship wheedles us with colorblindness and codes of silence. This is most apparent when it is folded into forms of racial awareness that, according to C. R. Squires (2014), rely "on a desire to remain 'innocent' of racism," whether in a real or, shall we say, performative sense (p. 230). In tandem with this desire for innocence is what Squires calls the "post-racial mystique," which is predicated upon an aura of fascination and fantasy about those who are "in the know" and those who are not when it comes to deficiencies in racialized representations (p. 12). In *Represent and Destroy: Rationalizing Violence in the New Racial Capitalism*, J. Melamed (2011) similarly argues that postracialism revolves around issues of rhetorical control over what counts as racism and what does not and thereby how that judgment can be deployed in the name of anything from show running to a solatium. Postracial whiteness reorganizes the racist trappings of "supremacy" by making a show of racialism (at best) and racism (at worst) as the fertile grounds for festivity and fun—or violent fervor when things get real.

Things got real on January 6, 2021. After Trump lost his bid for reelection, a horde of his supporters stormed the US Capitol convinced of the "Big Lie" that the president's power was somehow stolen from him—from *them* (Jefferson, 2021; see also Bush, 2011, p. xvi; K.-Y. Taylor, 2021). It was a festal display of Old Guard cavaliers at a political carnival. Insurrectionists donned various forms of white-nationalist and racist regalia. They flew the Confederate battle flag. They exhibited a makeshift gallows to evoke the "Day of the Rope." One of the leaders, hailed as the "QAnon Shaman," dressed up as a Nordic symbol of Odinism, bared his chest and Valknot tattoos and even sported a fur hat with horns. Others just wore Marvel superhero costumes. The Capitol insurrection was festive. It was fervent. The milieu was chaotic, but the mood was giddy. "They were having fun," as one reporter saw it, "entertaining *themselves* [emphasis added]" (Ismail, 2021). But Trumpism is not the sole driving force of troublesome color lines in resurgent populism, reactionary conservatism, alt-right rhetorical cultures, and means-ends cultural politics. On the contrary, the symbols and outfits and their histories and historiographies all gesture to the ghosts of racism's present (Belcher, 2016). The poltergeist of postracialism that reveals itself as a "ghostly haunting by the racial of the social supposedly rid of race" (Goldberg, 2015, p. 82)—the ghost of Jim Crow (Higginbotham, 2013). This is a specter that has long haunted US public culture.

More than just a set of policies and principles, Jim Crow embodies the long shadow of a "real" person fabricated as the first "Black" stage character in the late 1820s by the "father of American minstrelsy," Thomas D. "Daddy" Rice. Zip Coon. Sambo. Mammy. Lucy Long. These and other caricatures grew up along with Jim Crow and became staples of the minstrel troupes of Daniel Decatur Emmett and Edwin P. Christy in the 1840s and others that came after. By the turn of the twentieth century, minstrel comics, singers, dancers, and actors garnered a reputation for racial caricature that traversed films, music, television shows, and cartoons. The tripartite of "black political mimicry, exaggerated African inspired plantation dances, and dialect songs" rounded out choreography organized by an interlocutor who was almost always a "civilized, well-dressed, white man who dictated the show's progression" and regulated "the actions of the incoherent Blackface endmen" (Barnes, n.d.). They comprise "a stain of Blackness" that Lee abhors and that persists in what M. Erigha (2019) brands "the Hollywood Jim Crow" (p. 3). The historical conundrum for Black performers is the Baldwin-esque black-and-white fallacy of choosing to either "resist blackface stereotypes and be ignored" or "play the minstrel and gather some power and profit" under the watchful eyes of white masters of ceremonies (Roberts, 2017, p. 270). The blackface minstrelsy normalized mimicry, mockery, and malice in good fun as sources of ascendency and amusement in the antics of stock characters during *olios*; the malapropisms, solecisms, and slips of the tongue in comic stump speeches; and the turnarounds of those acting out caricatures of Blackness. Blackface accommodates a "black comic sensibility" (Cole, 2020, p. 119). George Walker and Bert Williams are prime examples of how folk laughter was infiltrated into the minstrelsy by Black performers. Black laughter offered a comic escape from the minstrel formula (Fauset, 1925, p. 166). But it also gave "white viewers permission to laugh at the coon show" (Y. Taylor & Austen, 2012, p. 304). Jim Crow, and his original bid for *white* laughter, prefigured the conformity of Black performers to the wiles of whiteness and its ruinous racial imaginations.

This is why minstrel comicality anticipated what D. Enck-Wanzer (2011) characterizes as "born again racism" (as in the title of this work). According to B. Roberts (2017), it undercuts postracialism by revivifying a "humor-based racism" (p. 6) that is "quintessentially American" (p. 93), with Jim Crow as the standard for judging "the authenticity of blackness *relative* to whiteness" (Sammond, 2015, p. 283). In the blackface minstrelsy of old, audiences were often rowdy and eager to be entertained. They "hollered, cheered, and booed with the intensity and fervor of today's football fans"—or, we might say, with the élan of Trump supporters and New Right apologists at MAGA rallies, of those watching *Gutfeld!* Or *Hannity*, taking in reports from the One America News Network and Newsmax, or reveling in an insurrection at the Capitol. The blackface minstrelsy is dead; long live the blackface minstrelsy. The white minstrelsy, which is underwritten by the very "whiteness of blackness" in Black caricature, is alive and well (Ellison, 1973, p. 61). Black *and* white minstrelsies betoken racial phantasms "transparent to nostalgic racists and anti-racist scourges alike" (Lott, 1993, p. 249). The specifically postracial joke shown and told in *Bamboozled* is that blackface is a paradigm case for those who *humor* Black caricature to live and let die.

BAMBOOZLING BLACK REPRESENTATION

When he pitches his minstrelsy *en vogue*, Delacroix pegs it as a satire for "racial healing." He urges Dunwitty to picture "this very American tradition of entertainment" as the resource for creating a comic simulacrum of Black

Fig. 6.2. Would-be Mantan tap dances when auditioning for *Mantan: The New Millennium Minstrel Show* in *Bamboozled* (New Line Cinema, 2000), directed by Spike Lee.

life. Alone, at home, Delacroix stares at a blank television screen and baits himself to feed the idiot box. In a private meeting with Dunwitty, he pitchs an idiotic satire that was sure to be a ratings failure. Dunwitty ultimately loves the idea—all the more when Delacroix sets the show on a plantation with the Alabama Porch Monkeys for a house band (ironically played by blues- and jazz-infused hip-hop band, The Roots). He loves it more still when he introduces the stars of the show, Mantan and Sleep 'n Eat, "two real coons" who will don blackface to "lend authenticity" in their dramatization of the ignorance, dull-wittedness, balefulness, and indolence so characteristic of Black caricatures, and yet more still when, much to the dismay of Delacroix's assistant, Sloan (played by Jada Pinkett Smith), a supporting cast of laugh- ably "three-dimensional characters" is put on the table. Honeycutt. Topsy. Rastus. Little N****r Jim. Sambo. Aunt Jemima. All of this precedes an ad hoc performance by Mantan (figure 6.2), who tap dances on the conference room table to Dunwitty's delight.

The show lives up to expectations. It is the racist outrage that Sloan pre- dicts. It meets Dunwitty's demand for "cutting-edge" content that nonetheless "examines blackness by cutting its target and stabbing itself" (Black, 2003, p. 19). It feeds into fantasies about "the blackening of America"—again (Lott, 1993, pp. 4, 92–111). It earns Mantan the fortune and fame he sought in "hoof- ing." Unfortunately, it sells Blackness short by reducing the very real richness of Black folk art and cultural artistry to a comic production wherein "the fascination of blackness could be enjoyed" (Ellison, 1973, p. 58). Womack, or

Sleep 'n Eat, can only stomach it for so long before pronouncing how the minstrelsy makes "the white man's relish" into "the black man's gall" (Ellison, 1973, p. 59), especially when playing to the follies *of* white audiences is not enough to get away from playing the fool *for* white audiences. *This* is what Delacroix misrecognized, and misrepresented, in the Blackness of comic traditions. This notion that, as Jim Crow once sang to his "brodder niggers," it is never going to be enough to "laugh at dem / Who happen to be white" (Rice, 2009, p. 25). Even satire that satirizes satire can lead to uncritical laughter (Kopp, 2014). Blackface can be satirical when it locates some humanity in "black men mimicking white men who were pretending to be black" (Powell, 2020, p. 109). To keep 'em laughing is to forego the idea that anyone could actually satirize blackface, a comic icon of whiteness.

Consider some of the flashpoints from the film, and note that they are recounted in the following manner to emphasize the fragmented and fractured nature of Blackness as performance as well as to encapsulate the various ways that Lee makes this very point across the film.

•

In the writer's room before the pilot, Delacroix works with a group of predominately white writers (save for one Jewish man), who reiterate stereotypes of Blackness less as resources for satire than for realistic points of reference for Black experience. Delacroix advises them to translate these sensibilities into material for sketches and skits.

•

Delacroix ends up writing the pilot himself. However, a white male writer coordinates with Dunwitty to revise it—to make it funnier, they say, by blackening it up. In a scene preceding the first taping, Sloan narrates as Mantan and Sleep 'n Eat burn cork and carefully apply their blackfaces (figures 6.3 and 6.4). Their arrival on stage is framed as a return to a "simpler time" when "n****rs knew their place," when they were back on the plantation with no poverty, rap music, urban decay, or nouveau riche Black athletes. The house band plays, dressed in jailhouse garb. The emcee, Honeycutt (played by Thomas Jefferson Byrd), warms the crowd. Sleep 'n Eat leads the comic discourse. Mantan establishes himself as a dancing fool. The mostly white audience is aghast, until they are entertained.

•

Figs. 6.3 and 6.4. Mantan and Sleep 'n Eat apply blackface in *Bamboozled* (New Line Cinema, 2000), directed by Spike Lee.

On the eve of his show's debut, Delacroix visits his father, Junebug (played by Paul Mooney), a renowned stand-up comedian of the Black underground. Junebug appears onstage, seated, dapper, a microphone held loosely in his hand. He tells "street jokes." One involves a pretend film script about the last white man on Earth; another, the exploitation of Black personae in representations of what it means to "act Black" and "sound Black"—and the expropriation of a desire to be Black without *being* Black. Delacroix joins Junebug backstage after the performance. They bicker about the difference between making it by making a killing (i.e., Delacroix) and killing it by keeping it real (i.e., Junebug). Delacroix spurns his father's comedy, namely his unremitting use of the word "n****r," which Junebug mockingly attributes to his interest in keeping his teeth white. Crucially, Junebug outlines the root of a Black *commedia dell'virtù*. Real satire is not about ratings. It is not about going mainstream or keeping up appearances. It is about dislocating racial oppression by giving it a Black face. So it goes that bamboozlement in a time of resurgent, mainstream white supremacy is what Lee reveals as that haunting, peculiar problem of how to be Black without being a n****r.

•

Delacroix, Manray, Sloan, and Womack watch the first broadcast of the new minstrel show. The opening credits feature animated caricatures of Mantan and Sleep 'n Eat. The commercial sponsors include faux malt liquor, the Bomb, and pseudo–Tommy Hilfiger knockoff, Timmi Hiln****r. Advertisements for both are replete with Black stereotypes, and they complement Lee's comic provocation to beware of racial fantasies that move from festivity through fun to flagrancy.

•

After the first broadcast, a white female public-relations consultant is called in to head off any fallout from the overnight ratings. "Lighten up"—this is the core message she intends to convey to would-be critics. Beyond that, she recommends putting up a front. The network should hire Black workers for the set. Delacroix should remember that the audience is primarily white, so keep writing a nonthreatening, white-is-right view of Blackness. The "cultural police" should take a walk with their politically correct outrage. Plus, who defines Blackness? Whatever. It's satire, stupid. And "*f*" anyone who can't take a joke! So says the "N****rologist." Delacroix's words.

•

Sloan gets Delacroix a gift to celebrate his hit show. It's a Jolly N****r Bank. A piece of racist memorabilia, a collectible, that eats money and represents a historical moment when, says Sloan, "we were considered inferior, subhuman." Delacroix does a Black talk-radio show soon thereafter and defends the new millennium minstrelsy as a piece of televisual art that disrupts the "slave mentality" and shows people how the antiracist revolution will be televised. Representation meets reality, though, when the audience members present for live tapings are soon made up in blackface (even Dunwitty), displaying what happens when fun, festivity, and flagrancy meet fandom in Television Land. Delacroix profits from the fact that racism pays off (Collins, 2020). His show earns critical praise. Delacroix wins an Emmy. But during his acceptance speech, he becomes a "dancing fool" by turning into the "grateful Negro," fumbling and misspeaking just like his minstrel brethren.

•

The "slave mentality" transmogrifies into the "master mentality" in Delacroix and in Manray, who takes to treating choreography as a mechanism of control. Delacroix earns the disappointment of his mother. "A coon is a coon," she tells him over the phone, no matter if it is satirical. Womack quits but not before confronting Manray—Mantan—about the damage done by capitulating to the good ol' days of a new minstrelsy.

•

Self-mockery and self-deprecation are rooted in the Black comic tradition. But they are made foolish when what is laughed *at* becomes a comic mask for what is laughed *off* (Watkins, 1999, pp. 12–13). Manray finally comes to his senses: no more "blackening up." Delacroix insists that the show must go on. Julius, a.k.a. Big Blak Afrika (played by rapper Mos Def), who is Sloan's brother and a stand-in for the Black revolutionary spirit as the leader of an underground rap group, the Mau Maus, agrees. He and his posse concoct a plan to film Mantan's execution on live television: a true-to-life "Dance of Death." The last time Mantan goes on stage, he does so as himself. "I am sick and tired of being a n****r!" he shouts to the crowd before falling flat on his back. Dunwitty flies into a rage. Delacroix tries to pass it off as a joke—or a mere case of "coonitis." The audience is dismayed. In the end, the Mau Maus carry out their plan. Wearing blackface masks, members of the Mau Maus tie Mantan to a chair, mock his foolish gambol, and then fire gunshots at his feet as he tap-dances on top of a makeshift stage. Then they shoot him. Dunwitty delivers a televised public service announcement in defense of the American way of life. The police ambush the Mau Maus. Julius is killed.

If only it was satire.

•

Fig. 6.5. Delacroix lies dying in *Bamboozled* (New Line Cinema, 2000), directed by Spike Lee.

In the final scene, Sloan enters Delacroix's office to find him amidst his trappings of Black caricature. The Jolly N****r taunted him—an objet d'art, an *objet petit a* in Lee's comic vision, dancing out of impulse, out of routine. Delacroix destroys his office. When Sloan enters, he is slouched on the floor in blackface. Sloan has a gun. She is sobbing. The blackface is no longer funny looking. It is expressionless on Delacroix's face. Sloan compels Delacroix to play a video she created of Black minstrel caricatures on his television. She appeals to the blood on his hands, the responsibility he has for the death of Manray (her lover, we know by now) and her brother. She sobs and, finally, shoots Delacroix in the stomach. He dies on the floor. As he dies, he narrates his own death in a voice-over, quoting J. Baldwin—"people pay for what they do" and "what they become"—and providing a not-so-comic image of Blackness, with his bright red lips and tears streaming down his face (figure 6.5). À la Ellison, this ending evokes a Blues sense of humor. It goes with the territory of a racist heritage. It exemplifies "the great human joke" of tears and sufferance and song and dance in the death cult of laughter (Ellison, 2003, p. 25).

The show mustn't go on.

This was the main point of so many early critics of Lee's film. His representation of Black representations was simplistic, reductive, stereotypical, antiquated, backward, *bamboozled*. The film makes the blackface taboo into a touchstone for supposedly enlightened entertainment only to remake bygone racial oppressions into more overt displays of white supremacy. Furthermore, there is something to be said for the fact that the end of *Bamboozled* resembles the end of the 1976 Black comedy *Network*. In *Network*, a white male news anchor is slated to be canceled because of bad ratings until he performs an on-air outburst about the foolishness of commercial news that makes him into a "mad prophet of the airwaves." The anchor, Howard Beale, gets popular again, but his popularity is short-lived when he descends into apparent madness with diatribes that detail how bad life is when it is monetized. Higher-ups at the network conspire to eliminate Beale, affecting an ethic of keeping the corporate (or cultural) setup by killing whatever threatens it. In this case, they devise a plot to have Beale shot dead on live television, making his death a spectacle for all to see. It is striking how alike this is to the romanticism of racialism in the Blackface minstrelsy, centered as it is on "misery, death, indeed disappearance" (Lott, 2013, p. 190). Lately, the comic conditions of minstrelsy have obvious traces in twenty-first-century discourses of political correctness, wokeness, and cultural cancellation. If it was satirical, *Bamboozled* still kept Blackness in its place.

More recently, though, there has been recognition that there may be more to *Bamboozled* than meets the colorblind, postracial eye. A. Clark (2015), who curates the Criterion Collection and wrote the book on facing Blackness in Lee's film, proclaims that the grotesquely nightmarish (although utterly real) racial mythos makes *Bamboozled* more of a warning than an outmoded *film maudit* (see also Aftab, 2020; A. Clark, 2010; Dennis, 2020). Others note that it is so jarring because its revitalization of "old" ways of doing Black representation is a sign of the times, here and now. To keep 'em laughing—those who embody Black caricature, that is—is to keep 'em where they belong. That's the "dark farce" of *Bamboozled* (Patterson, 2000). Then again, it is also the dark joke that has been told for decades, even centuries, about the comedy of racial struggles. It is best to enjoy yourself when you can because sooner or later you will die in spite of your humanity (Coates, 2010).

This brings me to Ellison's notion of Black comicality as more than changing the joke to slip the yoke of racism. *Bamboozled*'s satirical take on the consequences of postracialism has to do with just how difficult it is "for a white observer to even imagine" a representational system that does not rely on images and ideas of Blackness framed for, by, and of whiteness (Ellison, 2003, p. 285). There is no need to change the joke of blackface. White people imagine that the joke is on Black people, on Blackness. The joke, however, is on us; the joke is on white people—on people who do not need to harbor any white-supremacist sentiments but nonetheless might inadvertently or unwittingly maintain a white-supranatural approach to the world. *Bamboozled* betrays a form of racial identity politics so ridiculous that it cannot actually be anything other than a foolish attempt by a feeble culture to confront its dark histories. Conventional wisdom about the comic sensibility suggests that satire "foregoes easy readings," that it destabilizes "the racial status quo" (Morgan, 2020, p. 4). In these ways, *Bamboozled* can be seen as "a mode of laughing at the laugh created by the minstrel stage" (Carpio, 2008, p. 410). It can be appreciated for its provocation of racial formations that foreground the very cultural politics of Blackness that resist any simple distinction between what J. L. Cole might call a "black comic sensibility" and the rhetorical force of white supremacy.

Our postracial moment is one "in which mutually constitutive and often contradictory conceptions of racial difference that have presented themselves in historically specific ways at other moments appear now as aggressive performances of the struggle over the relative value of authentic identity" (Sammond, 2015, p. 283). Lee's characters are not simplistic caricatures (Y. Taylor & Austen, 2012, p. 296). They are complex. They reveal Blackness as a rhetorical artifact of institutionalized racism that can persist without the presence of real, humanized Black people. This is what W. T. Lhamon (1998) means by the problem of "white identification with blackness" as the fetish inherent to motely alliances in matters of cultural production (p. 207). It is the basis as well for Ellison's reminders about the complexities of comic motives. Satire can facilitate more complicated views of Black selfhood. Even so, blackface taken at face value can be funny without being satirical. It can also be comical when seen for what it is—in this case, the burden of postracialism on people of color who are expected "to move *beyond* racial identity because only non-whiteness is racialized" (Morgan, 2020, p. 3). Mantan is a case in point in that he moves forward as a result of his racial identity, then moves beyond it before finally succumbing to the great beyond. To *get over it* by looking past the racial hierarchies embedded in fantasies of cultural difference is to see through the struggles at stake over the relative value of authentic identity. The stakes are changed when those struggles are over the *satirical* value of representational politics.

Hence, there is the problem with comic motives of representative figures like Dunwitty to preserve a racial hierarchy by "killing it" with ratings and figures like Delacroix (and even Lee), who want to kill off racism. As K. Burke (1969) says, "the *killing* of something is the *changing* of it, and the statement of the thing's nature before and after the change is an *identifying* [emphases original] of it" (p. 20). It is not the Other, the one that is killed, who is changed, though. It is the self. There is recognition here that an image of whiteness comes along with an image of Blackness insofar as both are "established by *common involvement* in a killing" (p. 265). Blackface is glaringly derivative and perverse. But it does good *satirical* work if it is *self*-directed rather than *Other*-directed. Burke and Ellison were very good friends, and Burke undoubtedly influenced Ellison's ideas about satire and cultural identity (Crable, 2012). Both posit satire as "a troublous form" (Burke, 2003, p. 54) in part because it leads to projections of what is in ourselves and in our collective sensibilities and senses of selfhood. *Bamboozled* pushes this trouble to the end of its line by utilizing satire not for comic reflection but rather for comic projection. *Bamboozled* reimagines postracial struggles with the comic image of a return of the oppressed in "new" approaches to race relations. He imagines the dangers of caricature becoming the "real thing" such that a representation, to be killed, requires the killing of actual human beings who embody it. What remains is a goad to reconsider the comic license to kill.

CONCLUSION: MISLED. HAD. TOOK.

In 1925, the activist, philosopher, dramatist, and founder of the Howard Play-ers, T. M. Gregory, imagined a performance space dedicated to Black life. It would make more of racial experiences than a laughingstock (Gregory, 1925, p. 159). *Bamboozled* recovers the legacies of racial caricature in post-racial fantasies that have made white supremacy entertaining again even as they have prefigured an end to the "comic-opera" that has long sustained a "delusion of whiteness" in the "stigma of blackness" (Baldwin, 1985, p. 123, see also p. 555). It was always going to be a matter of life and death. But it was supposed to be in the cri de coeur of satire, in an impassioned comic appeal, not just in racial jest.

Delacroix quotes Baldwin at the moment when his death seems a just desert. As a filmic device, this makes it as entertaining to see Delacroix killed as it is for characters in *Bamboozled* to watch Manray die at the hands of the Mau Maus. Black representations are transformed into reality TV. The satire bespeaks the entertainment value in seeing Black persons lose their capacity to stay in on the joke. From the beginning, Delacroix was writing for his life. He just did not know how much it would involve doing the Black thing in a way that white audiences would want to see. He did not know it would get him killed or that it would kill anyone else. It is the perfect, twisted satirical outcome: in the white-facing representation of Blackness, Black people do not just play themselves, they also kill each other. For some, this can affirm that nothing has changed—that there is nothing to see other than the "sheer WTF-edness and creeping feeling of progress being undone by violence and oppression" (Fear, 2020). For others, *Bamboozled* is either funny or unfunny, so take it or leave it. For others still, the same sort of racist festivity that makes *Mantan: The New Millennium Minstrel Show* a hit makes *Bamboozled* a comic horror show. It remakes white America again. What has changed? Everything. And nothing.

If *Bamboozled* makes whiteness into an object of ridicule, it also sustains Blackness as *the* cultural icon of racial mockery, hence why comicality à la Baldwin is so crucial alongside comicality à la Ellison. *Bamboozled* is a postracial film that merges a sense of hysteria with a sense of humor. Satire itself is the postracial fantasy. It is based on a recursive principle of reproducing racist stereotypes in order to perpetuate them. There are no laughing barrels here. Racial laughter resounds in the open air. *Bamboozled* confounds expectations as much as it makes white supremacy palatable in public spaces *as entertainment*. Laughter is flipped upside down, and when laughing barrels are emptied of their contents, what we find are Black tears. To make America bamboozled again is to make fun of the follies of postracial caricature—to see blackface as "black, benighted, brutal, consumed with hatred," not as its embodiments are "consumed with guilt," but rather as they are consumed with gaiety and glee (Baldwin, 1985, p. 84). In a Burkean sense, the dance of words and images is the dance of bodies, postures, and attitudes. Baldwin and Ellison provide the framework for bamboozlement in comic operatics, in the dance of Blackness as a "comic distortion," blighted by "burnt-corked, cotton-gloved cornballs" (Ellison, 2003, p. 171). A dark joke indeed.

REFERENCES

Aftab, K. (2020, May 15). Spike Lee's masterpiece about racism in the US. *BBC*. https://www
    .bbc.com/culture/article/20200515-spike-lees-masterpiece-about-racism-in-the-us
Anderson, C. (2016). *White rage: The unspoken truth of our racial divide*. Bloomsbury.
Baldwin, J. (1985). *The price of the ticket*. Beacon Press.
Barnes, R. L. (n.d.). *The birth of blackface minstrelsy and the rise of Stephen Foster*. US History Scene. https://ushistoryscene.com/article/birth-of-blackface/
Belcher, C. (2016). *A Black man in the White House: Barack Obama and the triggering of America's racial-aversion crisis*. Water Street Press.
Benjamin, R. (2018, October 27). The Trumpist white minstrel show. *Los Angeles Times*. https://www.latimes.com/opinion/op-ed/la-oe-benjamin-white-minstrel-20181027-story.html
Black, R. (2003). Satire's cruelest cut: Exorcising Blackness in Spike Lee's *Bamboozled*. *The Black Scholar: Journal of Black Studies and Research, 33*(1), 19–24.
Boyd, M. R. (2008). *Jim Crow nostalgia: Reconstructing race in Bronzeville*. University of Minnesota Press.

Burke, K. (1969). *A rhetoric of motives*. University of California Press.

Burke, K. (2003). Towards Helhaven: Three stages of a vision. In W. H. Rueckert & A. Bonadonna (Eds.), *On human nature: A gathering while everything flows, 1967–1984* (pp. 54–65). University of California Press.

Busack, R. (2000, October). Facing up to stereotypes. Jim Crow Museum. https://www .ferris.edu/HTMLS/news/jimcrow/links/essays/Bamboozled.htm

Bush, M. E. L. (2011). *Everyday forms of whiteness: Understanding race in a "post-racial" world*. Rowman & Littlefield.

Carpio, G. (2008). *Laughing fit to kill: Black humor in the fictions of slavery*. Oxford University Press.

Clark, A. (2010, March 17). Bamboozled: *New millennium, same bullshit*. Criterion Collection. https://www.criterion.com/current/posts/6862-bamboozled-new-millennium-same -bullshit

Clark, A. (2015). *Facing Blackness: Media and minstrelsy in Spike Lee's* Bamboozled. Critical Press.

Clark, S. (2020, July 1). *How white supremacy returned to mainstream politics*. Center for American Progress. https://www.americanprogress.org/issues/security/reports/2020 /07/01/482414/white-supremacy-returned-mainstream-politics/

Coates, T.-N. (2010, October 4). You been misled. You been had. You been took. *The Atlantic*. https://www.theatlantic.com/personal/archive/2010/10/you-been-misled-you-been -had-you-been-took/63999/

Coates, T.-N. (2017, October 15). Donald Trump is the first white president. *The Atlantic*. https://www.theatlantic.com/magazine/archive/2017/10/the-first-white-president-ta -nehisi-coates/537909/

Cole, J. L. (2020). *How the other half laughs: The comic sensibility in American culture, 1895–1920*. University Press of Mississippi.

Collins, K. A. (2020, March 23). Spike Lee's *Bamboozled* is still sharp, stinging, and utterly vital. *Vanity Fair*. https://www.vanityfair.com/hollywood/2020/03/spike-lee-bamboozled -criterion

Crable, B. (2012). *Ralph Ellison and Kenneth Burke: At the roots of the racial divide*. University of Virginia Press.

Dennis, D., Jr. (2020, January 8). *Bamboozled* 20 years later: We all shortchanged Spike's classic film. *Level*. https://level.medium.com/bamboozled-20-years-later-we-all -shortchanged-spikes-classic-film-6a2830d0bbc0

Dundes, A. (1973). Preface. In A. Dundes (Ed.), *Mother wit from the laughing barrel: Readings in the interpretation of Afro-American folklore* (pp. xiii–xvi). University Press of Mississippi.

Ebert, R. (2000, October 6). *Bamboozled*. RogerEbert.com. https://www.rogerebert.com /reviews/bamboozled-2000

Eckardt, A. R. (2017). *On the way to death: Essays toward a comic vision*. Routledge.

Ellison, R. (1973). Change the joke and slip the yoke. In A. Dundes (Ed.), *Mother wit from the laughing barrel: Readings in the interpretation of Afro-American folklore* (pp. 56–64). University Press of Mississippi.

Ellison, R. (1986). *Going to the territory*. Vintage.

Ellison, R. (2003). *The collected essays of Ralph Ellison* (J. F. Callahan, Ed.). Modern Library.

Enck-Wanzer, D. (2011). Barack Obama, the Tea Party, and the threat of race: On racial neoliberalism and born again racism. *Communication, Culture & Critique, 4*(1), 23–30.

Erigha, M. (2019). *The Hollywood Jim Crow: The racial politics of the movie industry.* New York University Press.

Fauset, J. (1925). The gift of laughter. In A. Locke (Ed.), *The new Negro: An interpretation* (pp. 161–167). Albert and Charles Boni.

Fear, D. (2020, March 28). *Bamboozled* is the forgotten gem in Spike Lee's career. *Rolling Stone.* https://www.rollingstone.com/movies/movie-features/bamboozled-spike-lee -criterion-972833/

Goldberg, D. T. (2015). *Are we all postracial yet?* Polity Press.

Gregory, M. (1925). The drama of Negro life. In A. Locke (Ed.), *The new Negro: An interpretation* (pp. 153–160). Albert and Charles Boni.

Grossberg, L. (2018). *Under the cover of chaos: Trump and the battle for the American Right.* Pluto Press.

Higginbotham, F. M. (2013). *Ghosts of Jim Crow: Ending racism in post-racial America.* New York University Press.

hooks, b. (2015). *Black looks: Race and representation.* Routledge.

Hughes, L. (1925). The new Negro. In A. Locke (Ed.), *The new Negro: An interpretation* (pp. 141–145). Albert and Charles Boni.

Hyman, S. E. (1973). The folk tradition. In A. Dundes (Ed), *Mother wit from the laughing barrel: Readings in the interpretation of Afro-American folklore* (pp. 45–56). University Press of Mississippi.

Ismail, A. (2021, January 7). What I saw inside the Capitol riot. *Slate.* https://slate.com /news-and-politics/2021/01/capitol-riot-photos-inside-trump.html

Jefferson, H. (2021, January 8). Storming the US Capitol was about maintaining white power in America. *FiveThirtyEight.* https://fivethirtyeight.com/features/storming -the-u-s-capitol-was-about-maintaining-white-power-in-america/

Johnson, E. P. (2003). *Appropriating Blackness: Performance and the politics of authenticity.* Duke University Press.

Kelly, C. R. (2020a). Donald J. Trump and the rhetoric of ressentiment. *Quarterly Journal of Speech, 106*(1), 2–24.

Kelly, C. R. (2020b). Donald J. Trump and the rhetoric of white ambivalence. *Rhetoric & Public Affairs, 23*(2), 195–223.

Kendi, I. X. (2021, June 22). Our new post-racial myth. *The Atlantic.* https://www.theatlantic.com/ideas/archive/2021/06/our-new-postracial-myth/619261/

Kopp, L. (2014). Satirizing satire: Symbolic violence and subversion in Spike Lee's *Bamboozled.* In D. C. Mau & J. J. Donahue (Eds.), *Post-soul satire: Black identity after civil rights* (pp. 214–227). University Press of Mississippi.

Kunzru, H. (2017). *White tears.* Alfred A. Knopf.

Lee, S. (n.d.). *Bamboozled.* Internet Movie Script Database. https://imsdb.com/scripts/Bamboozled.html

Lee, S. (Director). (2000). *Bamboozled* [Film]. New Line Cinema.

Lhamon, W. T. (1998). *Raising Cain: Blackface performance from Jim Crow to hip hop.* Harvard University Press.

Liebow, N., & Glazer, T. (2019). White tears: Emotion regulation and white fragility. *Inquiry: An interdisciplinary journal of philosophy, 66*(1), 122–142.

Lott, E. (1993). *Love and theft: Blackface minstrelsy and the American working class.* Oxford University Press.

Lumet, S. (Director). (1976). *Network* [Film]. Metro-Goldwyn-Mayer.

Mahar, W. J. (1999). *Behind the burnt cork mask: Early blackface minstrelsy and antebellum American popular culture.* University of Illinois Press.

McVeigh, R., & Estep, K. (2019). *The politics of losing: Trump, the Klan, and the mainstreaming of resentment.* Columbia University Press.

Melamed, J. (2011). *Represent and destroy: Rationalizing violence in the new racial capitalism.* University of Minnesota Press.

Morgan, D. F. (2020). *Laughing to keep from dying: African American satire in the twenty-first century.* University of Illinois Press.

Morrison, T. (2020). *The source of self-regard: Selected essays, speeches, and meditations.* Vintage Books.

Nussbaum, E. (2017, January 23). How jokes won the election. *New Yorker.* https://www .newyorker.com/magazine/2017/01/23/how-jokes-won-the-election

Omari, J. (2019, July 3). Seeing red: A professor coexisting with "MAGA" in the classroom. *ABA Journal.* https://www.abajournal.com/voice/article/coexisting-with-maga-in -the-classroom

Ott, B. L., & Dickinson, G. (2019). *The Twitter presidency: Donald J. Trump and the politics of white rage.* Routledge.

Parvulescu, A. (2010). *Laughter: Notes on a passion.* MIT Press.

Patterson, T. (2000, October 20). *Bamboozled. Entertainment Weekly.* https://ew.com /article/2000/10/20/bamboozled-4/

Powell, R. J. (2020). *Going there: Black visual satire.* Yale University Press.

Rice, T. D. (2009). Jim Crow, still alive! In W. T. Lhamon (Ed.), *Jim Crow, American* (pp. 9–26). Belknap Press.

Roberts, B. (2017). *Blackface nation: Race, reform, and identity in American popular music, 1812–1925.* University of Chicago Press.

Sammond, N. (2015). *Birth of an industry: Blackface minstrelsy and the rise of American animation.* Duke University Press.

Serwer, A. (2009, April 15). White nationalism's deep American roots. *The Atlantic.* https:// www.theatlantic.com/magazine/archive/2019/04/adam-serwer-madison-grant-white -nationalism/583258/

Smith, A. (2012). Indigeneity, settler colonialism, white supremacy. In D. M. HoSang, O. LaBennett, & L. Pulido (Eds.), *Racial formation in the twenty-first century* (pp. 66–90). University of California Press.

Squires, Catherine R. (2014). *The post-racial mystique: Media and race in the twenty-first century.* New York University Press.

Taylor, K.-Y. (2021, January 12). The bitter fruits of Trump's white-power presidency. *New Yorker*. https://www.newyorker.com/news/our-columnists/the-bitter-fruits-of-trumps-white-power-presidency

Taylor, Y., & Austen, J. (2012). *Darkest America: Black minstrelsy from slavery to hip-hop*. W. W. Norton & Company.

Toll, R. C. (1977). *Blacking up: The minstrel show in nineteenth-century America*. Oxford University Press.

Watkins, M. (1999). *On the real side: A history of African American comedy from slavery to Chris Rock*. Lawrence Hill Books.

Watkins, M. (2012). Foreword. In Y. Taylor & J. Austen (Eds.), *Darkest America: Black minstrelsy from slavery to hip-hop* (pp. xiii–xvi). W. W. Norton & Company.

Williamson, K. D. (2017, October 20). The white-minstrel show. *National Review*. https://www.nationalreview.com/2017/10/white-working-class-populism-underclass-anti-elitism-acting-white-incompatible-conservativism/

Wright, J. (2019, January 31). How the MAGA hat became a symbol of hate. *Harper's Bazaar*. https://www.harpersbazaar.com/culture/politics/a26099971/maga-hat-hate-jussie-smollet-tennessean-explained/

Wright, R. (2019, July 31). The rhetoric and reality of Donald Trump's racism. *New Yorker*. https://www.newyorker.com/news/our-columnists/the-rhetoric-and-reality-of-donald-trumps-racism

Chapter 7

THE POSTRACIAL FANTASYLAND OF LIVE-ACTION DISNEY REMAKES

ARTHUR D. SOTO-VÁSQUEZ

Amidst the racial reckoning following the police killing of George Floyd in the summer of 2020, many companies released statements recognizing the history of racial injustice in the United States. In its statement issued on May 30, representatives of the Walt Disney Company affirmed its "resolve to use our compassion, our creative ideas and our collective sense of humanity to ensure we are fostering a culture that acknowledges our people's feelings and their pain" (Chapek et al., 2020). Later that year, at the 2020 investor-day presentation, Executive Chairman (and former CEO) Bob Iger (2020) followed up by saying, "We are redoubling our efforts to create rich, diverse content that best represents . . . the consumers that we're making that content for. It's very important to us that when people watch our shows and movies, they see themselves and their experiences." These efforts were realized through an announced slate of products involving diverse artists in front of and behind the camera.

Absent from these public statements is the role the Walt Disney Company has played in portraying racist stereotypes, especially in its animated films (Brode, 2005; Cheu, 2013; Lugo-Lugo & Bloodsworth-Lugo, 2009). Prior to 2020, the company made some noteworthy attempts to reconcile this history. The 1946 film *Song of the South*, considered racist and offensive even in the 1940s, has never been released on home video in the United States (Inge, 2012). And in 2020, the company announced that the Splash Mountain attraction in multiple Disney parks would be rethemed, dropping the *Song of the South* theming in favor of *The Princess and the Frog*—the first Disney film with a Black princess (Barnes, 2020). On Disney+, a disclaimer now runs before films like *Dumbo* and *Peter Pan* that states, "This program includes negative depictions and/or mistreatment of people or cultures. These stereotypes were wrong then and are wrong now" (Lattanzio, 2020). And the company has been applauded for increasing diversity in its products since the 2010s (Desta, 2016). In this chapter, I will focus on another strategy the company has undertaken to respond to criticisms of their animated films. The remaking of their animated classics into live-action films, often with great success at the box office, has been an attempt to both respond to criticisms of racism in their animated features and also "retheme" the company's past. I will refer to the three main rhetorical moves used in the live-action films as "racial remembering and forgetting," the "multicultural cinematic universe," and "racial Imagineering."

To make this argument, I discuss three films as exemplars of each tactic. In *Dumbo* (2019), the racial critiques were sidestepped by removing the infamous crows and Black laborers from the film. In *The Lion King* (2019), Black and Latinx actors were hired as voice actors. And perhaps most interestingly, in *Lady and the Tramp* (2019), Black and white characters were depicted living in racial harmony in an ambiguously southern town at the turn of the twentieth century. Each film's plot will be critically summarized and analyzed in relation to the attempt to use the live-action films to both respond to criticisms and reflect the diversity and inclusion values that the company has pledged to uphold. To do so, I argue the live-action remakes construct a theme-park-like racial fantasyland where multiculturalism was always the norm and racial violence and strife never existed. Here, I advance a concept I call the "postracial fantasyland" to describe how a sanitized acknowledgement of race and celebration of multiculturalism reflects many of the practices of the Walt Disney Company through a process scholars have called "Disneyization" (Bryman, 2004).

Much like the use of historical theming at Disney parks, I argue that Disney's postracial fantasyland simultaneously sanitizes and obscures race as it commodifies racial progress into a consumable good. The outcome broadly informs a larger trend in the early 2020s in which large, multinational corporations often revise US history in their communications while also obscuring their own role in persistent inequalities through a veneer of diversity and inclusion. Indeed, the three rhetorical strategies I trace in this chapter—racial remembering and forgetting, multicultural representation, and racial Imagineering—not only ideologically reinscribe the postracial but are also emblematic of an emerging corporatized response to racial injustice.

THE HISTORY OF RACE REPRESENTATION
IN DISNEY ANIMATED FILMS

Far from harmless entertainment for children, animated films offer a means to read the racial (and gendered) terrain of society from a young age

(Lugo-Lugo & Bloodsworth-Lugo, 2009). Animated films made for children offer an easily consumable cultural education (Giroux, 1999), which can then be reinforced in the family and society at large. One might ask, How can race be present in animated films when many of the characters are anthropomorphic animals? As C. R. Lugo-Lugo and M. K. Bloodsworth-Lugo (2009) argue, it is through anthropomorphizing (giving animals human features and traits) that the characters in animated films can be read racially. Since giving animals human traits needs to be communicated in quick fashion for short attention spans, animators resort to stereotypes to quickly convey the traits of an animated character. Even in more recent films, like *Zootopia* (2016), there are several instances of stereotypes communicated through the essentialized features of animals: the shrews are coded as Italian American mafiosos, and a midriff-baring gazelle voiced by Shakira is coded as Latina. The racial heuristics present in many Disney films become the sites of cultural learning for young children (Giroux, 1999)

Beyond education for children, the racist stereotypes in Disney films have also aligned with political goals of the United States domestically and abroad. Black people, for example, are stereotyped as childlike primitives in the earliest Mickey Mouse cartoons, such as *Trader Mickey* (1932), and early films, such as *Fantasia* (1940) and *Dumbo* (1941). Scholars argue that this trope undergirded Jim Crow–era racial segregation (Willetts, 2013). K. R. Willetts notes that Disney did remove racist elements of the *Pastoral* Symphony segment of the 1969 theatrical release of *Fantasia*, representing one of the first Disney edits to its own history. *Trader Mickey* is also not currently available on Disney+, unlike many other Mickey shorts.

Disney films have also historically used racial stereotypes to either advance the interests of the United States or cope with anxieties related to the Other in the Cold War. *Saludos Amigos* (1943) and *The Three Caballeros* (1945), for example, were a part of the Good Neighbor policy, which was aimed at generating friendlier relations between Latin America and the United States after decades of intervention. The goal was to represent Latin America as a viable tourist destination and lucrative market as Europe descended into the chaos of World War II. Despite the intention of the policy, the films still reinforce gendered and racial stereotypes of Latin Americans. K. S. Goldman (2013) argues that the sexualization of Latinas, whom Donald Duck lusts over throughout *The Three Caballeros*, reflects the historically "gendered narrative of U.S. masculine-identified hegemony vis à vis a highly feminized representation of Latin America" (p. 25). This exemplifies how racializing and sexualizing the Other in the guise of representation can advance geopolitical goals. The same can also be said for the horribly Orientalist stereotypes at play with the Siamese cats from *Lady and the Tramp* (1955), which resonated with the moral panic over the Asian Other during the Cold War. These representations are not relics of the mid-twentieth century either, even as social norms change. The Disney renaissance of the 1990s, for example, showcased a racially diverse set of female leads in *Aladdin* (1992), *Pocahontas* (1995), and *The Hunchback of Notre Dame* (1996), but these characters were more sexualized than typical white Disney princesses (Lacroix, 2004). Disney's choice to diversify its lead characters, of course, also expands the company's viewing market (Valdivia, 2008). Perhaps in response to past criticism, Disney returned to traditional 2D animation with the 2008 film *The Princess and the Frog*, which features a conservatively dressed and hardworking Tiana, who spends most of the plot as a green anthropomorphic frog (Turner, 2013). When Disney began to reach into its catalog of classics to reinterpret for live-action films, it certainly had a lot of its own history to contend with. Next, I will discuss the strategies of the postracial fantasyland that inform that process.

CORPORATE MULTICULTURALISM

Corporate America's ongoing reckoning with race comes after a decades-long approach of "not seeing" race and denying its role in persistent inequalities (Bonilla-Silva, 2017). After the civil rights movements of the 1960s, a discourse emerged claiming that racism was "over." However, as E. Bonilla-Silva (2017) demonstrates in *Racism without Racists*, enduring racial gaps in wealth, education, and health remain. The ideological rationalization for these disparities cohered into what he calls colorblind racism. Colorblind ideology states that racism is individualized rather than systematic and that racial inequalities are the result of presumed cultural differences, such as work ethic and family support, rather than racially motivated public policies, such as housing or employment discrimination.

Indeed, our current moment is marked by colorblind ideologies, which posit we do not see race and a postracial periodization of racial progress that presumes that racism is in the past (Bonilla-Silva, 2015). H. Gray (2019) argues that this postracial periodization "implies a temporal sense of movement from one (unfair and unequal condition) to another (fair and equal)" (p. 25) that helps ideologically mystify the persistence of racial inequality and domination. This is accomplished through the disavowal of the social construction of race and the reaffirmation of essentialist understandings of race.

In our postracial era, even multinational corporations support social change in the form of multiculturalism and diversity initiatives. Indeed, as

R. A. Ferguson (2019) demonstrates, the embrace of multiculturalism is critical to postracial ideology since it forecloses more radical ideological alternatives to capitalism in the pursuit of an antiracist politics. The corporate embrace of multiculturalism achieves this very goal through the integration of (some, often highly educated) racialized minorities into the structures of capitalism as both avatars of progress and evidence that this system can accomplish racial progress. More recent terms like "diversity" and "inclusion" also follow a similar logic, especially as they appear in the Walt Disney Company statement quoted earlier. Stylistically, postracialism thus contains the radical in the name of reform.

The capitalist embrace of the postracial extends beyond the hiring and promotion of racial minorities. First, brands now actively integrate progressive social movements around race, gender, and sexuality into their marketing and advertising (Kanai & Gill, 2020), which serves to make consumption habits "feel good" ethically (Montez de Oca et al., 2020). Second, as A. Kanai and R. Gill (2020) argue, the prominence of historically marginalized people in corporate branding turns them into de facto "mascots" of progress for the capitalist system. Finally, corporations undertake their own revisionist histories, and in the next section, I will outline how Disney has strategically undertaken such a move.

THE DISNEYIZATION OF THE POSTRACIAL

Before delving into the specifics of each film, it is worth establishing why Disney's postracial tactics are so illuminating. We are living in a culture that some have argued has been Disneyized (Bryman, 2004). Disneyization can be summarized as the process of applying the very successful business practices of the Walt Disney Company to society at large. For A. Bryman (2004), this consists of applying Disney themes to shopping malls, restaurants (e.g., Hard Rock Cafe), music festivals, and Instagram pop-ups. Disneyization extends to customer-service jobs for which people are expected to perform "cheerful" emotional labor. But of most interest to this analysis is the sanitization of history and culture through films and other media. Disneyization of history, literature, and myth necessitates removing the unpleasant aspects of the past and then either sanitizing or sentimentalizing those aspects to make them more palatable and consumable to the audience (Walz, 1998). Dark European fairytales, for example, are translated by Disney into family-friendly entertainment with generally uncontroversial themes.

One illuminating example of the harm Disney can do to US history is the controversy over building a theme park in Virginia near a historic Civil

War battlefield (Synnott, 1995). The park was planned to have areas themed around historical periods where issues like war, slavery, and manifest destiny would be unavoidable. Historians opposed to the park doubted Disney could handle these issues appropriately. The risk, as D. McCullough says, would be "to replace what we have with [a] plastic, contrived history, mechanical history" (Janofsky, 1994). While the park never came to be, Disney's impact on US Americans' (lack of) knowledge of their own history remains. One only has to turn to Disneyland Park in California to see how the "Wild West" is recolonized through the symbolic elimination of Indigenous people in Frontierland (Francaviglia, 2011). Finally, Disney's approach to updating its attractions in the park is instructive here too. The term "Imagineering" is a portmanteau of "imagination" and "engineering" and is trademarked by the Walt Disney Company. Imagineers work on Disney theme-park attractions, often using state-of-the-art lighting, sound, set design, and ride systems to convey stories to theme-park guests. Imagineers are often in the process of adding thrilling new show elements to older attractions with the latest technology. When they do this, they also update attractions to remove problematic elements from midcentury attractions too. The revision of the Jungle Cruise to remove anti-Indigenous stereotypes is the most recent example (Prieur, 2021).

Here, the Disneyization of the postracial works at two levels that need distinction. First, as Disney's America theme park shows, the company often intervenes in and interprets broader United States and world history in its media production. Second, as the updating of attractions by Imagineers shows, the company also intervenes into its own corporate history too. The recent live-action remakes work on both of these levels, textually and metatextually. Through these multilevel sanitizing rearticulations of the past, Disneyization attempts to disavow America's racist past, including Disney's own contribution to this racist past, while also obscuring the persistence of racial difference. This is further accomplished by hiring diverse actors and directors to create new Disney projects. In this way, the strategies of Disney are broadly informative of corporate America's responses to the ruptures and reckonings in the last few years. The following analysis of three live-action Disney remakes further illustrates these three moves.

RACIAL REMEMBERING AND FORGETTING IN *DUMBO*

The live-action remake of *Dumbo* was released in 2019, almost eighty years after the original film was released in 1941. Among the films discussed in this chapter, it takes the most liberties with reimagining the story of the original film. The film refocuses the story away from the animals (who are stand-ins for human personalities in the original) as the drivers of dramatic action in the original film toward humans and how they treat the animals in a circus and each other. While the original film runs just sixty-four minutes, the remake runs over two hours. The film is directed by Tim Burton and features many actors who appear in his other films, which have been described as having a dark, gothic style that focuses on outsider characters. Burton also has a long and complicated history with Disney, never quite fitting into the Disney brand but also working with it on several successful films (Romano, 2019).

The second hour in the live-action remake centers on what happens after Dumbo discovers he can fly. As Dumbo becomes an overnight sensation, he draws the attention of a P. T. Barnum– / Walt Disney–esque entrepreneur and showman character named V. A. Vandevere who acquires the Medici Bros. Circus. This new plot element adds dramatic tension to the plot in a few ways. In contrast to the animated film, Jumbo is separated from her child, Dumbo, earlier in the film. It is then revealed later that Jumbo was unknowingly purchased by Vandevere's Dreamland (a gothic Disneyland stand-in). The remainder of the film involves the protagonists trying to break both elephants out of Dreamland and return them to the wild. This is in contrast to the original animated film, in which the dramatic tension of not being accepted by others is resolved by Dumbo learning to fly (with the help of a magic black feather) and becoming a top drawer for the circus. The original animated plot concludes with the new celebrity Dumbo reunited with his mother but remaining in the circus as a performer.

The change to the plot removes the need for Dumbo to learn how to fly. In the original film, Dumbo learns how to fly quite late in the film with the help of the infamous crows. The crows, led by a character actually named Jim Crow, are coded as Black Americans by their exaggerated "word choice, phonology, and mannerisms" that reference stereotypes of the time (Willetts, 2013, p. 19). The blithe use of the term "Jim Crow" to identify a character along with the crows using "boy" to address Dumbo, not to mention that the crows are voiced by white actors, exemplify the casually cruel racist attitudes of the moment. The crows gift Dumbo the "magic" feather, evoking the longstanding trope in Hollywood of which Black characters with unique wisdom or mystical insight aid white protagonists (Hughey, 2009). In the live-action remake, the crows are simply left out and not even addressed. Only some of their lines are referenced by a circus announcer.

The removal of the racist crows as a major plot element reflects a larger pattern of *racial remembering and forgetting* in postracial communication and media. "Racial forgetting" is the purposeful and strategic forgetting of racism. We saw instances of racial amnesia during the 2020 summer protests when corporations and conglomerates released statements acknowledging pain, suffering, and injustice but eliding their own part in representing harmful racial stereotypes or helping to produce divergent outcomes. Others have noted the power of cultural remembering and forgetting. For example, the exuberant postracial feelings after the election of Barack Obama were a result of a feeling of conclusion to the story of Black liberation since the civil rights movement—conveniently forgetting moments of conflict, violence, and political setbacks for equality in between (Gray, 2019; Hoerl, 2012). Thus, as Gray (2019) argues, this tactic also functions by remembering the "good" progressive elements in a story while ignoring the bad—periodizing racial disunion as something that happened in the past and that, importantly, society is constantly progressing away from.

Another instance of racial stereotyping is dropped in the live-action remake of *Dumbo*. In the beginning of the animated version, "Song of the Roustabouts" plays over a scene in which Black laborers and the animals set up the circus in a new city. The song contains statements from the roustabouts such as "We never learned to read or write." That the song occurs during a raging thunderstorm and the film is set during the early 1900s in the American South gives the scene even more menace. Even though both the crows and the roustabouts are dropped from the live-action film, there remain slight intertextual references to them in the live-action version, which function to signal to "in-the-know" audiences that the company is aware of its past. This Easter-egg acknowledgment of past racist representation is also a very specific instance of remembering and forgetting in postracial media, as the acknowledgments rely on the intertextual nature of a remake film. Contemporary audiences who are aware of the problematic elements in the original film recognize that they should not be included in the remake but also want affirmation that their reading of the original film is correct in our current racial milieu.

Here is where it becomes useful to also think of the live-action remakes as commodities. Embedding media with Easter eggs and allusions to previous media can also extend the influence of a product onto social media, where fans will decode the meaning of the references. As N. Haramis (2023) writes, "Scouring for these narrative tricks is addictive—for one thing, they flatter consumers' sense of themselves as nobody's fool." While the racial amnesia in *Dumbo* might go over the head of younger audiences, for adults in the know, it is both satisfying and affirming to *remember* the older depiction, periodize it in the regressive past, and identify the change. Just as with racially

progressive sport advertising, audiences can feel good (or even upset, depending upon partisanship) consuming this kind of media.

One last element of the *Dumbo* live-action film deserves mention. The
added hour, which focuses on Vandevere and Dreamland, also works as a
not-so-subtle metatextual reference to the Walt Disney Company and its
acquisition, conglomeration, and commercialization practices. As critics
note, the film makes Disney a villain in a Disney film (Wilkinson, 2019).
This message serves as another means to signal to the audience that Disney
is aware of its history and its media power—"an invitation from filmmaker
to audience to share a knowing chuckle over the essential soullessness of the
entire enterprise," as one critic puts it (Dessem, 2019, para. 6). Yet this ironic
acknowledgement seems to be there only to flatter the audience rather than
be a true critique or change in business. The film also accomplishes this by
reframing the ethical theme of the story away from bullying (original film)
and toward the mistreatment of animals, as L. Ellis (2019) points out. The
racial problems from the original film are replaced by the message of ending animal-led circuses, which also lends it a feeling of progress. It does so
by placing the racial stereotypes of the 1930s version as a distinct issue of
the past—whereas now, animal cruelty is presented as a more topical issue.
The ending of the film presents a solution to this problem with a return to
nature for Dumbo.

THE LION KING AND THE MULTICULTURAL
CINEMATIC UNIVERSE

In contrast to *Dumbo*, the live-action remake of *The Lion King* is almost an
exact retelling of the original animated film. The music, plot, dialogue, and
themes of the original film remain. The character of Mufasa is still voiced by
James Earl Jones. There are, however, two major changes in the live-action
version, one of which will be the focus of this section. The first change is
that the cartoon animation has been replaced by computer-generated images
(CGI), meaning this is technically not a live-action remake. The filmmakers
used CGI to create a *National Geographic*–style nature documentary simulacrum (Desowitz, 2019). Critics largely found this change less impactful than
the original animation, although they noted that the visuals are impressive.
The other major change I focus on here, which did receive praise from critics,
is the move to cast a more racially diverse group of voice actors in contrast
to the original (Parachuk, 2019).

In the original *Lion King*, almost all the lead characters are voiced by white actors. Simba is voiced by Jonathan Taylor Thomas as a cub and by Matthew Broderick as an adult, Nala is voiced by Moira Kelly as an adult, and Scar is voiced by Jeremy Irons. In the 2019 version, these characters are voiced by Donald Glover, Beyoncé Knowles-Carter, and Chiwetel Ejiofor, respectively. The voice acting of the hyenas was also changed, which serves to update their role in the film from symbolic of the US American racialized underclass to more general outsiders. Despite the original film being set in a vaguely African setting, the 1994 version can be read as an allegory of race and urban politics in postindustrial America (Gooding-Williams, 1995). Whoopi Goldberg as Shenzi and Cheech Marin as Banzai use US American Black and Chicano slang when they meet Simba and Nala after the lion cubs "lose themselves in the American inner city," symbolically represented as the elephant graveyard (Gooding-Williams, 1995, p. 375). Later in the film, Scar usurps the throne with the aid of the hyenas but, in the process, disrupts the natural order of the Pride Lands, leading to famine and ecological crisis. The message of the film, according to R. Gooding-Williams, is clear: racial integration is pollution and disrupts the natural order. Further, this unnaturalness is emphasized by the Nuremberg rally imagery invoked in the song "Be Prepared," which seemingly implies that the racial underclass presents a threat to the natural (read "white") order when mobilized by a cynical authoritarian.

Seemingly aware of this reading of the racialized-threat narrative from the original, in the live-action version, Disney tones down the role of the hyenas. Shenzi is characterized as a more independent leader of the hyenas, forming a partnership with Scar to dethrone Mufasa. Shenzi is also voiced by Ugandan-born actress Florence Kasumba. Banzai and Ed are sidelined and are now a bickering duo played for laughs. In this case, the racially problematic elements from the original film are not as easily ignored like in *Dumbo*. Rather, Disney pursues another strategy here: the casting of racially and nationally diverse actors to revise their Disney renaissance films from the 1990s. I call this practice the "multicultural cinematic universe," knowingly referencing Disney's other major intellectual property, which has also diversified its stable of superheroes. Here, something interesting simultaneously occurs; the characters are deracialized in the text of the film, but the discourse on the metatextual level is all about the multicultural project of casting diverse actors, affirming its postracial status. In essence, the diverse actors both give a sense of symbolic progress and help soften any claims of continuing harm.

Disney's current embrace of multiculturalism began in the 1990s when it began to draw source material beyond European fairy tales. *Aladdin* is based on the Arabic folklore of *One Thousand and One Nights. Mulan* (1998) is based on the Chinese legend of Hua Mulan. And as C. Lacroix (2004) notes, more nonwhite Disney characters are put to screen. However, despite the use of non-Western stories, many of these films utilize white voice actors to portray nonwhite characters. *Aladdin* is perhaps the most egregious case, with an all-white cast (Charity, 2017). Further, as A. Elmogahzy (2018) argues, *Aladdin, The Lion King*, and *Mulan* all feature main characters who value independence and end up rebelling against the repressive stand-ins for the non-Western societies they are set in. Jasmine and Mulan both resist traditional gender roles in their films. When *Aladdin, The Lion King*, and *Mulan* were all remade into live-action films, there was an effort to cast diverse actors—even if the underlying plots were only slightly revised. As such, diversity becomes the easy fix.

The Walt Disney Company's efforts to diversify their remakes and new content are part of a larger push for Hollywood and the entertainment industry to diversify. The Annenberg Inclusion Initiative, which tracks representation in media, notes there has been some progress since 2007 but unequal representation remains the norm (S. L. Smith et al., 2020). And as I. Molina-Guzmán (2016) notes, the increase in representation is often framed as an economic imperative by the entertainment press—due to increasing audience diversity, new venues for production in streaming, and diverse films making more at the box office—rather than as a moral one. That multicultural representation is often framed within a discourse of expanding audience markets also echoes the criticisms of woke washing by corporations that deployed racial justice as branding. In this way, corporate multiculturalism remains entrenched in the flexible accumulation logics of capitalism. And as Gray (2013) notes, the push for diversification and representation in media can also elide efforts to pursue full economic equality since symbolic progress becomes more visible than material progress. The 2019 *Lion King* remake is the highest grossing animated film of all time, seemingly confirming the idea that cast diversity equals higher returns.

Disney's postracial politics—ranging from diversifying its media catalogue and behind-the-camera talent to its family-friendly acknowledgment of race—provides a basic blueprint we can expect other companies to follow. The projects announced at the 2020 investor-day meeting from Walt Disney Studios, Marvel Studios, and Lucasfilm all promise more diversity. Yet, we should ask, Who is this multicultural cinematic universe really for? It will surely make lots of money for the company, but so would almost any film or

TV show that carries the Marvel or Disney brand. It will also make audiences *feel better* about consuming a product from a giant media conglomerate. And it will increase diversity and inclusion in media. All three elements can be true. All deserve close attention in the coming years as scholars continue to unpack changing rhetorical boundaries of American racial relations.

LADY AND THE TRAMP AND RACIAL IMAGINEERING

Of the films analyzed in this chapter, *Lady and the Tramp* is the only live-action remake not to see a theatrical release. It was instead released on the newly launched Disney+ streaming service on November 12, 2019. Like the live-action remake of *The Lion King*, the 2019 *Lady and the Tramp* sticks mostly to the original in characters, plot, and music. Also like the live-action remake of *Dumbo*, the film removes the racist elements from the original. In the 1955 animated version, two Siamese cats wreak havoc in a musical scene. The lyrics of their song broadly reflect the Cold War anxieties of the Asian Other, as K. Akita and R. Kenny (2013) describe. As they discuss, the Siamese cats are laden with Orientalist stereotypes and frame Asians as "inscrutable" and a "menace to the Western order of things" (p. 61). The wreckage is blamed on Lady, and she is taken to a pet store to be muzzled, which advances the plot of the film. In the live-action remake, two cats also wreck the living room, but their racial coding is removed, just like in *Dumbo*. In addition, the ethnic coding of different dog breeds (e.g., Chihuahua = Mexican American) is toned down or removed. The same can also be said for the Italian stereotyping of Tony from the original. So, forgetting the text of the original is present here, just like in the remake of *Dumbo*.

Curiously, the remake does more than remove racial elements from the original film. It changes the setting and the diversity of its cast to Imagineer the racial past of the United States. Some context is needed to explain this claim. Where the story is set is not clearly specified in the original film, but an official Disney website says the setting was inspired by Marceline, Missouri (Waggener, 2018). Marceline is Walt Disney's hometown and is also the inspiration for Main Street, USA, in Disneyland. In the animated film, the human characters speak with a mostly generic American midwestern accent. The live-action version changes the setting completely, as the film is clearly set in the American South at the turn of the twentieth century. There is jazz, cotton, and a riverboat. It was also shot on location in Savannah, Georgia (S. Smith, 2019).

The setting of the film in the South makes the other prominent aspect of the live-action film even more revisionist. Lady's owners are an interracial couple. At the turn of the twentieth century in the US South, this would have been uncommon to say the least. It was not until the 1967 US Supreme Court decision *Loving v. Virginia* that every state in the former Confederacy had its antimiscegenation laws overturned. Black and white people are shown socializing in a baby-shower scene later in the film. There are Black store owners and nonwhite authority figures. In other words, segregation seems to have never existed here, and there is no racial conflict presented in the film. The past that is portrayed is a highly idealized one. This is different from revising Disney's corporate history; instead, the 2019 remake revises race relations in the turn-of-the-century American South.

Like other films in the multicultural cinematic universe, the 2019 remake's cast is diverse, featuring Yvette Nicole Brown, Ken Jeong, and the voice talents of Tessa Thompson, Janelle Monáe, and Benedict Wong. Yet the cast is only tangential to the larger issue of racial Imagineering seen in the film. As mentioned earlier, in recent years, Disney Imagineers have updated older attractions. Many are based in the original Disneyland, opened the same year (1955) that *Lady and the Tramp* was released. In Disney parks, the historical exploits of colonization (Jungle Cruise), piracy (Pirates of the Caribbean), Reconstruction (Splash Mountain), and westward expansion (Big Thunder Mountain Railroad) are either so sanitized or abstracted that the history and settings the attractions reference are only vaguely familiar to the guest. Disney has, in recent years, removed outdated portrayals in its attractions. While this move is likely the right one, it does feel more problematic when applied to cinematic depictions of US history rather than theme-park rides. As one critic of the live-action *Lady and the Tramp* says, "The entire movie feels like it was made inside a Disney theme park . . . as the movie swaps away turn-of-the-century racial politics for more family-friendly sources of tension" (Radulovic, 2019, para. 5). The film's idealized mid-American setting resembles Main Street, USA, more than any realistic historical setting. Indeed, moments when conflict might have become racialized, such as Aunt Sarah losing Lady and letting the cats make a mess of the living room while also criticizing Jim Dear's profession, are instead presented as a minor annoyance.

Disney is no doubt in a difficult spot when it comes to films set in the past—it cannot fully acknowledge the past without turning off parts of its audience. And while it might be able to ride a fine line by removing references to racist elements in the original films, by employing multiracial casts and engaging in revisionism, Disney risks further entrenching a sanitized and limited understanding of the preeminence of race in US history. Part of the postracial ruptures since Ferguson have particularly focused on how we remember, understand, and commemorate the history of the United States. So far, these tensions have emerged in the classroom, around Confederate monuments, and historically informed investigative journalism, like the 1619 Project. The postracial fantasyland of the *Lady and the Tramp* remake, where conflict and strife never existed, may end up doing more harm than good for future generations of children. Perhaps most destructive, it transplants a contemporary idealized postracial world into the past. The characters act much like they would in family-friendly entertainment set in the 2020s, just with corsets, sleeve garters, and Model Ts.

CONCLUSION

In a video essay on the failure of the planned Disney's America theme park, K. Perjurer (2018) keenly says, "Disney is America, and America is Disney." Acknowledging the shortcomings of either is hard because we want to "celebrate both for their power, glory, and magic but are often uncomfortable with the ways in which they were obtained." Criticizing Disney can often be uncomfortable because of its close association with our childhoods and positive memories of family and nostalgia. At the same time, the Walt Disney Company is the largest media conglomerate ever, setting trends and normalizing practices. In 2019, the company accounted for nearly 40 percent of box-office proceeds, while its closest competitor earned only slightly over 13 percent (Whitten, 2019). In a time when there are endless streaming options and hyperpartisan news sources, Disney remains the closest thing we have in the United States, besides arguably sports, to a shared culture across ideological divides. Because of the preeminence the company maintains and its power to influence children, the way Disney presents race, racism, and its own racial history remain pertinent. In this chapter, I have discussed how the live-action remakes of classic animated Disney films resonate with the ongoing struggle over race in the United States. So far, the company has acknowledged its racial history in a limited, sanitized, and ultimately Disneyized way. It has labeled some of its older products with disclaimers contributing to the periodization of racism. In films like *Dumbo* (2019), the tactic was racial forgetting and remembering, purposively forgetting past harmful depictions and remembering positive intertextual elements. In films like *The Lion King* (2019), the tactic was instead to use a multiracial cast to demonstrate progress. And in films like *Lady and the Tramp* (2019), the tactic was to revise the racial past, setting the film in a theme-park-like racial fantasyland where racial hierarchy and segregation do not exist. Ultimately, this chapter has identified three strategies—racial remembering and forgetting, the multicultural cinematic universe, and racial Imagineering—to better explain the rhetorical strategies of reckoning with race in a Disneyized way. These tactics of the postracial deserve mention and scrutiny precisely because they make us *feel good*, and progress appears to be happening before our eyes, even amidst resurgence of white-nationalist ideologies, continued racial violence, and inequality.

REFERENCES

Akita, K., & Kenney, R. (2013). A "vexing implication": Siamese cats and Orientalist mischief-making. In J. Cheu (Ed.), *Diversity in Disney films: Critical essays on race, ethnicity, gender, sexuality and disability* (pp. 50–66). McFarland.

Barnes, B. (2020, June 25). Disney's Splash Mountain to drop *Song of the South* depictions. *New York Times*. https://www.nytimes.com/2020/06/25/business/media/disney-splash -mountain-princess-frog.html

Bonilla-Silva, E. (2015). The structure of racism in color-blind, "post-racial" America. *American Behavioral Scientist, 59*(11), 1358–1376. https://doi.org/10.1177/0002764215586826

Bonilla-Silva, E. (2017). *Racism without racists: Color-blind racism and the persistence of racial inequality in the United States*. Rowman & Littlefield.

Brode, D. (2005). *Multiculturalism and the mouse: Race and sex in Disney entertainment*. University of Texas Press.

Bryman, A. (2004). *The Disneyization of society*. Sage.

Chapek, B., Iger, B., & Newton, L. (2020, May 31). *Resolve in a time of unrest: A message to fellow employees*. Walt Disney Company. https://thewaltdisneycompany.com/resolve -in-a-time-of-unrest-a-message-to-fellow-employees

Charity, J. (2017, July 18). Can Disney get *Aladdin* right? *The Ringer*. https://www.theringer .com/2017/7/18/16077838/aladdin-disney-remake-casting-whitewashing-debate -5f06580a85b5

Cheu, J. (Ed.). (2013). *Diversity in Disney films: Critical essays on race, ethnicity, gender, sexuality and disability*. McFarland.

Desowitz, B. (2019, July 20). *The lion king*: How Jon Favreau pushed "live action" animation to a new frontier. *IndieWire*. https://www.indiewire.com/2019/07/the-lion-king-live -action-animation-jon-favreau-virtual-vfx-1202159304

Dessem, M. (2019, March 28). Tim Burton's *Dumbo* tries to have its Disney-satirizing cake and profit off it too. *Slate*. https://slate.com/culture/2019/03/dumbo-review-2019 -remake-satirizes-disney-fox-michael-keaton-villain.html

Desta, Y. (2016, November 23). The year Disney started to take diversity seriously. *Vanity Fair*. https://www.vanityfair.com/hollywood/2016/11/disney-films-inclusive

Ellis, L. (2019, September 19). *Woke Disney* [Video]. YouTube. https://youtu.be/xU1ffHa47YY

Elmogahzy, A. (2018). A "whole new world": Race and representation in Disney's live-action remakes of Aladdin, The lion king, and Mulan [Master's thesis, Auburn University]. ProQuest.

Ferguson, R. A. (2019). On the postracial question. In R. Mukherjee, S. Banet-Weiser, & H. Gray (Eds.), Racism postrace (pp. 72–85). Duke University Press.

Francaviglia, R. (2011). Frontierland as an allegorical map of the American West. In K. M. Jackson & M. I. West (Eds.), Disneyland and culture: Essays on the parks and their influence (pp. 59–86). McFarland.

Giroux, H. A. (1999). The mouse that roared: Disney and the end of innocence. Rowman & Littlefield.

Goldman, K. (2013). Saludos amigos and The three caballeros: The representation of Latin America in Disney's "good neighbor" films. In J. Cheu (Ed.), Diversity in Disney films: Critical essays on race, ethnicity, gender, sexuality and disability (pp. 23–37). McFarland.

Gooding-Williams, R. (1995). Disney in Africa and the inner city: On race and space in The lion king. Social identities, 1(2), 373–379. https://doi.org/10.1080/13504630.1995.9959442

Gray, H. (2013). Subject(ed) to recognition. American Quarterly, 65(4), 771–798. https://doi.org/10.1353/aq.2013.0058

Gray, H. (2019). Race after race. In R. Mukherjee, S. Banet-Weiser, & H. Gray (Eds.), Racism postrace (pp. 19–36). Duke University Press.

Haramis, N. (2023, January 13). When did we all become pop culture detectives? New York Times. https://www.nytimes.com/2023/01/13/t-magazine/easter-eggs-taylor-swift.html

Hoerl, K. (2012). Selective amnesia and racial transcendence in news coverage of President Obama's inauguration. Quarterly Journal of Speech, 98(2), 178–202. https://doi.org/10.1080/00335630.2012.663499

Hughey, M. W. (2009). Cinethetic racism: White redemption and Black stereotypes in "magical Negro" films. Social Problems, 56(3), 543–577. https://doi.org/10.1525/sp.2009.56.3.543

Iger, B. (2020). [Speech transcript]. Investor Day, Walt Disney Company. https://thewaltdisneycompany.com/app/uploads/2020/12/Disney_Investor_Day_2020_transcript.pdf

Inge, M. T. (2012). Walt Disney's Song of the South and the politics of animation. Journal of American Culture, 35(3), 219–230. https://doi.org/10.1111/j.1542-734X.2012.00809.x

Janofsky, M. (1994, May 12). Learned opposition to new Disney park. New York Times. https://www.nytimes.com/1994/05/12/us/learned-opposition-to-new-disney-park.html

Kanai, A., & Gill, R. (2020). Woke? Affect, neoliberalism, marginalised identities and consumer culture. New Formations, 102, 10–27. https://www.muse.jhu.edu/article/787072

Lacroix, C. (2004). Images of animated Others: The Orientalization of Disney's cartoon heroines from The little mermaid to The hunchback of Notre Dame. Popular Communication, 2(4), 213–229. https://doi.org/10.1207/s15405710pc0204_2

Lattanzio, R. (2020, October 15). Peter Pan, Aristocats among Disney+ titles getting new disclaimer for "negative depictions" of race. IndieWire. https://www.indiewire.com/2020/10/disney-plus-disclaimer-films-negative-depictions-race-1234593225

Lugo-Lugo, C. R., & Bloodsworth-Lugo, M. K. (2009). "Look out new world, here we come"? Race, racialization, and sexuality in four children's animated films by Disney, Pixar, and DreamWorks. Cultural Studies ↔ Critical Methodologies, 9(2), 166–178. https://doi.org/10.1177/1532708608325937

Molina-Guzmán, I. (2016). #OscarsSoWhite: How Stuart Hall explains why nothing changes in Hollywood and everything is changing. *Critical Studies in Media Communication, 33*(5), 438–454. https://doi.org/10.1080/15295036.2016.1227864

Montez de Oca, J., Mason, S., & Ahn, S. (2020). Consuming for the greater good: "Woke" commercials in sports media. *Communication & Sport, 10*(6), 1165–1187. https://doi.org/10.1177/2167479520949283

Parachuk, T. (2019, August 27). The lion king *live action cast—Diversity in voice over.* Voices. https://www.voices.com/blog/the-lion-king-diversity-in-voice-over

Perjurer, K. (2018, July 4). *Defunctland: The war for Disney's America* [Video]. YouTube. https://youtu.be/-oqDqnQR5Aw

Prieur, D. (2021, February 1). Disney revamps Jungle Cruise ride to remove racist depictions of Indigenous people. *NPR.* https://www.npr.org/2021/02/01/962772012/disney-revamps-jungle-cruise-ride-to-remove-racist-depictions-of-indigenous-peop

Radulovic, P. (2019, November 12). The live-action *Lady and the tramp* feels like a theme-park version of real life. *Polygon.* https://www.polygon.com/reviews/2019/11/12/20961761/lady-and-the-tramp-review-disney-plus-remake

Romano, A. (2019, April 17). Tim Burton has built his career around an iconic visual aesthetic: Here's how it evolved. *Vox.* https://www.vox.com/culture/2019/4/17/18285309/tim-burton-films-visual-style-aesthetic-disney-explained

Smith, S. (2019, November 12). *Disney+ exclusive* Lady and the tramp *filmed on location in Savannah, Georgia.* The Location Guide. https://www.thelocationguide.com/2019/11/disney-exclusive-lady-and-the-tramp-filmed-on-location-in-savannah-georgia

Smith, S. L., Choueiti, M., & Pieper, K. M. (2020). *Inequality in 1,300 popular films: Examining portrayals of gender, race/ethnicity, LGBT & disability from 2007 to 2019.* USC Annenberg Inclusion Initiative. http://assets.uscannenberg.org/docs/aii-inequality_1300_popular_films_09-08-2020.pdf

Synnott, M. G. (1995). Disney's America: Whose patrimony, whose profits, whose past? *Public Historian, 17*(4), 43–59. https://doi.org/10.2307/3378384

Turner, S. E. (2013). Blackness, bayous and gumbo: Encoding and decoding race in a color-blind world. In J. Cheu (Ed.), *Diversity in Disney films: Critical essays on race, ethnicity, gender, sexuality and disability* (pp. 83–98). McFarland.

Valdivia, A. N. (2008). Mixed race on the Disney Channel: From *Johnny Tsunami* through *Lizzie McGuire* and ending with *The cheetah girls.* In M. Beltrán & C. Fojas (Eds.), *Mixed race Hollywood* (pp. 269–289). New York University Press.

Waggener, A. (2018, February 7). *10 things you didn't know about* Lady and the tramp. Oh My Disney. https://ohmy.disney.com/movies/2016/06/22/things-you-didnt-know-about-lady-and-the-tramp

Walz, G. (1998). Charlie Thorson and the temporary Disneyfication of Warner Bros. cartoons. In K. S. Sandler (Ed.), *Reading the rabbit: Explorations in Warner Bros. animation* (pp. 49–66). Rutgers University Press.

Whitten, S. (2019, December 29). Disney accounted for nearly 40% of the 2019 US box office. *CNBC.* https://www.cnbc.com/2019/12/29/disney-accounted-for-nearly-40percent-of-the-2019-us-box-office-data-shows.html

Wilkinson, A. (2019, March 28). Tim Burton's *Dumbo* is a charming-enough remake—and a biting Disney critique. *Vox.* https://www.vox.com/culture/2019/3/28/18282877/dumbo -review-tim-burton-disney

Willetts, K. R. (2013). Cannibals and coons: Blackness in the early days. In J. Cheu (Ed.), *Diversity in Disney films: Critical essays on race, ethnicity, gender, sexuality and disability* (pp. 9–22). McFarland.

Part 4

Crafting Memory in the Postrace Era

Chapter 8

STRATEGIES OF MEMORY CONSTRUCTION IN SPIKE LEE'S *BLACKKKLANSMAN*

A. SUSAN OWEN AND PETER EHRENHAUS

Spike Lee's *BlacKkKlansman* was released in August 2018 to mostly positive popular reviews and box-office success. The film received widespread artistic recognition, scoring multiple nominations from the 2019 Golden Globe Awards, the Academy Awards, the British Academy Film Awards, and the Screen Actors Guild, among others. *BlacKkKlansman* won an Oscar and a British Academy of Film and Television Arts (BAFTA) award for Best Adapted Screenplay and the 2018 Cannes Grand Prix.

The project was not initially Lee's. He inherited it from Jordan Peele, who subsequently became one of the film's producers. The story is based loosely upon a memoir by undercover detective Ron Stallworth, who, in 1972, became the first African American police officer in the Colorado Springs Police Department.

The film is quintessential Spike Lee, opening with a famous scene from *Gone with the Wind* (Fleming, 1939) followed by a frenetic pastiche within which Alec Baldwin plays a 1950s-style segregationist, practicing his lines for an anti-Black propaganda short film. As Baldwin's character spews out "toxic race theory" (Cooper, 2018, p. 31), Lee superimposes scenes from *The Birth of a Nation* (Griffith, 1915) across his face. At the end of the rant, Baldwin's character says, wistfully, "we had a great way of life."

The film then moves into the primary narrative diegesis about Ron Stallworth becoming a police detective in Colorado Springs and setting up a complex undercover operation where he and his white Jewish partner, Flip Zimmerman, successfully infiltrate the local chapter of the Klan. Stallworth initiates a phone conversation with the local Klan, using his actual name. When he is invited to meet members of the local chapter, Zimmerman steps in and impersonates Stallworth. At the same time, Ron is ordered to infiltrate the Black Student Union (BSU) at the local Colorado College in order to monitor Black "agitation" (Edelstein, 2018). This part of the narrative reveals Ron's conflicted feelings about spying on Black activists, who, in turn, press him to explain how he can "be Black" and "a pig" at the same time. The two storylines merge with Ron successfully duping the Klan and thwarting a deadly plot to bomb the Black Student Union. The film narrative ends with a comedic scene in which Ron reveals to David Duke that he has been duped by a Black man. Then, the film jump-cuts to documentary footage of the August 2017 white-nationalist rally and riot in Charlottesville, Virginia, including comments by the actual David Duke and President Donald Trump. The abrupt transition is jarring and sobering. A reviewer for *Commonweal* remarks, "the movie closes with bitter gravity and witness" (Cooper, 2018, p. 32). Another reviewer describes the transition as "a gut punch" (Browne, 2018).

Despite overwhelmingly positive popular reviews, some criticize the character development of Ron Stallworth, his positive relationship with white police officers, and the parodic portrayal of the Klan. Nevertheless, Lee's film has been lavishly praised by writers who describe him variously as a cultural critic (Mayo, 2018), teacher (Browne, 2018; Cooper, 2018; Ebiri, 2018), historian (Browne, 2018; Scott, 2018), and popular political artist (Scott, 2018). Several reviewers offer glowing commentary on the forcefulness of Lee's parallel editing (Cooper, 2018; Lane, 2018; Scott, 2018). In one example, Lee crosscuts between Harry Belafonte, as a fictional character, talking to the Black Student Union about a historical lynching, and the local chapter of the Klan inducting new members and viewing *The Birth of a Nation* (Boyd, 2018; Ebiri, 2018). A. O. Scott (2018) argues that Lee's crosscutting "unravel[s] the deep ugliness of [D. W.] Griffith's hymn to the heroes of white supremacy." Reviewers also praise Lee's adroit manipulation of film genres, finding pleasure in a pastiche of police procedural, male buddy film, comedy, melodrama, tragedy, Blaxploitation, and documentary (Boyd, 2018; Browne, 2018; Bugbee, 2018; Cooper, 2018; Lane, 2018; Scott, 2018; Tillet, 2018). As one reviewer notes, "Lee manages to crack the codes of genre storytelling, confronting audiences by placing the black experience at the center of familiar narratives" (Bugbee, 2018, p. 26).

African American film director and rap artist Boots Riley is one of the most vocal critics of *BlacKkKlansman*, taking exception to Lee's depiction of Stallworth and white cops as allies. Moreover, Riley claims that Lee fabricated this relationship (Easter, 2018; Real, 2018; "Boots Riley," 2019). Riley also raises questions about Stallworth's real-life infiltration of a Black radical organization, claiming that Stallworth sought to undermine Black activism (Easter, 2018; Real, 2018). Other reviewers sharply criticize Lee's decision to portray the Klan as "really pathetic" (Wilkinson, 2018). These critics feel that such a portrayal let white audiences off the hook by permitting them to disassociate from contemporary white supremacy (Ebiri, 2018; S. Williams, 2019). One reviewer suggests that the film would have been richer had Lee "dramatized the real Stallworth's reservations about black militancy" (Edelstein, 2018). These reservations reveal deep ideological contestation over the politics of representation, a point to which we shall return later in the chapter.

One theme common to virtually all reviews is an appreciation of how the film connects the past to our present moment, linking slavery and Jim Crow to the overt expression of white supremacy today. Most reviewers are deeply impressed with the scene where Belafonte's character offers eyewitness testimony to the Black Student Union about the 1916 lynching of Jesse Washington in Waco, Texas. However, no reviewer discusses the significance of Belafonte and the students holding enlarged photos of the charred, dismembered body of Washington, a striking element of the mise-en-scène.

We take this absence as our point of departure for a critical investigation of what L. Raiford (2009) labels "critical black memory." Through "historical interpretation and political critique" (p. 113), Raiford invites us to examine Black uses of lynching photographs—a "black visual hermeneutics"—that involves "visual re-representations and iconographic re-inscriptions" (p. 114), a reappropriation of the historical abject Black body that motivates contemporary Black agency. Through the film, Lee critiques white supremacy and lynching culture, calling attention to the history of American anti-Black policies and practices, policies and practices that also characterize the history of American mainstream cinema.

We develop our argument in two major sections. First, we explicate the historical context of white supremacy *for* the film and, thus, for its representation *in* the film by discussing Lost Cause mythology and lynching culture. Second, we provide a close reading of the key scene with Belafonte with particular attention to the display of enlarged lynching photographs. We conclude with observations about the film's relevance for understanding the attack on the United States Capitol building on January 6, 2021.

LOST CAUSE MYTHOLOGY AND LYNCHING CULTURE

Lee's decision to open the film with a short clip from *Gone with the Wind* reveals an incisive understanding of the discourse of Lost Cause mythology, which was central to the successful post-Reconstruction reconfiguration of white-supremacist rule. In that scene, Scarlett O'Hara frantically searches the Atlanta trainyard for Doctor Meade, whom Scarlett insists must return with her at once to deliver Melanie Hamilton's baby. The scene at the train station depicts the utter defeat of the Confederate Army, unable to stop the advance of Union troops upon Atlanta. Scarlett's face is tight with fear and anxiety due to both the approaching Yankee army and Melanie's vulnerable condition. Doctor Meade is bitter that the Yankee blockades have interdicted supplies he needs to treat the deluge of desperately wounded Confederate soldiers. As the scene ends, the camera cranes up and out to reveal hundreds of bodies lying prostrate on the ground, finally settling on a tattered Confederate flag waving mournfully; playing in the background is Steven Foster's minstrel song "Old Folks at Home."

This scene articulates five foundational myths of the Lost Cause. First is the primacy of the victimization and suffering of Confederate loyalists, especially white women and heroic wounded men (Blight, 2001; Clinton, 1995). Second, as the tattered flag and title of the film signify, is the wanton destruction by federalism of a graceful, idyllic civilization (Barker & McKee, 2011). Third, and closely related, is the myth that the Civil War was fought over states' rights and Southern honor, not slavery (Blight, 2001; Dray, 2002; Jack, 2019). Fourth is the sentimentalizing of slavery through the premises that slaves were well treated (Blight, 2001), they loved their white masters (Blight, 2001; Thurber, 1992), and needed the moral guidance of white civilization (Blight, 2001; Jack, 2019; Barker & McKee, 2011). And fifth is the memorialization of Confederate heroes and control of the public story of Southern dignity in defeat. White Southern women, such as the United Daughters of the Confederacy, participated fully in crafting public memory of the war (Blight, 2001; McPherson, 2003), including the virtue and frailty of white women in the context of dangerous freed Black men (Hall, 1979). Historian D. W. Blight (2001) observes adroitly, "the verdicts to be rendered in history and memory were not settled at Appomattox" (p. 261).

The Birth of a Nation preceded *Gone with the Wind* by twenty-four years. However, both films visualize and articulate Lost Cause mythology: faithful slaves, infantile and dangerous Black folk, Southern misery and sorrow, and a romanticized longing for a "lost racial utopia" (Blight, 2001, p. 281). They are also similar in their solutions for the post-Reconstruction era: repression of Black freed men and women, white reunification, and endorsement of lynching culture. These films are valuable for Lee's project because he "perceives that the powerful forces of mass media and popular culture are living artifacts of a history of lynching" (Jackson, 2008, p. 118). Embedded in these two films are the cultural and ideological principles of race lynching, which will, by the 1930s, be sublimated into more generalized Hollywood themes of mob violence and justice undone (Wood, 2009). As A. L. Wood

(2009) points out, "Hollywood was loath to release any pictures that would flout Jim Crow convention or impugn white southern character" (p. 228). It is unsurprising, then, that Lee chose to make *The Birth of a Nation* prominent in *BlacKkKlansman*. One of the most critical scenes in the film, which we shall discuss in greater detail, positions viewers as critical voyeurs to watch from the point of view of Ron Stallworth while members of the Colorado Springs Klan and their wives view *The Birth of a Nation*.

Several popular reviewers note Spike Lee's outspoken loathing for *The Birth of a Nation*, which is said to have begun when he was a film student at New York University (Browne, 2018; Tillet, 2018). Lee and others argue that the film is praised as a technological breakthrough in the history of cinema without subsequent discussion of its virulently anti-Black ideological content (Baldwin, 1976; Dray, 2002; Guerrero, 1993). Blight (2001) argues that the film "forged in story form[s] a collective memory of how the war may have been lost but Reconstruction was won—by the South and by a reconciled [white] nation" (p. 111). R. Jackson (2008) describes the film as the *"summa ungibled* of pro-lynching films" (p. 108).

What, then, makes this film so significant to the story of Ron Stallworth in Lee's *BlacKkKlansman*? We answer that question by examining how *The Birth of a Nation* functioned rhetorically in the context of the early and mid-twentieth century. We identify four rhetorical uses germane to Lee's project of developing a cinematic "critical Black memory" (Raiford, 2009): recruitment, inspiration and nostalgia, teaching, and white reunification.

Several historians note that *The Birth of a Nation* was used as a recruitment tool for the Klan, which often recruited in the lobbies of movie theaters where the film was being screened (Dray, 2002; Wood, 2009). The Klan sold hats, robes, and souvenirs at the screenings, further popularizing the ideological perspective of the film (Dray, 2002; Guerrero, 1993; Wood, 2009). The film was also used to fortify the resolve of recruits to enforce anti-Black ideology. Many of the Klan members involved in the murder of Michael Schwerner, James Chaney, and Andrew Goodman during the 1964 Mississippi Freedom Summer "had, within the preceding twelve months, been shown the old film *Birth of a Nation*" (Huie, 1965, p. 234).

The Klan was inspired and transfixed by the visual aesthetic of the film. For example, the Klan learned from *The Birth of a Nation* to burn crosses as quasi-religious signifiers, linking the intimidation and murder of African Americans with religious fervor and moral justification (Dray, 2002; Ehrenhaus & Owen, 2004; Patterson, 1998; Wood, 2009). In fact, the "sadism and bloodletting" that characterized the spectacle of sacrificial lynching was "a performative affirmation of fundamentalist Christian faith in a white supremacist national community" (Ehrenhaus & Owen, 2004, p. 277). Sacrificial lynchings were "constitutive acts of the perpetrators' Christian faith" and "functioned . . . as acts of devotion and defense, as blood sacrifices to a God whose covenant with the white Christian community had been violated by the intrusion of blackness into the sacred spaces of that covenant" (Ehrenhaus & Owen, 2004, p. 277). As we shall discuss in our analysis of a key scene of *BlacKkKlansman*, Lee juxtaposes the Klan members' Christian ardor and nostalgic longings for the return of white-supremacist rule of civil society against Black resistance and witnessing through the retelling of the sacrificial lynching of Jesse Washington in May 1916—the month following the premiere of *The Birth of a Nation* in that city (Bernstein, 2006).

Wood (2009) argues that the film teaches white viewers to become lynching spectators, positioning them as voyeurs within a cinematic white-supremacist gaze, which enables vicarious experience of lynching. Central to the white-supremacist gaze is one of the most pernicious myths in Lost Cause ideology: the "violated and suffering white woman" (Wood, 2009, p. 153) by beastly Black rapists (Hall, 1979). In *The Birth of a Nation*, Gus, a Black Union soldier, spies on a young white Southern girl, Flora, as she goes about her chores. Gus stalks Flora; she glimpses him and flees in terror. In response to this scene, Wood (2009) reports that in Spartanburg, South Carolina, men in the audience "shot up the screen in a valiant effort to save Flora Cameron from her black pursuer" (p. 166). Gus chases Flora until they come to a cliff edge from which she cannot retreat. In desperation and to save her honor, she jumps to her death rather than submit to Gus's sexual appetites. Similarly, in the 1992 film *Last of the Mohicans*, the pursuing male is Native American, another example of the enduring potency of the myth that men of color are dangerous predators of virtuous white women (Keller, 2001, p. 39).

Film historian R. Dyer (1996) notes that the vulnerability of "white women [is] the central focus of *Birth*. What is at stake in the film is the survival of the white race" (p. 172). Griffith uses innovative lighting and crosscut editing (i.e., moving back and forth between two scenes occurring simultaneously) to differentiate between white innocence in peril (Flora) and the threat of Black male sexuality (Dyer, 1996). Flora is centered in the frame with a halo of light around her image; Gus (played by a white actor in blackface) skulks in the shadows, hiding behind foliage. The crosscutting between the pursuer and the pursued builds tension and suspense. The scene teaches white audiences the cost of white female honor in the face of rapacious Black desire. Moreover, the myth of the beastly Black male rapist is visualized for white viewers through a powerful new medium with a heretofore unimaginable realist aesthetic. Later, Gus is lynched off camera and his body is dumped at the doorstep of the biracial villain Silas Lynch as a warning to those supporting Northern occupation. Vigilantism by white Christian men is presented as "honorable justice" (Wood, 2009, p. 152), the only path to saving the South, and, indeed, the nation. Blight (2001) argues that the lynching of Gus via the heroic vigilantism of the Klan "re-births" the nation (p. 395). Certainly, the film reenergized the Klan (Dray, 2002; Simcovitch, 1972; Wood, 2009) and was instrumental in a resurgence of Klan activity in the 1920s and 1930s (Blight, 2001; Wood, 2009).

One key difference between *Gone with the Wind* and *The Birth of a Nation* is the rhetorical appeal to reunification of white citizenry after the Civil War. M. Mitchell imagined her Southern characters as forever bitter about the Civil War and Union occupation, whereas Griffith imagined that marriage between Northern and Southern white families would provide a pathway to reunification. Both Mitchell and Griffith emphasize the absolute need for repression of Black education, civic participation, and economic prosperity. Griffith offers a vision of white Christian kinship and shared heritage that enables the ideology of white supremacy to flourish at a national level. Perhaps one of the best illustrations of the rhetorical success of Griffith's film in this regard was the screening of the film at the White House, the first feature film to be thus honored. Of the film, President Woodrow Wilson reportedly exclaimed, "It's like writing history with lightning. . . . And my only regret is that it is all so terribly true" (Dray, 2002, p. 198). During his presidency, contrary to his campaign promises, Wilson permitted his southern cabinet appointees to *re*segregate "federal employees in Washington agencies" and to install "Jim Crow bathrooms" in all federal buildings (Dray, 2002, p. 198).

Lynching culture developed rapidly during the period of Reconstruction and became pervasive during the first six decades of the twentieth century. The rhetorical efficacy of *The Birth of a Nation* and *Gone with the Wind* enabled the mass circulation of shared commitments of white-supremacist communities. Resonant with Lost Cause mythology, these commitments included beliefs that slavery was not morally wrong, emancipation was a disaster for the welfare of the nation, and white vigilantism against African Americans was both necessary and justified to protect the nation from the pollution of nonwhite blood (Ore, 2019; Patterson, 1998). The pragmatic goals of lynching culture concerned racial solidarity and a "racial caste system" (Wilson, 2002, p. 198; see also Alexander, 2010; Tolnay & Beck, 1995), the repression of African American suffrage (Litwack, 1998), and economic recovery from the collapse of the plantation economy (Alexander, 2010; Brundage, 1997a; McPherson, 2003). Within this cultural and historical context, "the question of labor—who performs it and who owns its result—is quietly excused" (Barker & McKee, 2011, p. 8).

Despite the best efforts of white Evangelical Christians to reconfigure postbellum white supremacy, African Americans enacted numerous strategies for resistance to white-supremacist control and lynching culture, even though that resistance could produce deadly consequences (Litwack, 1998). As W. F. Brundage (1997b) writes, "the hegemony of white supremacy was never complete" (p. 275). This historical context illuminates Lee's cinematic project, which weaves together white-supremacist threats *and* Black resistance throughout *BlacKkKlansman*. The title of the film itself is a nod to the Black Panther Party's modified spelling of America as "AmeriKkKa" (Boyd, 2018). Postbellum resistance to white rule included Black citizens refusing to work for known lynch-mob leaders (Brundage, 1997b), mass migration of Black labor to the north (Brundage 1997b; Dray, 2002), and antilynching campaigns organized by the NAACP (Zangrando, 1980) and aided by the efforts of Black journalists, most notably Ida B. Wells-Barnett (Royster, 1997; Schechter, 1997). Additionally, W. E. B. Du Bois's pioneering work with *The Crisis* offered "an African American countermemory" to Lost Cause mythology, creating an antilynching visual aesthetic, which critically reinterpreted lynching performances and photographs (Kirschke, 2007, p. 16). In the arts, African Americans and their allies created antilynching plays (Mitchell, 2011), novels and poetry (Jackson, 2008), and music (Perry, 2013). Billie Holiday's rendition of "Strange Fruit" was prominent among musical expressions of dissent; her performance of the song "invited audiences to thoroughly understand the repulsive nature of white supremacist violence" and to "dispute white supremacist interpretations of the lynched [Black] body" (Perry, 2013, p. 471).

African American resistance to *The Birth of a Nation* was vociferous and persistent (Dray, 2002; Wood, 2009). Black moviegoers, segregated into the balcony section, sometimes cheered for the supposedly villainous Black characters in the film, causing consternation for white audiences below (Wood, 2009). Similarly, *Gone with the Wind* was publicly denounced through protest and picketing. Black newspapers such as *New York Amsterdam News* and the *Los Angeles Sentinel* renounced the film for its melodramatic appeal to Lost Cause mythology and anti-Black sentiment (Owen, 2000).

American history and cinema have systematically erased or minimized the persistence of Black resistance to white-supremacist culture. Spike Lee has addressed these erasures through *Malcolm X* (1992), *4 Little Girls* (1997), and *When the Levees Broke* (2006). *BlacKkKlansman* is yet another countermemory project, addressing the persistence of anti-Black discourses, institutionalized practices of racism, and race violence in the United States. In an interview with *Time* about the film, Lee says, "The United States of America's foundation is genocide of native people and slavery" (Browne, 2018).

CRITICAL BLACK MEMORY CONSTRUCTION
IN *BLACKKKLANSMAN*

Throughout the primary narrative of *BlacKkKlansman* are reminders that lynching culture was a reality for Black citizens in the 1970s. The narrative suggests that "racism is highly adaptable" (Alexander, 2010, p. 21). The past is prologue for white-supremacist activity in the United States. Lee uses figurative recall of historical racial subordination and violence, such as racial stereotypes and epithets, bombings, armed citizen militia, the threat of disappearance lynching, and the infiltration of national security and the military by the Klan. For example, Ron Stallworth is persistently disrespected by other (white) police officers. His white undercover partner, Flip Zimmerman, must conceal his Jewish identity when he infiltrates the local chapter of the Klan lest he be injured or killed. Black college students are pulled over and harassed by the local police. The Klan plots to bomb the residence of the most outspoken member of the BSU. Near the end of the interior narrative, the Klan burns a cross to intimidate the Black citizens of Colorado Springs.

The film also emphasizes the resolve of Black resistance to white supremacy, including the Colorado College Black Student Union, led by Patrice Dumas, whose character construction pays homage to Angela Davis. Patrice and the BSU invite Kwame Ture (previously, Stokely Carmichael) to campus to speak to students who are riveted by his words. Reaction shots of their faces underscore Ture's powerful words about Black self-love and Black power. Stallworth's assignment to "monitor" Ture's speech initiates Ron's conflict between his desire to be a police officer and his identification with Black liberation. His relationship with Patrice creates the dialogic space for arguments about whether oppressive systems should be changed from the inside or "dismantled" (Cooper, 2018, p. 32). Stallworth exhibits defiance whenever he is confronted by subtle or vulgar forms of white discrimination and exclusion. Most notably, he taunts David Duke by entrapping him in a compromising photograph. We now turn to the scene that critics cite but then fail to elaborate on the display of lynching photographs.

WITNESSING THROUGH LYNCHING PHOTOGRAPHS

As we have claimed, the emotional and melodramatic center of *BlacKkKlansman* is the scene in which Harry Belafonte, playing a character named Jerome Turner, recounts, for the BSU, his terrifying experience of witnessing and surviving the May 15, 1916, lynching of Jesse Washington in Waco, Texas.

The students hold poster-sized enlargements of Washington's burned, hanging corpse. The film crosscuts between this action and the Klan initiation ceremony presided over by David Duke (played by Topher Grace). The film editing also includes reaction shots of Stallworth who is secretly spying on the Klan initiation ceremony. (He has been assigned to security detail for David Duke.) There are twenty-three crosscuts in the scene; Belafonte and students appear in eleven subscenes, Stallworth in six, and the Klan in six. This three-way editing structure privileges the perspective of Belafonte, the BSU, and Stallworth in three ways. First, Black experience and perspective literally dominate the scene. Second, Stallworth's point of view frames the white-supremacist ceremony. Third, sound editing supports a Black point of view. For example, Belafonte's voice carries over into three of the Klan subscenes (a sound bridge), framing their activity from a Black perspective. The mournful music used to set the tone for telling the story about Jesse Washington continues to play throughout the Klan initiation ceremony. In this way, Lee subverts and inverts the melodrama of Lost Cause mythology, constructing a critical Black gaze. This visual and auditory composition enables the possibility of critical Black memory by positioning both the interior audience (Stallworth and the BSU) and viewers within a critical Black gaze.

Constructing a critical Black gaze is an affirmation of Black agency and an act of resistance. b. hooks (1992) observes that "an effective strategy of white supremacist terror and dehumanization during slavery centered [upon] white control of the black gaze" (p. 168). hooks explains further that prohibiting Black looking (i.e., prohibiting direct observation of white people and of the world), effectively stripped Black people of subjectivity. She writes, "to fully be an object then was to lack the capacity to see or recognize reality" (p. 168). White rules for relations of looking functioned to produce "less threatening servants" (p. 168) and thus curtailed Black agency in the world. This white-dominated structure of looking was foundational to American cinema in its early years, as we have seen, and continues to dominate (English, 2019). hooks (1992) offers a corrective to L. Mulvey's white feminist theory of the cinematic gaze through her discussion of an "oppositional gaze" (pp. 115–131). "There is power in looking," she writes (p. 115). Central to its development is resistance to erasure of past terrors. "It is the telling of our history," she asserts, "that enables political self-recovery in contemporary society" (p. 176). We now turn to the key scene in *BlacKkKlansman* that instantiates hooks's claim.

Belafonte's character, Jerome Turner, is an esteemed elder, an embodied site of memory, dedicated to reclaiming memory of past terrors so that young African Americans might foster the "political self-recovery" of which hooks (1992) writes (p. 176). His firsthand witness narrative transports the

BSU members from Colorado Springs to Waco and from 1972 to 1916. As A. Douglass and T. A. Vogler (2003) observe, "acts of witness are required to establish an event as worthy of witnessing" (p. 10). Moreover, bearing witness requires an empathetic audience capable of and willing to listen (Brison, 1999; Kopf, 2009). E. A. Kaplan and B. Wang (2004) caution that cinema about trauma can oversimplify, vicariously traumatize, or create a numbing spectacle. They concur that "being a witness" (p. 10) involves constructing a coherent narrative for listeners capable of "empathic identification" (p. 10). Lee's editing strategy positions the viewing audience as moral witness to the terror of past racial violence and the spectacle of "euphoric hate" (Bugbee, 2018, p. 29) that comprises contemporary Klan activity. The crosscutting between Turner's story and the ludicrous pseudoscience of the Klan's actual eugenic-based discourse (Brady, 1955) inverts and subverts the romanticism and moral superiority of Klan self-representation as exemplified both in early cinema and contemporary white nationalism.

The Turner subscene begins with him explaining that a "slow" seventeen-year-old Jesse was accused of raping and murdering a white woman named Lucy Fryer. "They put Jesse on trial, and he was convicted by an all-white jury after they deliberated for only *four* [emphasis original] minutes." Students gasp audibly at the injustice of the trial as editing crosscuts to Grace's David Duke discussing eugenic theory of white superiority. Interspersed with this and other crosscuts are shots of Stallworth's clandestine observation of the Klan proceedings.

Turner next describes the actions of the mob: The mob wrapped a chain around Jesse's neck and dragged him into the street. He was brutally beaten and stabbed. Then, "finally in a bloody heap, they held him down in the street—and cut off his testicles." The students are horrified, transfixed by the recounting. They gasp and moan in concert as editing crosscuts to Duke articulating the superiority of good white Christian men.

Turner continues. Despite the presence of police, the mob "cut off his fingers, and threw coal oil all over his body. They lit a bonfire, and raised and lowered him over these flames over and over, and over again." Convulsive gasps of horror and dismay fill the room as editing crosscuts to the Klan initiation ritual.

Turner tells the students that a professional photographer chronicled the torture; these images were sold as postcard souvenirs. At this point, numerous students in unison hold up enlarged images of Washington's lynched body. Belafonte's character holds an enlarged photo of his own. As the camera moves in, Belafonte looks at the camera, breaking the "fourth wall" in the film's only moment of direct address to viewers.

Belafonte concludes by talking about the power of *The Birth of a Nation*, tying its influence directly to the murder of Jesse Washington. Two points are significant about Turner's subscene. First, the potency of Belafonte's performance is magnified by his lived experience during the voter-registration campaign in the 1964 Mississippi Freedom Summer. As M. Sturken (1997) explains, "even bodies themselves" can "generate memory" (p. 10). T. Branch (1998), historian and chronicler of the civil rights era, writes that Belafonte, along with Sidney Poitier, flew to Greenwood, Mississippi, to speak at a rally sponsored by the Student Nonviolent Coordinating Committee (SNCC) and to donate funds that they raised for the campaign. They entered one of the waiting cars, both of which had been sanded to a matte finish to avoid reflecting light from pursuing Klan vehicles' headlights. On their drive to the rally, Belafonte "expressed relief" when he saw a long line of headlights only to be informed by SNCC leader James Forman that they were being pursued by the Klan. Branch reports, "silence gripped the passengers through a swerving chase over back roads" (p. 450). The driver of their escort car was able to absorb the "ramming blow" from one of the pursuing Klan vehicles. Unhurt but shaken, Belafonte and Poitier "retained the image of a heavy piece of lumber strapped to the attacker's front bumper" (p. 450). Later that night, they heard gunshots shattering a staff car's windshield and "overheard two-way radio dispatches about a volunteer being followed" (p. 451). Neither slept soundly that night.

Second is the significance of the enlarged lynching photographs held by members of the BSU and Belafonte. Sturken (1997) explains that "the [still] image . . . remains the most compelling of memory objects" (p. 11). S. P. Perry (2013) and E. J. Ore (2019) describe lynching images as a "visual vocabulary" of racial hierarchy. Since the publication of *Without Sanctuary: Lynching Photography in America* (Allen, 2000), lynching photos have been a highly contested site of cultural struggle. As P. J. Williams (2000) observes, "The history preserved in those pictures . . . is one of the more complicated public secrets of this nation's past" (p. 9). Raiford (2009) and Ore (2019) argue that while the relations of looking constructed by the original production are complex and lacking an "innocent" viewing position, they are also constitutive of historical Black experience. Ore (2019) in particular argues that appropriate contextualization of the images render them useful for drawing attention to contemporary structured relationships in law, policing, and justice, which continue to "lynch" Black people (see also Hoyt, 2019). Lynching photos, she explains, function rhetorically as "a visual vocabulary for the 'deep rule' of democracy" regarding race and citizenship (Ore, 2019, p. 84). A brief review of the *original* form and function of lynching photography illuminates Ore's point.

As we have explained, racial lynching itself was a performance of white-supremacist communal cohesion, civic duty, and racial solidarity (Ehrenhaus & Owen, 2004; Tolnay & Beck, 1995). The photographic medium provides an extension of these relationships. As D. Apel and S. M. Smith (2007) explain, photographs are used for "imagining and contesting communities" for the purposes of "inclusion and exclusion" (p. 15). Lynching photographs "were primarily messages to other whites that amplified and solidified their own power and unity" (Wood, 2009, p. 209).

The composition of the photo typically displays an already-debased dead body; some photos show curious or festive white spectators looking at the body or white spectators deliberately posing with the body like a trophy photo (Apel & Smith, 2007). The photographs function to "freeze" time, thus preserving the objectification, debasement, and abjection of the Black body (Raiford, 2009). White spectators appear orderly and calm; white violence against the Black victim is kept outside the frame in order to perpetuate the myth of law and order in an extralegal context (Wood, 2009). Visual evidence of genital mutilation, such as that inflicted upon Jesse Washington, is typically concealed in some fashion. Finally, and significantly, almost never are Black Americans pictured at the lynching scene, a constructed absence that accelerates the utter desolation of the Black victim.

Lynching photographs were displayed in public venues, such as country stores and gas stations. White citizens sent them to their relatives, collected them and displayed them in their homes. White citizens sent them to Black leaders as a warning against violation of racial hierarchy. As an oppositional resource, lynching photography "is a constitutive element of black visuality since [the time when] these images began their intense circulation . . . following the end of Reconstruction" (Raiford, 2009, p. 118). Black activists used the photos in antilynching activism and midcentury civil rights struggle; from Ida B. Wells to the Black Panthers and Congress of Racial Equality (CORE), the images were used rhetorically to counter the rhetorics of white supremacy (Raiford, 2009; Zangrando, 1980).

The use of the photos in the scene with Belafonte merit careful consideration because Lee *transforms* the original function of the photos into "a site of mourning and remembrance" (Ore, 2019, p. 91). Jesse Washington is remembered, embraced (i.e., literally held by Black hands), and mourned within an empathic Black community. He is memorialized, his body reclaimed, at rest. Crosscuts to the Klan initiation ceremony provide an unsettling contrast in which David Duke espouses the very eugenics theory that undergirded race lynching, exemplified by the segregationist screed *Black Monday* (Brady, 1955). "God, give us true white men," Grace's Duke intones, raising his eyes heavenward, mimicking the visual and discursive traditions of Lost Cause mythology.

Lee's use of the enlarged photos, held by Black hands, evoke comparison to a 1994 *Newsweek* photo of James Cameron holding an enlarged photo of the 1930 lynching of his two friends in Marion, Indiana. Cameron survived and spent his adult life bearing witness to the horror (Apel & Smith, 2007; Raiford, 2009). The scene also evokes Mamie Till's defiance of the state of Mississippi by unsealing the casket bearing her son and inviting the local Black community in Chicago to look at Emmett's ruined face. A published photograph of Emmett Till in his casket circulated throughout the broader Black community, inspiring several well-known Black public figures, including Muhammad Ali, to become outspoken critics of American "democracy" (Harold & DeLuca, 2005). "Looking-back-at" from a position of agency and resistance, Cameron, Till, and the fictional characters in *BlacKkKlansman* wrest "possession of the past, reclaiming the black body in pain" (Raiford, 2009, p. 121). These are powerful examples of how reinterpretation of lynching photos constitutes a critical Black memory that subverts and inverts the rhetoric of white supremacy.

CODA: FROM CHARLOTTESVILLE TO THE US CAPITOL

The American experience seamlessly unites the material and representational histories of white supremacy, white Christian nationalism, and lynching culture. Spike Lee's *BlacKkKlansman* coalesces these histories into a site for witnessing and resisting—and thus for developing critical Black memory. Lee concludes the film with nearly seven minutes of footage of the alt-right, white-supremacist Unite the Right Rally in Charlottesville, Virginia, August 11–12, 2017. The footage begins with a nighttime torch parade with white supremacists chanting, "Jews Will Not Replace Us!" It segues to counterdemonstrators chanting, "Black Lives Matter!" followed by a violent melee between the two groups. In these clips of rioting, white supremacists carry Nazi and Confederate flags; some wear Nazi Iron Cross patches. Two brief scenes of Trump follow, separated by counterdemonstrators chanting, "Nazis Go Home." Then, explicitly linking the interior diegesis of *BlacKkKlansman* to the concluding documentary footage, the film introduces a clip of the actual David Duke telling his audience in Charlottesville, "This is the first step toward taking America back." Viewers then see footage of one white supremacist plowing his car into counterdemonstrators, killing Heather Heyer and injuring nineteen others. The film concludes with counterdemonstrators' ad hoc shrine to Ms. Heyer, which fades into an inverted US flag, a symbol of distress.

The release of *BlacKkKlansman* followed the Charlottesville riot by one year; it preceded the seditious insurrection at the US Capitol by almost two and a half years. Nevertheless, the film's argument is prescient. As armed and violent insurrectionists breached the Capitol on January 6, 2021, they defiantly waved the Confederate battle flag and the Christian flag, even as they wrapped themselves in the nation's flag. A noose on scaffolding stood at the ready. Some carried zip ties to make "citizens arrests," hold "people's trials," and execute verdicts. Of these "persons unknown" (as in the title of Dray, 2002), one columnist writes, "They were disturbingly normal: normal the way some faces in the crowd look normal in the old photos of lynchings" (Kesich, 2021).

Expanding on G. Kesich's observation, public intellectual M. Duster (2021) writes, "The mob action that took place at the US Capitol . . . was a reminder that most White and Black Americans live in different worlds with vastly different realities." Racial privilege distinguishes these realities. She notes that the white mob felt "free enough to assemble in large numbers armed with assault weapons . . . storm federal buildings, crash through windows, roam around a seat of power, take selfies, brandish flags with racist symbols—and leave unharmed." For Duster, these actions resonate with "the unbridled barbarism and oppression my great-grandmother Ida B. Wells lived through over 100 years ago," when the "progress of Black people was met with rage and violence" and "hate groups formed and reigns of terror were unleashed." In the most sadistic moments of lynching culture, "Black people were murdered with impunity for minor infractions or accusations of crimes." Then and now fuse together. "The idea that they were 'taking their country back' was the motivation for rolling back the gains achieved by Black Americans back then—and it echoed in 2021." As David Duke declared, Charlottesville was the first step in "taking [*our*] America back."

Echoing Charlottesville, the storming of the Capitol fused the violence of lynching culture with the signifiers of Lost Cause mythology and white Evangelical Christian nationalism. The Confederate battle flag has long been a key signifier of "white insurrection" and "white resistance to increasing Black power" (Brasher, 2021) from its original use in secessionist manifestos to affirm the "truths" of racial hierarchy, inequality, and slavery to Strom Thurmond's segregationist Dixiecrat movement (1948) to riots opposing federal mandates for integration (1950s to the 1960s) to the murder of nine Black congregants at Emanuel African American Church in Charleston, South Carolina (2015), and on to Charlottesville (2017) and the US Capitol (2021).

White supremacy, white Christian nationalism, and lynching culture are deeply entangled. This worldview defines "a sacred covenant . . . between that community and their god" (Ehrenhaus & Owen, 2004, p. 278). The crisis to this "covenantal social order" is the "federally mandated intrusion of blackness into the now defiled sacred public space." The crisis persists despite this sacred community's "best efforts . . . to manage that public space" through Jim Crow legislation. Although public-spectacle lynchings, such as that of Jesse Washington, are relics of our past, "the ideological fervor of salvation through Christ's sacrifice remains potent," shaping "domestic and foreign policy" agendas of white Evangelical Christians (Ehrenhaus & Owen, 2004, p. 278). Among the banners held high at the Capitol, some bore this slogan inscribed upon the nation's flag: "Jesus Is My Savior. Trump Is My President."

Democratic pluralism is a threat to Christian nationalists "because doctrines of inerrancy do not allow for difference of religious or political opinion" (Perry, 2020, p. 121). In this Manichean dualist worldview, religion and politics are inseparable, a struggle between good and evil, between spiritual light and the forces of darkness. Robert Jones, founder of the Public Religion Research Institute, explains that Christian nationalism "seeks to affirm and codify America's identity as an explicitly Christian country, by leveraging the religion's influence in the public sphere" (Kuruvilla, 2021). It is "a potent mix of nationalism, Christianity and white supremacy," and it "has been complicit in legitimizing and baptizing white supremacy throughout the entire American story" (Kuruvilla, 2021). Regarding the events of January 6, 2021, Perry does not mince words: "The Capitol insurrection was as Christian Nationalist as it gets" (Edsall, 2021), an extension and elaboration of the violent Unite the Right spectacle in Charlottesville.

Spike Lee's *BlacKkKlansman* opens a space for viewers to envision practices of resistance and witnessing in furtherance of developing "critical black memory" (Raiford, 2009). Using *The Birth of a Nation* and Charlottesville as bookends, the film showcases Lee's attention to the relationships between and among history, memory, photography, cinema, and race in America. *BlacKkKlansman* invites viewers to move beyond the comfort of entertainment spectatorship to the more challenging terrain of proactive citizenship. His message is even more urgent today than when it was issued.

REFERENCES

Alexander, M. (2010). *The new Jim Crow: Mass incarceration in the age of colorblindness.* New Press.

Allen, J. (2000). *Without sanctuary: Lynching photography in America.* Twin Palms.

Apel, D., & Smith, S. M. (2007). *Lynching photographs.* University of California Press.

Baldwin, J. (1976). *The devil finds work*. Dial Press.

Barker, D., & McKee, K. (2011). *American cinema and the southern imaginary*. University of Georgia Press.

Bernstein, P. (2006). *The first Waco horror: The lynching of Jesse Washington and the rise of the NAACP*. Texas A&M University Press.

Blight, D. W. (2001). *Race and reunion: The Civil War in American memory*. Belknap Press.

Boots Riley: Spike Lee yelled at me after *BlacKkKlansman* criticism, but we're good now. (2019, February 23). *Variety*. https://variety.com/2019/film/news/boots-riley-spike-lee -yelled-at-me-after-blackkklansman-criticism-but-were-good-now-1203147183/

Boyd, H. (2018, August 5). *BlacKkKlansman* [Review of *BlacKkKlansman*, directed by S. Lee]. *Cineaste*, *43*(4), 41–43.

Brady, T. P. (1955). *Black Monday: Segregation or amalgamation . . . America has its choice*. Association of Citizens' Councils.

Branch, T. (1998). *Pillar of fire: America in the King years, 1963–65*. Simon & Schuster.

Brasher, J. (2021, January 14). The Confederate battle flag, which rioters flew inside the US Capitol, has long been a symbol of white insurrection. *The Conversation*. https://the conversation.com/the-confederate-battle-flag-which-rioters-flew-inside-the-us-capi tol-has-long-been-a-symbol-of-white-insurrection-153071

Brison, S. J. (1999). Trauma narratives and the remaking of the self. In M. Bal, J. Crewe, & L. Spitzer (Eds.), *Acts of memory: Cultural recall in the present* (pp. 39–54). University Press of New England.

Browne, R. (2018, August 20). Spike Lee wants you to wake up. *Time*, *192*(7), 48–54.

Brundage, W. F. (1997a). Introduction. In W. F. Brundage (Ed.), *Under sentence of death: Lynching in the South* (pp. 1–20). University of North Carolina Press.

Brundage, W. F. (1997b). The roar on the other side of silence: Black resistance and white violence in the American South, 1880–1940. In W. F. Brundage (Ed.), *Under sentence of death: Lynching in the South* (pp. 271–291). University of North Carolina Press.

Bugbee, T. (2018). It happened here. *Film Comment*, *54*(4), 24–29.

Clinton, C. (1995). *Tara revisited: Women, war & the plantation legend*. Abbeville Press.

Cooper, R. R. (2018, October 19). Spike Lee's American seminar. *Commonweal*, *145*(17), 31–32.

Douglass, A., & Vogler, T. A. (2003). Introduction. In A. Douglass & T. A. Vogler, (Eds.), *Witness and memory: The discourse of trauma* (pp. 1–54). Routledge.

Dray, P. (2002). *At the hands of persons unknown: The lynching of Black America*. Random House.

Duster, M. (2021, February 3). My great-grandmother exposed lynchings: This is what she would say about the Capitol riot. *CNN*. https://www.cnn.com/2021/02/03/opinions /what-ida-b-wells-would-say-about-capitol-riot-duster/index.html

Dyer, R. (1996). Into the light: The whiteness of the South in *The birth of a nation*. In R. H. King & H. Taylor (Eds.), *Dixie debates: Perspectives on southern cultures* (pp. 165–192). New York University Press.

Easter, M. (2018, August 18). Director Boots Riley issues a sharp critique of Spike Lee's *BlacKkKlansman*. *Los Angeles Times*. https://www.latimes.com/entertainment/movies /la-et-mn-boots-riley-criticism-blackkklansman-20180818-story.html

Ebiri, B. (2018, May 15). Spike Lee's *BlacKkKlansman* seizes the moment (and the American past). *Village Voice.* https://www.villagevoice.com/2018/05/15/spike-lees -blackkklansman-contains-multitudes/

Edelstein, D. (2018, August 6). *Spike Lee's* BlacKkKlansman *is an entertaining and effective piece of melodrama.* Vulture. https://www.vulture.com/2018/08/spike-lee -blackkklansman-movie-review.html#_ga=2.203142161.1473474559.1615502466 -1284533906.1615502465

Edsall, T. B. (2021, January 28). The Capitol insurrection was as Christian Nationalist as it gets. *New York Times.* https://www.nytimes.com/2021/01/28/opinion/christian-nation alists-capitol-attack.html?searchResultPosition=1

Ehrenhaus, P., & Owen, A. S. (2004). Race lynching and Christian evangelicalism: Perfor mances of faith. *Text and Performance Quarterly, 24*(3–4), 276–301.

English, M. (2019). *The Hollywood Jim Crow: The racist politics of the movie industry.* New York University Press.

Fleming, V. (Director). (1939). *Gone with the wind* [Film]. Metro-Goldwyn-Mayer.

Griffith, D. W. (Director). (1915). *The birth of a nation* [Film]. David W. Griffith Corporation.

Guerrero, E. (1993). *Framing Blackness: The African American experience in film.* Temple University Press.

Hall, J. D. (1979). *Revolt against chivalry: Jessie Daniel Ames and the women's campaign against lynching.* Columbia University Press.

Harold, C., & DeLuca, K. M. (2005). Behold the corpse: Violent images and the case of Emmett Till. *Rhetoric & Public Affairs, 8*(2), 263–286.

hooks, b. (1992). *Black looks: Race and representation.* South End Press.

Hoyt, K. D. (2019). #Handsupdontshoot: Connective images and ethical witnessing. *Criti cal Studies in Media Communication, 36*(2), 103–121.

Huie, W. B. (1965). *Three lives for Mississippi.* WCC Books.

Jack, B. M. (2019). Introduction. In B. M. Jack (Ed.), *Southern history on screen: Race and rights* (pp. 1–10). University Press of Kentucky.

Jackson, R. (2008). A southern sublimation: Lynching, film and the reconstruction of American memory. *Southern Literary Journal, 40*(2), 102–120.

Kaplan, E. A., & Wang, B. (2004). From traumatic paralysis to the force field of modernity. In E. A. Kaplan & B. Wang (Eds.), *Trauma and cinema: Cross-cultural explorations* (pp. 1–22). Hong Kong University Press.

Keller, A. (2001). Generic subversion as counterhistory: Mario Van Peeble's *Posse.* In J. Walker (Ed.), *Westerns: Films though history* (pp. 27–46). Routledge.

Kesich, G. (2021, January 17). Fringe theories go mainstream in GOP Maine Republican party. *Portland Press Herald.* https://www.pressherald.com/2021/01/17/the-view-from -here-fringe-theories-are-mainstream-in-the-gop/

Kirschke, A. H. (2007). *Art in crisis: W. E. B. Du Bois and the struggle for African American identity and memory.* Indiana University Press.

Kopf, M. (2009). Trauma, narrative and the art of witnessing. In B. Haehnel & M. Lutz (Eds.), *Slavery in art and literature: Approaches to trauma, memory and visuality* (pp. 41–58). Frank & Timme.

Kuruvilla, C. (2021, January 15). White Christian radicalization is a violent threat. *Huffington Post.* https://www.huffpost.com/entry/white-christian-nationalism-capitol-riot_n _5ff73916c5b612d958ea19db?ncid=txtlnkusaolp00000616

Lane, A. (2018, August 20). Spike Lee does battle with *BlacKkKlansman. New Yorker.* https://www.newyorker.com/magazine/2018/08/20/spike-lee-does-battle-with -blackkklansman

Lee, S. (Director). (1992). *Malcolm X* [Film]. Warner Brothers.

Lee, S. (Director). (1997). *4 little girls* [Film]. Home Box Office.

Lee, S. (Director). (2006). *When the levees broke* [Film]. Home Box Office.

Lee, S. (Director). (2018). *BlacKkKlansman* [Film]. Universal Pictures.

Litwack, L. F. (1998). *Trouble in mind: Black southerners in the age of Jim Crow.* Alfred A. Knopf.

Mayo, K. (2018). The re-birth of a nation. *Essence, 49*(4), 76–77.

McPherson, T. (2003). *Reconstructing Dixie: Race, gender, and nostalgia in the imagined South.* Duke University Press.

Mitchell, K. (2011). *Living with lynching: African American plays, performance, and citizenship, 1890–1930.* University of Illinois Press.

Ore, E. J. (2019). *Lynching: Violence, rhetoric, and American identity.* University of Mississippi Press.

Owen, A. S. (2000). The Great War as Civil War: Rhetorics of memory in *Gone with the wind.* In T. A. Hollihan (Ed.), *Argument at century's end: Reflecting on the past and envisioning the future* (pp. 553–561). National Communication Association.

Patterson, O. (1998). *Rituals of blood: Consequences of slavery in two American centuries.* Basic Books.

Perry, S. [P.] (2013). "Strange Fruit," ekphrasis, and the lynching scene. *Rhetoric Society Quarterly, 43*(5), 449–474.

Perry, S. P. (2020). *Rhetorics of race and religion on the Christian right.* Lexington Books.

Raiford, L. (2009). Photography and the practices of critical Black memory. *History & Theory, 48*(4), 112–129.

Real, E. (2018, August 24). Spike Lee responds to Boots Riley's *BlacKkKlansman* criticism. *Hollywood Reporter.* https://www.hollywoodreporter.com/news/spike -lee-responds-boots-rileys-blackkklansman-criticism-1137276

Royster, J. J. (Ed.). (1997). *Southern horrors and other writings: The anti-lynching campaign of Ida B. Wells, 1892–1900.* Bedford / St. Martin's Press.

Schechter, P. A. (1997). Unsettled business: Ida B. Wells against lynching, or, how anti-lynching got its gender. In W. F. Brundage (Ed.), *Under sentence of death: Lynching in the South* (pp. 292–317). University of North Carolina Press.

Scott, A. O. (2018, August 9). Review: Spike Lee's *BlacKkKlansman* journeys into white America's heart of darkness [Review of *BlacKkKlansman*, directed by S. Lee]. *New York Times.* https://www.nytimes.com/2018/08/09/movies/blackkklansman-review-spike -lee.html?searchResultPosition=1

Simcovitch, M. (1972). The impact of Griffith's *Birth of a nation* on the modern Ku Klux Klan. *Journal of Popular Film, 1*(1), 45–54.

Sturken, M. (1997). *Tangled memories: The Vietnam War, the AIDS epidemic, and the politics of remembering.* University of California Press.

Thurber, C. (1992). The development of the mammy image and mythology. In V. Bernhard, B. Brandon, E. Fox-Genovese, & T. Perdue (Eds.), *Southern women: Histories and identities* (pp. 87–108). University of Missouri Press.

Tillet, S. (2018, August 5). Spike Lee takes on the Klan. *New York Times.* https://www.nytimes.com/2018/08/02/movies/spike-lee-blackkklansman.html?searchResultPosition=1

Tolnay, S. E., & Beck, E. M. (1995). *A festival of violence: An analysis of southern lynchings, 1882–1930.* University of Illinois Press.

Wilkinson, A. (2018, August 9). Spike Lee's *BlacKkKlansman* draws a ham-fisted line from white supremacy's past to its present. *Vox.* https://www.vox.com/culture/2018/5/15/17355432/blackkklansman-review-spike-lee-david-duke-charlottesville

Williams, P. J. (2000, February 14). Without sanctuary. *Nation, 270*(6), 9.

Williams, S. (2019, January 27). The problem with spike Lee's Oscar-nominated *BlacKkKlansman. Daily Beast.* https://www.thedailybeast.com/the-problem-with-spike-lees-oscar-nominated-blackkklansman

Wilson, K. H. (2002). *The reconstruction desegregation debate: The politics of equality and the rhetoric of place, 1870–1875.* Michigan State University Press.

Wood, A. L. (2009). *Lynching and spectacle: Witnessing racial violence in America, 1890–1940.* University of North Carolina Press.

Zangrando, R. (1980). *The NAACP crusade against lynching, 1915–1950.* Temple University Press.

Chapter 9

THE NECROPOLITICS OF MEMORY

How Subjects (Don't) Matter in *Crazy Rich Asians* Discourse

EUNI KIM

With the release of *Black Panther* and *Crazy Rich Asians*, 2018 became a banner year for representation of racial minorities in Hollywood. Unsurprisingly, these films prompted many comparisons between them, for instance that *Crazy Rich Asians* was "the Asian *Black Panther*." Yet proof of these comparisons is suspiciously absent: one article argues that "*Crazy Rich Asians* comparisons to *Black Panther* [are] not quite fair" but provides no evidence that such claims had been made (Cheng, 2018); yet another that declares "no, *Crazy Rich Asians* isn't the 'Asian *Black Panther*'" in its headline only guides its reader to broken Twitter links that one can only assume also made the comparison (Han, 2018).[1]

The apophatic ability to locate a discourse only in its disavowals animates the central problem addressed in this chapter—the central problem, indeed, of Asian America writ large. After the release of the *Crazy Rich Asians* trailer, several Asians and Asian Americans criticized the absence of "brown" faces and the overrepresentation of "the nouveau white": East Asians (Truong, 2018). Though pre- and postrelease discourse largely centers on the "groundbreaking" nature of the film (Haynes, 2018), several point out the erasure and tokenization of the darker-skinned South and Southeast Asians, prompting the hashtag campaign #BrownAsiansExist (Tseng-Putterman, 2018). The recurring prominence and predominance of East Asians in media discourse and major film roles in conjunction with the subordination and absence of Southeast Asians have long haunted Asian America throughout its nearly constant quest for identity stability and uniformity (Chuh, 2003). These issues also closely mirror a "post-racial mystique," which celebrates the end of racism as it insidiously perpetuates it (Squires, 2014). But the problem of erasure raises distinct challenges: How do you critique that which does not exist? How do you make substantive claims you cannot substantively prove? I approach these questions by drawing from rhetorical studies, Asian American studies, and memory studies to explore how Asian America participates in the ethnic repetition and exclusion that comprise its legibility in the broader US body politic. Following K. A. Ono (1995) and K. Chuh (2003), I interrogate the self-signification of "Asian America(n)" as a signifier that emerges through the constitutive rhetorical practices of memory and amnesia. In the following section, I discuss how remembering and forgetting are necessarily constitutive rhetorical processes (Charland, 1987) that call audience members into being through certain political subject positions. I then connect these rhetorical processes to the production of Asian America as a racialized signifier amidst contemporary logics of postracialism. Next, I conduct a critical reading of texts pertaining to the representational politics of *Crazy Rich Asians*, which exemplifies the "amnesiac acts" that underscore the purported stability of Asian America and Asian American identity (Chuh, 2003, p. 32). I conclude by discussing possible ramifications of Southeast Asian American erasure through rhetorical amnesia within the broader signifier of "Asian American" as a racial term of identification.

MEMORY, AMNESIA, AND THE
BOUNDARIES OF ASIAN AMERICA

The Rhetoricity of Memory and the Postracial

"Memory" can be understood as the socially negotiated web of meanings about the fact or fiction of particular historical events, trends, beliefs, artifacts, and people (Halbwachs, 1992). As such, memories are malleable, uncertain, and often—like many psychosocial phenomena—indicative of deeper underlying ideologies. Additionally, memory and amnesia have long been considered two sides of the same coin (Browne, 1995; Foucault, 1997). M. Sturken (1997) goes so far as to say that amnesia is only "*misinterpreted* [emphasis added] as forgetting" (p. 2). Similarly, B. Zelizer (1998) argues that the very process of producing memories facilitates amnesia. Memories, particularly in visual formats, such as photographs—taken-for-granted, re-presented truths of our past—congeal and ultimately become definitive narratives of history. What is present is continually reinscribed by the very nature of memory work (e.g., photographs, news clippings), while what is absent is gradually erased by our continued reliance on it.

Media function as powerful repositories of memory around which communities, publics, or nation-states coalesce. Ono (2000) shows how Japanese American memories of incarceration during World War II are shaped through reflexive cinematic practices and spectatorship. He demonstrates both the elastic nature of memory as a rhetorical construct and memory as less a particular moment and more a negotiated process materializing through film and television. It is therefore crucial to explore discourses within which filmic representations of communities are embedded, particularly marginalized communities with less access to mainstream modes of representation (e.g., Hollywood cinema).

M. Foucault (1975) reminds us that "people are shown not what they were, but what they must remember having been" (p. 25). Thus the stakes of memory as a rhetorical construct are not merely symbolic but also constitutive. M. Charland (1987) contends that prior to persuasion (i.e., the Aristotelian standard for rhetoric), a discourse interpellates individuals into particular group subjectivities, inviting them to recognize themselves and their peers as members with a shared identity and goal. The narrative processes that "naturalize the arbitrary selection of memories" function as memories that discursively construct particular representational forms of nations and the subjects within it (Choi, 2008, p. 372). Audiences, therefore, can be understood as *effects* emerging from rhetoric rather than its receptacles.

Memory, when understood as a constitutive rhetoric, takes on a distinctly necropolitical dimension (Mbembe, 2019). A. Mbembe's theorization of the necropolitical focuses on how social relations are structured with a clear aim of protecting those who should live and sacrificing those "destined" to die. Here, I extend his theory to encompass the logic of representation and memory: those who are remembered continue to live in memory, and those who are forgotten die there. In other words, memory work is deeply invested in the enforced death or destruction of some memories (e.g., artifacts, histories, languages) and the tacit acceptance of others. The necropolitics of memory refers to the representational politics by which living bodies are preserved or absented and hinges on both the material and discursive effects of memory. Indeed, history is comprised of who, among the dead, are remembered. Memory work is often concerned with the means by which we preserve memories, but the ways we destroy or forget memories are just as significant. Beyond what K. Hoerl (2012) calls "selective amnesia," or the omission of counternarratives within public memory, necropolitical memory work seeks the total erasure of counternarratives.

When used to discursively bound race and racial identities, necropolitical memory work becomes a powerful tool of postracialism, or the belief that contemporary society has freed itself of the pesky problem of race. Despite the nearly infinite number of media, policies, and deaths that prove otherwise, postracialism has rapidly become the "racial common sense" that dominates race-based discourses (Mukherjee et al., 2019). The widespread insistence on racism's historic existence and contemporary absence creates fruitful space within which necropolitical memory work can function. E. K. Watts (2017) argues that postracialism is a "fantasy" that leans on its own tautologies to continue perpetuating racist discourses in new or repackaged forms. Rather than overtly racist actions or words that explicitly denigrate differences attributed to race (e.g., appearance, intelligence, sexuality), postracialism thrives in doublespeak. This often occurs through explicit invocations of race that are used to deny racism: "race is claimed as irrelevant, but Blackness must be differentiated anyway" (p. 327). Society no longer must remain "pure"; rather, it should celebrate the ever-increasingly abstract notions of "diversity" and "multiculturalism." All races are equal! But, much more importantly, all races are *different*. Necropolitical memory work thus flourishes under the simultaneously disciplinary and disavowing auspices of postracialism and bears careful scrutiny and critique.

By positing memory as necropolitical, I question how memory and amnesia, presence and absence, act as intentional acts of preservation or destruction that implicate the discursive as a condition of the material. Thus the discursive erasure of certain bodies or memories from historical narratives creates the conditions for their physical, material erasure. It is not a coincidence that empires destroy the artifacts, histories, and languages of those they conquer. You cannot remember that which is not there. And before long, those artifacts, histories, and languages will go from "no longer being there" to "never having been there at all." Thus the paradox of memory: If something is not there—if it was never there at all—how do you recover it? How do you critique its absence if you cannot prove its presence?[2]

While exclusion and misrepresentation are common tactics of postracial discourses, as C. Banks (2018) and K. D. Brown (2011) argue, connecting postracial memory work to necropolitics illuminates how such rhetorics strategically absent and affirm different racial identities in service of the larger project of postracialism. Multiculturalism can only be tolerated insofar as it meets the conditions of a "racial state" that "invisibly legislates and mandates specific race definitions—and racial inclusions and exclusions—without referring to 'race'" (Halualani, 2011, p. 249). By focusing on the violence wrought by necropolitical memory work, critics can make visible the disciplinary practices of the racial state. Having demonstrated the significance of memory as a rhetorical device through which to negotiate identity claims,

I will now theorize how Asian America as a racial formation is constituted through necropolitical memory work.

The Memory of Asian America

The "co-constitutive processes" of remembering and forgetting are crucial to the realization of Asian Americans as a racialized group within the US American body politic (Sturken, 1997, p. 2). In some ways, this is incredibly obvious: it took nearly forty years of Japanese American activism for the US government to admit that its incarceration of Japanese Americans during World War II was based on "a bogus theory that the ethnic Japanese could not or would not assimilate to become 'American'" that was driven in part by white backlash against the immigrant Japanese labor force arriving to the West Coast (Commission on Wartime Relocation and Internment of Civilians, 1982, p. 4). In other ways, this formation is more insidious: V. T. Nguyen (2002) and Y. Chang (2010), for instance, critique the Asian American intellectual and literary traditions, respectively, for discursively erasing the class-based origins of Asian American politics and Asian America's perpetuation of capitalism in favor of race- and culture-based identification. Their arguments suggest that sustaining class amnesia is central to Asian American self-identification as a racialized political identity, and they importantly call attention to the ways external economic and sociopolitical pressures influence how Asian Americans discursively (dis)articulate themselves in the contexts of race and class. This attention to what Ono and J. M. Sloop (1995) call "vernacular discourses" reveals the myriad and nuanced ways in which marginalized subjects identify or disidentify (Muñoz, 1999) with dominant discourses, as well as the means through which they create new discursive practices of identity. It is through such critiques of vernacular discourse that Asian Americanists poignantly identify how, for instance, Asian America's reliance on underrepresentation of Southeast Asians undergird Asian American racial identity (Chuh, 2003; David, 2013).

In the following sections, I examine vernacular discourses about Asian American identity with respect to *Crazy Rich Asians* to theorize how rhetorical memory and amnesia are often central to contemporary instantiations of racialized Asian American identity. Through a critical analysis of texts *about* the film rather than the film itself, I argue that "Asian America" becomes configured as a predominantly East Asian formation through implicit and overt associations between East Asia and Asian American identity, as well as an aphasia or refusal to address the limits of "Asian American" as a signifier. The film's success—not to mention the overt racial and class signifiers throughout

the film—produced a fruitful discourse that exemplifies processes of rhetorical remembering and forgetting. I argue that although *Crazy Rich Asians*
may announce Asian Americans as a discrete *presence* in a whitewashed,
"postracial" media landscape, it also participates in the continued *absence*
of Southeast Asians that sustains "Asian America(n)" as a racial signifier.

CRAZY RICH ASIANS AND THE RHETORICAL POLITICS OF ASIAN AMERICAN IDENTIFICATION

As the first Hollywood film since *The Joy Luck Club* (1989) to feature a predominantly Asian and Asian American cast and production, *Crazy Rich
Asians* is unsurprisingly perceived by many as an Asian American "arrival"
to Hollywood (e.g., Fang, 2018; Ho, 2018). The sense of urgency and pride
surrounding the film's release was, for many Asian Americans, exacerbated
by the casting of white actresses Emma Stone, Tilda Swinton, and Scarlett
Johansson as Asian characters in *Aloha* (2015), *Doctor Strange* (2016), and
Ghost in the Shell (2017). Twitter was flooded with nearly one million tweets
by Asian Americans and non-Asian Americans alike in the months leading
up to the premiere, with 350,000 of those tweets posted during the film's
opening weekend (Jenkins, 2018). While *Crazy Rich Asians* merits attention
for its portrayal of Asians and Asian Americans, particularly within global
contexts of capitalism, the response to the film is just as interesting. Following Ono and Sloop (1995), I interrogate vernacular discourses of/about Asian
American identity to illustrate one way that racial signifiers are rhetorically
constructed through necropolitical practices of memory and amnesia.

Importantly, while I explore a particular discourse of Asian American
subjectification (Foucault, 1998), this does not preclude the existence of other,
even contradictory, discourses. Indeed, as Y. Ding (2020) illustrates, the complexities of representation qua capital necessitate nuanced readings of how
different and distinct discourses interact with larger structures of power, such
as neoliberalism and white supremacy.[3] The following analysis is one such
reading that is particularly attentive to how race operates to homogenize the
nuances of racial identity in rhetorical articulations of identity as memory.
If "memory is a narrative rather than a replica of an experience that can be
retrieved and relived," then what is the narrative of Asian American group
membership and identity (Sturken, 1997, p. 7)?

Crazy Rich Asians, based on a novel by Kevin Kwan (2018), (ostensibly)
reflects Kwan's own upbringing in the "very real world" of Singaporean
opulence. The story follows Rachel Chu, a Chinese American economics

professor at New York University, and her boyfriend, Nick Young, to Singapore, where Rachel meets Nick's family for the first time. Unbeknownst
to Rachel, who was raised by a single, presumably working-class mother,
Nick's family is "crazy rich . . . 'old money' rich" (Chu, 2018). Rachel's time
in Singapore is fraught with culture- and class-based clashes with members
of Nick's family, particularly his mother, Eleanor, who considers Rachel's
Americanness incompatible with the future she desires for her son.

To supplement existing research on the film, which largely critiques the
film's reliance on the Orientalist dichotomy of East and West and the tacit
endorsement of neoliberal hedonism (Ding, 2020; Phruksachart, 2020; Vijay,
2020), I examine the discourse preceding and following the film's release to
demonstrate how Asian Americans participate in meaning-making processes
that construct "Asian America" as a signifier of race-based identity. Given
its ability to survive "impossible representation standards," it is unsurprising
that *Crazy Rich Asians* prompted political commentary from the director,
cast, and members of the Asian American community (Scaife, 2018). In what
follows, I explore the "representational logics" through which Asian America
takes shape in the director's and cast members' public statements, as well as
popular social-media posts pertaining to the relationship between Asian
American media representation and identity (Shome, 2011, p. 389). I take up
a critical rhetorical orientation (McKerrow, 1989) in my analysis, keeping in
mind the way these textual fragments (McGee, 1990) participate in power
relationships regarding intra-Asian racialization and class ignorance. Such a
contextual approach connects recurrences of certain representational logics
across texts in a diffuse media landscape. This illuminates how rhetorical
practices of memory and amnesia are not bound within any particular text,
but rather diffuse across texts (e.g., interviews, messages to/for non-Asians).

And It Was All Yellow: Remembering (East) Asian America

One way the film remembers Asian America is through the continued association between Asian America(ns) and East Asia or East Asian American
experiences. Toward the end of the film, as Rachel is preparing to leave
Singapore for New York, a cover of the song "Yellow" by Coldplay swells in
the background. The song evokes the color of stars for its title and became
popular after its release in 2000, even being nominated for two Grammy
Awards. Instead of the original song, however, the film uses a cover sung
entirely in Mandarin. Shortly after premiering, news of the song's significance circulated across social media and news outlets: initially, Coldplay
rejected the request to feature the song in the film, with some suspecting this

was due to previous mishaps with Asian cultural appropriation (Sun, 2018; J. Yang, 2018). In December 2017, however, director Jon M. Chu wrote a letter to Coldplay asking for permission to use their song, noting an element of racial signification to the otherwise generic love song. Chu (2017) describes how, as a child, he associated the color yellow with "being called the word in a derogatory way throughout grade school," but "Yellow" represented a way he and his friends could "reclaim the color for ourselves" (para. 1). He closes by impressing upon Coldplay the cultural and personal significance of their song, writing that its appearance in the film "will give a whole generation of Asian-Americans . . . the same sense of pride I got when I heard your song" (para. 3).

Use of the term "yellow" represents how Asian Americans are constituted as a "community of memory" based on particular historical moments of racism and reclamation (Owen & Ehrenhaus, 2010). Chu's "complicated relationship with the color yellow" extends beyond his own childhood experiences of racism (Chu, 2017, para. 1). Indeed, the term "yellow peril," which refers to an Orientalist (Said, 1978) fear of cultural, economic, or physical invasion by Asia, rose to prominence after the 1895 painting *Die Gelbe Gefahr* (literally, "The Yellow Peril") became "the most influential political illustration of the late nineteenth century" (Lee, 2015, p. 123). The yellow-peril stereotype was a common fixture of early Asian and Asian American representation in film and television (Hamamoto, 1994; Ono & Pham, 2009) and continues today, particularly in depictions of futuristic Western societies that have been unmistakably "Orientalized" (Park, 2010). At the other end of this spectrum is "yellow fever," which refers to non-Asian (usually white male) sexual desire for (usually female) Asians and Asian Americans, often represented as a repackaged form of yellow peril in early Hollywood cinema (Marchetti, 1995).[4] Chu's hope of rhetorical reclamation echoes similar attempts by Asian Americans, most notably the Yellow Power movement, to change what "yellow," as a referent to the Asian body, means.

A relatively consistent trend in the use of "yellow" in both dominant (e.g., yellow peril/fever) and vernacular discourses (e.g., Yellow Power) is East Asian and East Asian American centrality.[5] Indeed, such centrality has prompted scholars such as E. J. R. David (2016) to identify "Brown Asians" (i.e., Filipinos and South and Southeast Asians) as a distinct subset of Asians and Asian Americans. Furthermore, these attempts to reclaim "yellow" as an Asian American signifier obscure the term's inherent limits to capture the diverse nationalities of Asian America that, ironically, form its foundations. Chu's assumption that the color yellow would be meaningful to "a whole generation of Asian-Americans" points to this very pattern as central to the rhetorical constitution of Asian America as, in fact, *East Asian America.*

Another example of this conflation between Asian America and East Asia is a series of viral tweets appearing after the film's release. As of this writing, the tweets have amassed a combined total of almost 175,000 retweets and nearly one million likes. The tweets, posted by Kimberly Yam, describe her relationship to her Chinese identity through a series of vignettes that take place at ages eight, nine, sixteen, seventeen, twenty, and twenty-five years old. She writes in the second person, quite literally interpellating her audience into her own subject position and inviting them to recall her own memories as their own. The thread begins with a photo of a Chinese character tattooed on her wrist along with the following words: "You're 8 years old. Your 3rd grade class orders Chinese food & your father delivers it. You are so excited to see your pops in school. He's your hero. But apparently other kids don't think he's so cool. They laugh at him and mimic his accent. You don't want to be Chinese anymore" (Yam, 2018b). At seventeen years old, "for the 1st time, you want to be Chinese" (Yam, 2018a). At twenty, "you get your family's name inked into your skin. . . . You won't let anyone make you feel the way you did all those years ago. You love being Chinese" (Yam, 2018d). Then, at twenty-five, "You see a movie with an all-asian [*sic*] cast at a screening and for some reason you're crying and you can't stop. You've never seen a cast like this in Hollywood. Everyone is beautiful. You're so happy you're Chinese. #CrazyRichAsians #RepresentationMatters" (Yam, 2018c).

Like Chu, Yam juxtaposes the affective dimensions of her childhood experiences with racism against current feelings of racial pride. Her emphasis on Chinese (American) identity makes sense: both Yam and Rachel, the film's protagonist, are Chinese American, and the film's plot centers Chinese characters (a fact strongly reflected in the cast as well). However, I read Yam's tweets within the broader context of *Crazy Rich Asians* being considered a "watershed moment" for Asian America (W. Yang, 2018). Though the tweets may have been written as a way for Yam to convey personal affection through eloquent prose, her tweets were quickly taken up to represent broader Asian American sentiments regarding the film. Articles about the thread's popularity stress its ability to "brilliantly [capture]" or "perfectly [show]" the significance of *Crazy Rich Asians* for Asian Americans writ large (Ke, 2018; Perry, 2018), and several reports describe how the tweets encourage Asians and non-Asians to reconnect with cultural practices they had abandoned or lost (e.g., Chen, 2018; Katzowitz, 2018). The positioning of Yam's tweets as a beacon for the culturally dispossessed, particularly Asians and Asian Americans, abstracts Yam's Chinese American experience to a broader Asian American experience in order to demonstrate the film's psychosocial impact.

This rhetorical coalescence of the specific and the general suggests that the second persona (Black, 1970) evoked by Yam is *Asian* American rather than *Chinese* American. Who, then, is the third persona: the audience(s) who falls outside the set of the second persona and are thus ignored by the speech act (i.e., Yam's tweets) at best or entirely negated by it at worst (Wander, 1984)? In contradistinction to the Chinese Americans explicitly hailed in Yam's tweets, the third persona ultimately represents the same brown Asians who criticize the film's representational politics but receive significantly less attention, both on social media and in traditional press. Thus, in the same way Chu's use of "yellow" forgets "brown," the rhetorical collapse of signification between Chinese American experiences and Asian American sentiment forgets how experiences of racism differ for Asian American groups across US geopolitical history (David, 2013).

I Know, I Know, I Know: Aphasic Representation

In addition to "East Asian American" standing in metonymically for "Asian American," a curious rhetorical elision occurs when members of the Asian diaspora realize their group's diversity. Notably, viral social-media posts by members of the cast outwardly admit that *Crazy Rich Asians* does not and/or cannot represent every Asian or Asian American but do not name the Asians and Asian Americans who are most excluded—let alone the consequences of the doubled form of exclusion that arises from being both unrepresented and unnamed. Two weeks before the film's premiere, Constance Wu, who played Rachel, tweeted about the importance of the film for Asian American media. One week after the premiere, Gemma Chan, who played a significant supporting character, shared a similar post on her Twitter and Instagram. Both actresses' statements followed a similar script in which they openly admit and accept that the film, revolutionary as it may be, is imperfect in its representational limits: Wu (2018) writes, "I know CRA won't represent every Asian American," while Chan (2018) admits, "I know that this is just one film . . . and that it can't be all things to all people." Then, they gestured toward the capacity for *Crazy Rich Asians* to create the conditions for more or better representations, with both of them hoping that the film would pave the way for "immigrant stories" (Wu, 2018) and "authentic storytelling . . . [from] any group which has been underrepresented in the past" (Chan, 2018) to make their way to mainstream media. Their statements suggest that what *Crazy Rich Asians* lacks in representational *capacity*, it makes up for in representational *possibility*.

Both Wu's and Chan's comments propose that longing for better representation is a suitable replacement for unhappiness with existing representation and thus exemplify an aphasia—an inability to name or express—that upholds Asian American racial signification. While the previous section of analysis reflects Chuh's (2003) critique of Asian America's preoccupation with uniformity, Wu and Chan's comments seem to suggest the opposite. Surely, their acknowledgement of the limits of representation affirms the inherent heterogeneity of Asian America (Lowe, 1996), does it not? Perhaps it would if they did actually affirm the inherent heterogeneity of Asian America at any point. Both actresses signal the general value of diversity in media: Wu through an evocation of an immigrant melting pot and Chan through the explicit nod toward underrepresented groups. These signifiers of diversity, however, neither register Asian America's heterogeneity nor are the primary (or even secondary) concerns those very underrepresented groups (i.e., brown Asians) had with the film.

As a matter of fact, both statements seem to point *away* from Asian America's heterogeneity in favor of a broader form of a neutral, postracial diversity. Wu (2018) calls for "stories of dreams, of love, of sacrifice, of courage, of honor," which she suggests are best told through the lens of immigration. She does not call for unique, Asian American "stories of dreams" or even Asian American immigrant stories, but rather simply "immigrant stories." More troublesome, though, is Chan's (2018) invitation for "more diverse, inclusive . . . storytelling, *not just from other Asian perspectives* [emphasis added] but any group which has been underrepresented." At best, she reiterates Wu's appeal to a(ny) race-neutral increase in media diversity. At worst, she implies that *Crazy Rich Asians* has effectively represented "Asian perspectives" and, in doing so, has set the stage for non-Asian perspectives to accomplish the same.

The signifier of "Asian America(n)," as leveraged by Wu and Chan, functions as an effective way to distinguish between representations of different *racial* groups within Hollywood, such as whites or Asians. However, it also obfuscates a more focused vocabulary that acknowledges the presence of the many *ethnic* groups that comprise Asia and Asian America, functioning almost catachrestically (Spivak, 1993). Like the film itself, Wu's and Chan's comments foreground the presence of Asians and Asian Americans within a dominant visual and racial landscape of non-Asians and Asian Americans yet continue to absent the same Asians and Asian Americans who already struggle to be recognized under the moniker of "Asian American" (e.g., the #BrownAsiansExist Twitter campaign).

Wu's and Chan's elision of Asian America's heterogeneity and tacit refusal to engage with the central problematics of the film's representational politics as articulated by brown Asians function as an aphasic act of forgetting that constructs a narrative of memory (i.e., presence) through amnesia (i.e., absence). Allusions to the inability of *Crazy Rich Asians* to represent "every Asian American" or "all people" name the limits of Asian American representation but not the bodies these limits implicate. This reflects the "simultaneous presence of a thing and its absence" that animate aphasic acts of exclusion and denial (Stoler, 2011, p. 145). In doing so, such statements act as a form of memory work that lays the foundations for future acts of amnesia. For if, indeed, Wu's and Chan's hopes for a nebulously "diverse" media landscape are realized, then the film's representational politics will be resolved. If the problem was never Southeast Asian erasure or misrepresentation, then it will never be one that continues to trouble Asian American signification and identification. After all, if something is not there—if it was never there at all—how do you recover it? How do you critique its absence if you cannot prove its presence?

This aphasia and the use of "Asian American" as a catachrestic signifier for East Asian Americans highlight how necropolitical memory work, particularly as a tool of postracial fantasizing, functions so insidiously. Memories are easy to identify insofar as they exist as identifiable texts. A monument, no matter how battered and worn, is a monument nonetheless. A recorded history, no matter how obscure or ignored, is a history nonetheless. However, when historical narratives or ongoing projects of racial subjectification do not contain even the traces of presence, how do we recover those we *know* to be present? Like a bandit brushing away their footsteps, necropolitical memory work eliminates not only explicit presences in repositories of memory (e.g., media) but also the traces of such exclusion. The ability for necropolitical memory work to produce amnesia, to disavow, without having to name the symbol or body that must *be* disavowed bolsters postracialism by rhetorically eliding any mention of race to simply assert that equality, in the form of national, ethnic, or immigrant identity, ought to be prioritized.

ASIAN AMERICAN ABSENCE AND ABSENTING

Although my theorization and analysis focus primarily on how the necropolitics of memory are implicated in contemporary postracial logics, Asian

America is also inherently intertwined with other racial projects, especially transnationally. For instance, a Southeast Asian's criticism of the prominence of East Asians in *Crazy Rich Asians* as akin to "replacing white people with . . . the nouveau white" poignantly addresses the way wealth and whiteness are intimately intertwined within the racial signification of Asian America (Sa'at, 2018). Representations of Asian Americans as the "nouveau white," then, function as a form of "glocalized whiteness" (Asante, 2016) that reproduces the ideological underpinnings of whiteness, like the valorization of pale skin, along localized discursive contexts, such as the prominence of ethnic Chinese in Singapore.

T. S.-T. Wong (2022) further illustrates how the film's casting politics problematically represent Asianness as closer to whiteness—or *desiring to be* closer to whiteness—through subtle and overt acts of intra-Asian yellowface logics, or "co-ethnic yellowface ambivalence." In doing so, the film discursively draws artificial boundaries between US Asians and non-US Asians, participating in the problematics of transnationality alluded to earlier in this essay. Transnationality and postracialism, however, are not in tension. The use of coethnic yellowface ambivalence draws attention to how *Crazy Rich Asians* entertains postracial fantasies of abstract diversity while maintaining structural and systemic norms of whiteness. Even if one were to ignore US involvement in Asian geopolitics, the discourse traced throughout this essay also decidedly forgets the geo- and sociopolitical conditions that produce the reality of an ethnically Chinese, nouveau riche family in Singapore with servants and bodyguards who are, statistically, either Malay (Singapore's indigenous ethnic group) or Indian and, as such, are disenfranchised as ethnic minorities in the state. While the film's US context might establish the country's commitment to the postracial, it does not even minimally acknowledge active racial divisions within the country in which the film takes place. As Wong's study indicates, there is much to investigate regarding transnational negotiations of Asian/American subjectivity.

A. L. Stoler (2011) emphasizes that "*to forget*, like *to ignore* [emphases original], is an active verb. . . . It is an achieved state" (p. 141). Popular texts surrounding *Crazy Rich Asians* circulated affirmations of Asian American identity, helping audiences discover how "Asian America" becomes an "achieved state" of amnesia predicated on an aphasia of brown Asians (David, 2016) as Asians. While these practices are discursive in nature, they are also implicated in discourses of inequality and oppression with material effects. Thus, when I propose that memory must be considered as both constitutive and necropolitical, I encourage critics to seek out discursive absences in memory qua representation and connect them to absences in, for instance, resource distribution and access. Given the dramatic differences in the material distribution of resources and capital (both cultural and monetary), particularly as these differences are maintained by postracial rhetorics, it is imperative to conduct materialist readings of rhetorical phenomena within the practice of Asian American criticism and continue to problematize the stability of Asian American subjectivity (Nguyen, 2002; Chuh, 2003). In doing so, we can hope to avoid contributing to the postracial "amnesia" that obfuscates these differences in material conditions and perpetuates ongoing occurrences of structural violence.

NOTES

1. Twitter presented the same trend. Some of the most popular tweets on the subject suggest that the "Asian *Black Panther*" characterization had been rampant on social media or in their personal networks (e.g., K. Nguyen, 2018; D. Wong, 2018).

2. G. C. Spivak's (1988) theory of the subaltern as a subject who can only be recognized through their death is a useful corollary here. Spivak uses examples of individuals discursively and materially erased from society, though "subaltern" also refers to groups that are relegated to a state of social and corporeal death. Similarly, necropolitical memory work might refer to individual events or people absented from the soon-to-be-historical narrative, but it also refers to the ritual, repetitive, and power-based absence of particular groups as a form of structural amnesia.

3. b. hooks (1992) and J. Medina (2008) argue similarly.

4. Ono and V. N. Pham (2009), drawing from H. K. Bhabha (1994), also provide a helpful explanation of how this dialectic of fear and desire operates within stereotypes about Asians and Asian Americans.

5. This is not to say that East Asian Americans are not invested in panethnic liberation for Asian Americans, as Y. L. Espiritu (1992) has crucially argued.

REFERENCES

Asante, G. (2016). Glocalized whiteness: Sustaining and reproducing whiteness through "skin toning" in post-colonial Ghana. *Journal of International and Intercultural Communication, 9*(2), 87–103.

Banks, C. (2018). Disciplining Black activism: Post-racial rhetoric, public memory and decorum in news media framing of the Black Lives Matter movement. *Continuum: Journal of Media & Cultural Studies, 32*(6), 709–720.

Bhabha, H. K. (1994). *The location of culture.* Routledge.

Black, E. (1970). The second persona. *Quarterly Journal of Speech, 56*(2), 109–119.

Brown, K. D. (2011). Race, racial cultural memory and multicultural curriculum in an Obama "post-racial" US. *Race, Gender, & Class, 18*(3–4), 123–134.

Browne, S. H. (1995). Reading, rhetoric, and the texture of public memory. *Quarterly Journal of Speech, 81*(2), 237–265.

Chan, G. [@gemma_chan]. (2018, August 15). *Happy opening day* [heart emoji] *#crazy richasians #goldopen #representation* [Image attached] [Tweet]. Twitter. https://twitter .com/gemma_chan/status/1029832162797936645

Chang, Y. (2010). *Writing the ghetto: Class, authorship, and the Asian American ethnic enclave.* Rutgers University Press.

Charland, M. (1987). Constitutive rhetoric: The case of the *peuple Québécois. Quarterly Journal of Speech, 73*(2), 133–150.

Chen, T. (2018, August 21). A woman shared an emotional personal story of reconnecting with her identity inspired by *Crazy rich Asians. BuzzFeed News.* https://www.buzzfeed news.com/article/tanyachenwoman-shared-an-emotional-personal-story-inspired -by-crazy

Cheng, R. (2018, August 22). *Comparisons between* Crazy rich Asians, Black Panther *not quite fair.* CNET. https://www.cnet.com/news/crazy-rich-asians-comparisons-to-black -panther-not-quite-fair/

Choi, S. (2008). Silencing survivors' narratives: Why are we *again* forgetting the No Gun Ri story? *Rhetoric & Public Affairs, 11*(3), 267–388.

Chu, J. M. (2017, December 8). Jon M. Chu to Chris Martin, Guy Berryman, Jonny Buck-land, and Will Champion [Letter]. *Hollywood Reporter.* https://static.hollywoodreporter .com/sites/default/files/2018/08/letter_to_coldplay-compressed.jpg

Chu, J. M. (Director). (2018). *Crazy rich Asians* [Film]. Warner Bros.

Chuh, K. (2003). *Imagine otherwise.* Duke University Press.

Commission on Wartime Relocation and Internment of Civilians. (1982). *Personal justice denied.* US Congress, National Archives. https://www.archives.gov/research/japanese -americans/justice-denied

David, E. J. R. (2013). *Brown skin, white minds: Filipino-/American postcolonial psychology.* Information Age Publishing.

David, E. J. R. (2016, October 25). The marginalization of brown Asians. *Seattle Globalist.* https://seattleglobalist.com/2016/10/25/ejr-david-marginalization-brown-asians/57763

Ding, Y. (2020). "Asian pride porn": Neoliberal multiculturalism and the narrative of Asian racial uplift in Kevin Kwan's *Crazy rich Asians* trilogy. *Multi-Ethnic Literature of the United States, 45*(3), 65–82.

Espiritu, Y. L. (1992). *Asian American panethnicity: Bridging institutions and identities.* Temple University Press.

Fang, J. (2018, August 22). Celebrating my Asian face and American spirit, at last. *Washing-ton Post.* https://www.washingtonpost.com/opinions/celebrating-my-asian-face-and -american-spirit-at-last/2018/08/22/1dd1567a-a5b5-11e8-b76b-d513a40042f6_story.html

Foucault, M. (1975). Film and popular memory: An interview with Michel Foucault. *Radical Philosophy, 11*(11), 24–29.

Foucault, M. (1997). *"Society must be defended": Lectures at the Collège de France, 1975–1976* (D. Macey, Trans.). Picador.

Foucault, M. (1998). *Ethics: Subjectivity and truth* (p. Rabinow, Ed.). New Press.

Halbwachs, M. (1992). *On collective memory* (L. A. Coser, Trans.). University of Chicago Press.

Halualani, R. T. (2011). Abstracting and de-racializing diversity: The articulation of diversity in the post-race era. In M. G. Lacy & K. A. Ono (Eds.), *Critical rhetorics of race* (pp. 247–264). New York University Press.

Hamamoto, D. Y. (1994). *Monitored Peril: Asian Americans and the politics of TV representation*. University of Minnesota Press.

Han, K. (2018, April 27). No, *Crazy rich Asians* isn't the "Asian *Black Panther*." Teen Vogue. https://www.teenvogue.com/story/crazy-rich-asians-black-panther-comparisons

Haynes, S. (2018, August 10). *Crazy rich Asians* is more than glitz and glamour: It's groundbreaking for people like me. *Time.* https://time.com/5363724/crazy-rich-asians-representation-meaning/

Ho, K. K. (2018, August 15). *Crazy rich Asians* is going to change Hollywood: It's about time. *Time.* https://time.com/longform/crazy-rich-asians/

Hoerl, K. (2012). Selective amnesia and racial transcendence in news coverage of President Obama's inauguration. *Quarterly Journal of Speech, 98*(2), 178–202.

hooks, b. (1992). *Black looks: Race and representation*. South End Press.

Jenkins, A. (2018, August 20). Crazy rich Asians *is a box office hit and social media is a big reason why: Here are the numbers behind it.* Yahoo! https://sports.yahoo.com/apos-crazy-rich-asians-apos-203236459.html

Katzowitz, J. (2018, August 18). *This* Crazy rich Asians *Twitter thread has the internet sobbing.* Daily Dot. https://www.dailydot.com/irl/crazy-rich-asians-twitter-thread/

Ke, B. (2018, August 20). *One woman's Twitter story brilliantly captures the massive influence of* Crazy rich Asians. NextShark. https://nextshark.com/one-woman-tweets-crazy-rich-asians-influence/

Kwan, K. (2018, August 9). Meet the real family that inspired *Crazy rich Asians. Town & Country.* https://www.townandcountrymag.com/leisure/arts-and-culture/g22143613/kevin-kwan-interview-family-crazy-rich-asians/

Lee, E. (2015). *The making of Asian America: A history*. Simon & Schuster.

Lowe, L. (1996). *Immigrant acts: On Asian American cultural politics*. Duke University Press.

Marchetti, G. (1995). *Romance and the yellow peril: Race, sex, and discursive strategies in Hollywood fiction*. University of California Press.

Mbembe, A. (2019). *Necropolitics* (S. Corcoran, Trans.). Duke University Press.

McGee, M. C. (1990, Summer). Text, context, and the fragmentation of contemporary culture. *Western Journal of Speech Communication, 54*, 274–289.

McKerrow, R. E. (1989). Critical rhetoric: Theory and praxis. *Communication Monographs, 56*(2), 91–111.

Medina, J. (2008). Whose meanings? Resignifying voices and their social locations. *Journal of Speculative Philosophy, 22*(2), 92–105.

Mukherjee, R., Gray, H., & Banet-Weiser, S. (2019). *Racism postrace*. Duke University Press.

Muñoz, J. E. (1999). *Disidentifications: Queers of color and the performance of politics*. University of Minnesota Press.

Nguyen, K. [@knguyen]. (2018, April 25). *Asian Twitter:* Crazy rich Asians *is *our* Black*

Panther / *me: cRaZy rIcH AsIAnS iS OuR bLaCk PaNtHer* [Image attached] [Tweet]. Twitter. https://twitter.com/knguyen/status/989137922246041600

Nguyen, V. T. (2002). *Race and resistance: Literature and politics in Asian America.* Oxford University Press.

Ono, K. A. (1995). Re/signing "Asian American": Rhetorical problematics of nation. *Amerasia Journal, 21*(1–2), 67–78.

Ono, K. A. (2000). Re/membering spectators: Meditations on Japanese American cinema. In D. Y. Hamamoto & S. Liu (Eds.), *Countervisions: Asian American film criticism* (pp. 129–149). Temple University Press.

Ono, K. A., & Pham, V. N. (2009). *Asian Americans and the media.* Polity Press.

Ono, K. A., & Sloop, J. M. (1995). The critique of vernacular discourse. *Communication Monographs, 62*(1), 19–46.

Owen, A. S., & Ehrenhaus, P. (2010). Communities of memory, entanglements, and claims of the past on the present: Reading race trauma through *The green mile. Critical Studies in Media Communication, 27*(2), 131–154.

Park, J. C. H. (2010). *Yellow future: Oriental style in Hollywood cinema.* University of Minnesota Press.

Perry, T. (2018, August 20). *This viral Twitter thread perfectly shows why* Crazy rich Asians *is so important.* Upworthy. https://www.upworthy.com/this-viral-twitter-thread-perfectly-shows-why-crazy-rich-asians-is-so-important

Phruksachart, M. (2020). The bourgeois cinema of boba liberalism. *Film Quarterly, 73*(3), 59–65. https://doi.org/10.1525/fq.2020.73.3.59

Sa'at, A. (2018, April 20). From the trailer of the movie *Crazy rich Asians*: Crazy rich EAST Asians and their brown backdrop people; Does a [Image attached] [Status update]. Facebook. https://www.facebook.com/photo.php?fbid=10155488413932371&set=a.1015 1269765892371.1073741826.649992370&type=3&theater

Said, E. (1978). *Orientalism.* Random House.

Scaife, S. N. (2018, August 28). *Crazy rich Asians has survived impossible representation standards. The Verge.* https://www.theverge.com/2018/8/28/17788198/crazy-rich-asians -movie-representation-diversity-constance-wu-henry-golding-awkwafina

Shome, R. (2011). "Global motherhood": The transnational intimacies of white femininity. *Critical Studies in Media Communication, 28*(5), 388–406.

Spivak, G. C. (1988). Can the subaltern speak? In C. Nelson & L. Grossberg (Eds.), *Marxism and the interpretation of culture* (pp. 271–313). University of Illinois.

Spivak, G. C. (1993). *Outside in the teaching machine.* Routledge.

Squires, C. R. (2014). *The post-racial mystique: Media and race in the twenty-first century.* New York University Press.

Stoler, A. L. (2011). Colonial aphasia: Race and disabled histories in France. *Public Culture, 23*(1), 121–156.

Sturken, M. (1997). *Tangled memories: The Vietnam War, the AIDS epidemic, and the politics of remembering.* University of California Press.

Sun, R. (2018, August 19). *Crazy rich Asians:* Read the letter that convinced Coldplay to allow "Yellow" in the movie. *Hollywood Reporter.* https://www.hollywoodreporter.com /news/read-crazy-rich-asians-director-s-letter-coldplay-yellow-1135826

Truong, A. (2018, April 24). *The trailer for* Crazy rich Asians *has some asking: Where are the brown faces?* Quartz. https://qz.com/quartzy/1260412/crazy-rich-asians-trailer-south-asians-criticize-film-for-lack-of-ethnic-diversity-and-singaporean-accent/

Tseng-Putterman, M. (2018, August 23). One way that Crazy rich Asians is a step backward. *The Atlantic.* https://www.theatlantic.com/entertainment/archive/2018/08/asian-amer icas-great-gatsby-moment/568213/

Vijay, D. (2020). *Crazy rich Asians*: Exploring discourses of Orientalism, neoliberal feminism, privilege and inequality. *Markets, Globalization & Development Review, 4*(3). https://doi.org/10.23860/mgdr-2019-04-03-04

Wander, P. (1984). The third persona: An ideological turn in rhetorical theory. *Central States Speech Journal, 35*(4), 197–216.

Watts, E. K. (2017). Postracial fantasies, Blackness, and zombies. *Communication and Critical/Cultural Studies, 14*(4), 317–333.

Wong, D. [@XpertDemon]. (2018, April 24). *I've noticed a lot of Asian Americans, specially East Asians, commenting about* Crazy rich Asians *as being a landmark for* [Tweet]. Twitter. https://twitter.com/XpertDemon/status/988839963478429697

Wong, T. S.-T. (2022). Crazy, rich, when Asian: Yellowface ambivalence and mockery in *Crazy rich Asians. Journal of International and Intercultural Communication, 15*(1), 17 pp. https://scholarsphere.psu.edu/resources/02155681-082d-4c4a-bdb2-cdc50a72634f

Wu, C. [@ConstanceWu]. (2018, July 31). *#CrazyRichAsians opens August 15th. Read below to understand why it means so much to so many people. All love. @CrazyRichMovie* [Image attached] [Tweet]. Twitter. https://twitter.com/ConstanceWu/status/102444 9682766852096

Yam, K. [@kimmythepooh]. (2018a, August 17). *But you know you rejected your culture a long time ago. You know you refused to speak Chinese & you* [Tweet]. Twitter. https:// twitter.com/kimmythepooh/status/1030606417588363264

Yam, K. [@kimmythepooh]. (2018b, August 17). *You're 8 years old. Your 3rd grade class orders Asian food & your father delivers it. You are so excited* [Tweet]. Twitter. https://twitter .com/kimmythepooh/status/1030606419857469440

Yam, K. [@kimmythepooh]. (2018c, August 17). *You're 25 years old. You see a movie with an all-Asian cast at a screening and for some reason you're* [Tweet]. Twitter. https://twitter .com/kimmythepooh/status/1030606419857469440

Yam, K. [@kimmythepooh]. (2018d, August 17). *You're 20 years old. You've spent the past several years repatriating yourself. You get your family's name inked into your* [Tweet]. Twitter. https://twitter.com/kimmythepooh/status/1030606418905391105

Yang, J. (2018, August 15). *How Coldplay's "Yellow," in Chinese, ended up on the* Crazy rich Asians *soundtrack.* Quartz. https://qz.com/quartzy/1356129/crazy-rich-asians-how -coldplays-yellow-in-chinese-made-it-into-the-soundtrack/

Yang, W. (2018, August 6). Why *Crazy rich Asians* could be a watershed moment for Asian representation in Hollywood. *Vanity Fair.* https://www.vanityfair.com/hollywood /2018/08/crazy-rich-asians-casts-portfolio

Zelizer, B. (1998). *Remembering to forget: Holocaust memory through the camera's eye.* University of Chicago Press.

Chapter 10

THE HATEFUL EIGHT AS A CONTEMPORARY ALLEGORY OF ANTI-BLACKNESS AND POSTRACIAL RIFTS

ERIKA M. THOMAS AND MAKSIM BUGROV

For years, film critics have called our attention to representations of whiteness, colonialism, and forms of racial domination projected on our screens. Often, these representations take the form of recurring racialized stereotypes, but in recent decades, a more insidious postracial ethos of clichéd racial "progress" has taken hold to capture the imagination of a largely white American audience. As J. Sexton (2017) observes, American media culture has been ideologically shaped by "both neoliberal multiculturalism and neoconservative colorblindedness" especially since "the presidential election of Barack Obama in 2008" (xxiii).

In this chapter, we examine the ways Afropessimism offers an allegorical disruption of the postracial ethos of our times. We examine Quentin Tarantino's *The Hateful Eight* (2015) to show how the film's aesthetic and narrative characteristics challenge optimistic and comforting cinematic representations of American racial politics. Following Sexton (2017), R. Poll (2018), and F. B. Wilderson III (2010, 2015, 2020), we analyze the film's visual rhetoric, symbolic imagery, and plot devices to argue that *The Hateful Eight* counters the postracial aspiration of (Afro)optimistic conditions of possibility. The film instead exposes a deeply embedded racist relationship that reveals society's exploitive and structural ontological dependence on Black suffering. Ultimately, our critique reveals how Tarantino's allegory of our postracial times maps the way postracial rhetorics remain inherently parasitic on Blackness.

THE RISE OF THE POSTRACIAL

Most scholars understand the term "postrace" as an ideology that deempha-
sizes the significance race plays in structuring American life (Dunn, 2016;
Halualani, 2011; Lacy & Ono, 2011; Love & Tosolt, 2010; Mukherjee, 2011;
Squires, 2014). Some scholarship connects the rise of postracial attitudes to
the popular embrace of terms such as "multiculturalism" and "diversity" in
the 1990s (Halualani, 2011). Others, like R. Mukherjee (2011), argue that the
term describes a society in which "neither cultural practices nor political solidarities cohere predictably along racial lines" and where political coalitions
that once aspired for racial justice have been fragmented by neoliberalism's
cult of colorblind individualism and self-interest (p. 178). The transition to a
"postracial" society has been attributed to numerous developments, including the presumed achievements of progressive political movements since
the 1960s and the cultural visibility of nonwhite celebrities, such as Oprah
Winfrey or Barack Obama, whose careers suggest that race is not a barrier
for individual success or social progress in the United States (Cloud, 1996;
Craig & Rahko, 2021).

The postracial is a "power-laden representation" that ideologically circulates through media discourses that portray diverse racial and ethnic groups
as either present and equal or equally different (Halualani, 2011, p. 248). In
both instances, the disavowal of racial inequality and structural racism fails
to take seriously widespread xenophobia and implicit biases, such as anti-
Blackness, and undermines the sincerity of efforts to achieve genuine racial
reconciliation. Similarly, C. R. Squires (2014) critiques popular postracial
rhetorics that conflate postracism with antiracism and argues that we need
"to attend seriously to culture and the stories we tell ourselves—or ignore"
(p. 195). Indeed, postracial narratives, as in recent popular films like *The Blind
Side* (2009), *The Help* (2011), or *Green Book* (2018), often celebrate the role
of white saviors in the triumph of racial progress. Since American popular
culture is replete with postracial fantasies that pander to the sensibilities
of white audiences, Squires claims that "community-centered, multi-racial"
strategies are needed to alter collective memories and understandings of
the past (p. 206).

If postracial films perpetuate comforting narratives of racial progress
that disavow the lived experience of racism and anti-Blackness, then what
cultural artifacts and textual strategies might best disrupt or resist them? In
the remainder of this chapter, we commence our contribution to the critique
of America's postracial condition through a review of Afropessimism and
an analysis of *The Hateful Eight* (2015). Appearing at the end of the Obama

presidency, the film can be understood as a response to popular postracial ideologies that presume America has achieved equality or shared access to opportunity regardless of racial differences. As we shall demonstrate, *The Hateful Eight* breaks from and disrupts postracial narratives that began to circulate after Obama's election in 2008.

ANTI-BLACKNESS AND THE POSTRACIAL

To examine *The Hateful Eight*, we have chosen to apply theories of anti-Blackness to the aesthetics and subtext of the film through a paradigmatic analysis, which identifies patterns of opposition or antagonisms (Wilderson, 2010, 2021). Influenced by such scholars as F. Fanon, S. Hartman, Sexton, and H. Spillars, among others, the methodology maps how the constituent components, assumptions, and logics of dispossession of certain subjectivities (such as "slaves" and "savages") manifest in libidinal, political-economic, and cinematic practices.

Anti-Blackness, an ideology that is pervasive and all-encompassing, is understood as a paradigmatic structuring force within civil society. Whereas an Afrocentric analysis embraces the self-determination of Africans in relation to an examination of Pan-African history, philosophy, and culture, Afropessimism contends that Blackness is the antithesis of human. The "human" subject position is "that which the slave lacks" (Wilderson, 2010, p. 8)—a divide between the acquisition of "social life" compared to an accessibility to only "structural violence" premised on "social death" (Wilderson, 2020, p. 223). Though anti-Blackness is a global phenomenon, anti-Blackness in the context of US civil society identifies three explicit positionalities, the human (white, settler, master), the antihuman (the Black or the slave), and the savage (the Indigenous or red) (Wilderson 2010, p. 29). These positions provide a semantic field by which we imagine/unimagine or make legible/illegible subjecthood to reveal the norms and structures of society.

For Afropessimists, chattel slavery is illustrative of the ways anti-Blackness underlies the very condition of modernity. They argue that dehumanization through chattel slavery is categorically different from the dehumanization experienced by other racial and ethnic groups, thereby constructing a binary opposition between Blackness as a necessary precondition for enslavement and whiteness as compulsory for humanness (Wilderson, 2010, p. 15). Slaves, or Black people, "are objects and implements to be possessed (accumulated) and exchanged (made fungible) in the material and psychic life of Human subjects" (Wilderson, 2021, p. 41). Furthermore, the positionality of a slave is that of social death, which entails "genealogical isolation, dispossession, and [being] subject to gratuitous violence" (Sexton 2010, p. 14). Societies are thereby premised on an exclusionary, ontological condition of suffering inherent to Blackness and reproduced through the destruction of the Black body (Wilderson, 2010, p. 31). In short, the act of giving life back to the slave (due to the absent subject and its differential plane of existence) is inconceivable and requires the dismantling of white civil society. Blackness cannot give meaning back to the historical category or ontological position of a Black subject since the Middle Passage stripped all sense of identity (Watts, 2015). It exists in a Manichean, divided zone that ingrains colonialism and a gratuity of violence, making the (impossible) destruction of civil society a necessity for the contingent restructuring required (Wilderson, 2003, pp. 19–20). Accordingly, for Afropessimists, contemporary society in the (post)modern era should be understood as a reproduction of chattel slavery that shapes the deep socio-psychic structures of our popular and collective imagination.

We believe that the critique of anti-Blackness provides a theoretical lens that can achieve two ends. First, it can offer a methodological means for reading texts and discourse in American popular culture, which further broadens communication and rhetorical studies. Calls have been made upon the discipline of rhetorical studies to consider the radical theory related to contemporary political discourse even if there is tension between Afropessimism and the field's knowledge or theoretical investments (Corrigan, 2019; Kelsie, 2019; Law & Corrigan, 2018; Watts, 2015). For example, E. K. Watts (2015) contends that "thinking through Blackness as a condition of possibility for rhetorical action and social justice is a life-long pursuit that, given the tragic killing of Michael Brown in Ferguson, Missouri in August 2014, feels especially burning" (p. 276), and yet the incompatibility between anti-Blackness and concepts such as voice, "civil" dialogues, and normalized notions of humanism and citizenship grounded in the field remain unresolved. Nonetheless, scholars are engaging with anti-Blackness and recognizing the shortcomings that develop when we fail to engage with the specific decolonial and racial theory. For A. Kelsie (2019), recognizing stasis as starting point for the "ontologizing operations of" anti-Blackness identifies liberal sovereignty's refusal to acknowledge the limits of Blackness's generative and contingent conditions for life and possibility (p. 63). Other approaches suggest how concepts like K. Wilson's notion of "critical cosmopolitanism" may interrogate the same structural dynamics of anti-Blackness (Watts, 2015) or that a repositioning of anti-Blackness as a center can help scholars interrogate modernity's governmental and philosophical dimensions (Corrigan, 2019).

In addition to further informing rhetorical studies, we secondly contend that anti-Blackness as a methodological application can counter the myth of postracialism. Anti-Blackness reminds us that Blackness cannot be postracial if it is "a subject who is always already positioned a Slave" (Wilderson, 2010, p. 7). Poll (2018) similarly claims that an "inability to recognize that Black slavery structures modernity is the unacknowledged hallmark of post-Blackness" (p. 85). Post-Blackness, Poll explains, generally disavows the legacies of slavery and emphasizes social progress. In the horror film *Get Out* (2017), for example, the "lure" of adopting a postracial ideology is the setup for the terror that proceeds. In light of these positions and examples, it is our contention that Afropessimism and the ways the theory can be read allegorically in popular culture operate as both a critique of postracial fantasies and the failure to take seriously history and ontological conditions of slavery. The critique of anti-Blackness to understand cinematic cultural texts reveals how race relations originate and illuminates how these power structures operate.

To be sure, as Wilderson explains, Afropessimism is inherently critical of the postracial ethos of our contemporary moment.

The grammar of Black and Red suffering breaks in on this foreclosure, albeit like the somatic compliance of hysterical symptoms—it registers in both cinema and scholarship as symptom of awareness of the structural antagonisms. The election of President Barack Obama does not mitigate the claim that this is a taciturn historical moment. Neoliberalism with a Black face is neither the index of revolutionary advance nor the end of anti-Blackness as a constituent element of U.S. antagonisms. If anything, the election of Obama enables a plethora of shaming discourses in response to revolutionary politics and "legitimates" widespread disavowal of any notion that the United States itself, and not merely its policies and practices, is unethical. (Wilderson, 2010, pp. 4–5)

Though the label of "postracial" is not explicitly named in this passage, the cultural condition described by Wilderson is a postidentity politics and reference to the disavowals brought on by Obama's election. Likewise, T. R. Dunn (2016) makes a direct connection between the postracial as antithetical to anti-Blackness. Dunn identifies three strategies of postracialism—minimization, multiracialism, and inverting oppression—and argues the embrace of these characteristics or "charges only perpetuate antiblackness and discretely prevent its interrogation" (p. 275). The rhetorical patterns of postracial discourse—such as relegating racism to the past, postmodern notions of fluid identities, and blaming victims for their lack of social advancement—are hegemonic and exclusionary and thus operationally negate the ontological level of (anti-)Blackness.

The critique of anti-Blackness, however, reminds us that individuals cannot move beyond race or antagonistic structures through society's normal means of "acceptance" or "progress" and directly challenges the postracial notion that race is something that can be "escaped." Based on this similar justification, L. Corrigan (2019), in her review of African and Black decolonial literature, advocates the inclusion of anti-Blackness theory to assist rhetorical scholars in identifying the mystifying, subtle, and insidious strategies that modernist concepts and terms have applied to fuel colorblind approaches. Through readings of terms like "radical liberalism," Corrigan argues that rhetorical scholars serious about examining political and racial inequities embedded in practices and discourses require analyses of how colorblind and postracial approaches are actually sustaining and enforcing whiteness and anti-Blackness. Thus interrogations of postracial conditions remind scholars to similarly question the often persuasive and pervasive liberal models and ideals, critiques always and already assumed in Afropessimistic theories and literature.

ANTI-BLACKNESS IN FILM ANALYSIS

Following Wilderson (2010), we agree that a radical critique of race requires questioning the antagonisms underlying portrayals of identity formation, relationships, social allegories of the masters/whites and slaves / Black people and tracing the contradictory political demands within American texts.

The previous failures to recognize anti-Blackness as an epistemological and ontological filler for "our" world and the lack of attention to the way that film and mediated representations propagate anti-Blackness have left voids in discourse, theory, and film criticism. For example, Lacanian psychoanalytic approaches to film fail to account for the full ontological impact of the racial differences in subject formation derived from chattel slavery. Further, most films, especially those that are well known and mainstream, fail to mirror the condition of gratuitous suffering and instead dangerously further the mythic illusions that Black people can acquire the subjectivity of whites, dismissing the grammar of suffering. As Wilderson (2010) notes, "Both the films and the theory tend to posit a possibility of, and a desire for, Black existence, instead of taking cognizance of the ontological claim of the so-called

Afro-Pessimists that Blackness is both that outside which makes it possible for White and non-White (i.e., Asians and Latinos) positions to exist and, simultaneously, contest existence" (p. 65). The social obscurity of Blackness perpetuates the postracial theme of universalist, liberating, and multiracial colorblindness and thus forecloses a radical criticism and examination of identity structures that affirm the dominant norms of white politics. Social problems are framed contingently rather than as antagonisms, and "happy endings" perpetuate false hopes. Thus the most popular, mainstream cinema (regardless of its production by white or Black directors) reproduces society's racist and anti-Black underpinnings with representations that are inherently parasitic on those who are seen as nonhuman in society.

However, likely due to the influence of recent events, Black Lives Matter advocacy, and a growing awareness of the patterns of anti-Blackness and persistent racism, some films offer an honest assessment of the Afropessimistic condition. Wilderson (2015) and Poll (2018), for example, argue that Steve McQueen's *12 Years a Slave* (2013) and Jordan Peele's *Get Out* (2017) represent the conditions of slavery and social death as ontological structures that mark a critical shift in the techniques of film aesthetics.

In the next section, we draw upon paradigmatic analysis to examine *The Hateful Eight* as a site of cinematic antagonism. We argue that the film's aesthetics and setting during Reconstruction can be read as an allegorical critique of the postracial ethos that marked the Obama presidency and direct commentary on the persistence of anti-Blackness in the United States.

RACE, TARANTINO FILMS, AND THE AFROPESSIMISTIC DISRUPTION OF THE POSTRACIAL

The Hateful Eight is the eighth film directed by Quentin Tarantino. As a well-recognized auteur, Tarantino is known for his films addressing the topic of race. Numerous films by Tarantino and their representations and language have come under scrutiny by people in the industry, film critics, and scholars. Tarantino's directorial choices and his public persona are also criticized. For example, Tarantino's public commentary regarding issues of Blackness and his own identity are examined as emblematic of "race privilege," "an ability to say and do things that are offensive, even racist, without threat or fear of social reprisal" (Tierney, 2011, p. 83). Some of Tarantino's critics have called him racist for the repetitive and persistent use of the *n*-word in his films and a variety of various "Black" representations, including stereotypical roles (Nama, 2015). Furthermore, S. Tierney (2011) identifies Tarantino's rhetoric of whiteness through Tarantino's denial of his own race and ethnicity and his "knowledge" of others' experiences, his sweeping essentialism of African Americans, his claims of "accurate" representations despite the history of criminalizing characters, and his use of anti-Semitic as well as racially offensive dialogue. Despite these controversial elements that often surround his films, media critics also defend Tarantino, seeing value and progressive meanings in his works (Nama, 2015; Roche, 2018). D. Roche (2018), for example, argues that the focus in his films on social tensions "is evidence that our society is rife with them and that we have yet to move on to a post-racial, post-feminist world" (p. 13), and A. Nama (2015) recognizes these criticisms as often "reductive" (p. 9) and overlooking the "racial commentary woven throughout the body of his work" (p. 12). Like Roche and Nama, our analysis will show how Tarantino's allegory of Reconstruction's failures rebuke the optimistic, triumphant, and humanistic qualities found in the postracial rhetoric in mainstream film.

Despite its reputation as Tarantino's most prosaic film and its mixed reviews (Bradshaw, 2016; Sims, 2015), we view *The Hateful Eight* as significant and insightful because its subject matter and dialogue contributes to commentary on race relations by framing race discussions through the lens of anti-Blackness, thereby disrupting postracist assumptions. We believe the timing of the film's release, roughly three years after *Django Unchained* (2012), supports an Afropessimistic interpretation of his film. When read together, we can understand *The Hateful Eight* as a counterstatement to the postracial assumptions that underlie *Django Unchained*, which featured an overly optimistic ending marked by Django's triumph over slavery.

Django Unchained advances a postracial attitude toward American race relations since it celebrates the myth of racial progress. Django's escape from social death, his destruction of white, civil society, his triumphant rescue of Broomhilda, and the revenge he inflicts on the slave masters ultimately monumentalizes Django as human and erases the grammar of suffering. Wilderson (2010) argues that "films can be thought of as one of an ensemble of discursive practices mobilized by civil society to 'invite,' or interpellate, Blacks to the same variety of social identities that other races are able to embody without contradiction" (p. 24); but such portrayals are deceitful, false promises because the slave/Black is symbolically unable to occupy such subject positions (pp. 24–25).

When Django is given his "freedom," the narrative event encapsulates his transition to human. Shultz explains: "I'm obliged to help *you* on *your* [emphases added] quest to rescue your beloved Broomhilda." The narrative centers on Django and his journey, mission, or quest and inverts "the interracial buddy formula" (Winters, 2018, p. 9). Django and Schultz ride side by side like equals against landscapes containing majestic, rugged western mountains, symbolizing hope, free land, and the attainment of liberty in "unsettled" territory. Django is the protagonist, reinforced by the film's poster artwork and cover images that show Django front and center. Django is portrayed as a free man escaping the grammar of suffering, successfully destroying white civil society of Candyland, thereby attaining subjectivity and postracial idealism.

Unlike *Django Unchained*, *The Hateful Eight* directly disputes the fantasy that America has arrived at a postracial zenith. When read as cinematic strategy of anti-Blackness, the film serves to counter the postracial ideologies of the present day by providing an allegory that centers racial-based politics and the inevitable ontological state of Black people as slaves.

The film tells the story of eight strangers, including two bounty hunters, who all meet at a stopover while escaping a blizzard on their way to the city of Red Rock. John "the Hangman" Ruth and his driver, O. B., travel with the captured fugitive Daisy Domergue, a known murderer. They pick up the stranded Major Marquis Warren, an infamous bounty hunter with his own dead fugitives (and a past acquaintance), and eventually Chris Mannix, Red Rock's new sheriff, who also needs transportation. At the haberdashery, they meet four more guests: Bob, the alleged caretaker for Minnie, Oswaldo Mobray, the town's hangman, Joe Gage, a rancher, and Sanford Smithers, a former Confederate general with business pertaining to his presumed-dead son. As the storm persists and the evening progresses, tensions arise over Civil War politics and growing suspicions. Smithers is shot and killed by Warren after a provocation, and during that confrontation, someone poisons the coffee, killing O. B. and Ruth and leading to Warren teaming up with Mannix.

Warren eventually pieces together the mysterious circumstances of the poison and Minnie's disappearance. Bob is executed and a shoot-out occurs, leaving Warren shot and severely wounded by Domergue's brother, Jody, who has been hiding in the basement the entire time and responsible for the attempted heist and Minnie's murder. Warren and Mannix, both wounded, kill Jody, Mobray, and Gage and hang Domergue to her death. The film ends as Mannix and Warren lay dying after reading aloud a counterfeit "Lincoln letter."

The tale of heist gone bad in the setting of the Reconstruction era serves as an allegory for the state of America during the time of its release—that is, the revelation of anti-Blackness as shown by police killings and the persistence of racism in the post-Obama era. The film's allegory is a reminder that racism and anti-Blackness is the norm in America and serves as a refutation to the expectation, condition, and transcendence of postracial discourse deriving from the Obama administration (Haney Lopez, 2010; Love & Tosolt, 2010). In the following analysis, we identify four distinct themes of antagonisms in *The Hateful Eight*, creating an anti-Black allegory that disrupts postracial trends: Major Marquis as representative of the slave position, representations of gratuitous violence, the exclusionary condition of white civil society, and the representation of the requirement of inevitability of the slave's social death.

MAJOR MARQUIS WARREN AS SLAVE

Despite his role as a protagonist, Major Marquis Warren is related to a discourse and imagery that secures his inescapable position as slave, which is propagated by the history of slavery and "social death" and the conditions of the modern world. We contend that Warren's story is told paradigmatically rather than episodically, allowing the film to progressively push the limitations of cinema. Wilderson (2010) contends that episodic elements are grounded in most film narratives, inviting the Black person oxymoronically into the "fold of civic relations" even though "the three-point progression of a drama for the living cannot be applied to a being that is socially dead (naturally alienated, open to gratuitous violence and generally dishonored)" (p. 27). Instead, *The Hateful Eight*'s story, with continuous racism and suspicion directed at Warren, degrades his subject position, leaving him alienated, fungible, and subject to persistent gratuitous violence.

Despite the story occurring post–Civil War, Warren's literal slave/Black status is repeatedly acknowledged as each person fixates on his color and presumed character based on stereotypical beliefs and assumptions of inferiority. John Ruth first addresses him as "Black fella," while Daisy Domergue and Chris Mannix, call him "n****r."[1] Warren's marking as inferior is marked in language and continues with nearly all initial interactions. The most blatant racism comes from General Sanford Smithers who will not directly speak to Warren when he attempts to converse with Smithers about the war. Rather than answering Warren directly, Smithers instructs Mannix: "Inform the n****r in the cavalry officer's uniform that I had a division of Confederates under my command . . . in Baton Rouge," leading Mannix to derogatorily address Warren as "Major N****r!" Smithers continues to deny Warren's presence by explaining to Mannix, "I don't acknowledge n****rs in northern uniforms!"

Even before Warren enters the haberdashery, while he is busy completing stable work with Bob, news that Warren has arrived with the party circulates among the guests inside. The questions and suspicion surrounding Warren are openly addressed despite the subtle agitations and suspicious backgrounds or motives of the other guests. One of the most deplorable, racist lines of the film comes from Smithers, who, when asked if he knows Warren, responds: "I don't know that n****r. But I know he's a n****r, and that's all I need to know." The hatred expressed is jarring since Smithers does not even need to give a particular reason for dismissing him or justifying his racism as his racial identity implicitly provides all necessary justification. Likewise, when the topic that Warren is carrying an infamous letter from President Lincoln addressed to him is first brought up, disbelief is displayed by most individuals, including Oswaldo Mobray, whose formal, upper-class dress and British accent might imply a more progressive orientation than those guests from the South. Mobray shouts incredulously, "The n****r in the stable has a letter from Abraham Lincoln?" which results in Mannix repeating the same exact question in even greater astonishment. The question and the expression of incredulity reveal the shocked response to the idea that a slave has access to white civility. The contention that a slave would be accepted by the most powerful leader in the United States government seems impossible even for those individuals that seem most open to the Northern cause to "end" slavery.

The racist language in Tarantino films serves as a marker of historical views of race. Roche (2018), for example, argues that the rhetoric "underlines the mundanity of racist rhetoric, not just in the antebellum South . . . but in contemporary Los Angeles" (p. 63). Thus the film's discourse strategically operates as a disturbing reminder of how various identities relate to stigmatized Others. In a similar way, blatant representations of the ontological slave position operate to expose the postracial ethos as fictional and inaccurate.

Additionally, *The Hateful Eight* further reinforces the position of the slave as antihuman through the articulation of stereotypical constructions of and biases toward Warren / Black people that are held by the characters and eventually disclosed over the course of the story. Warren is consistently and overtly named or assumed to be the least trustworthy character in the room. Such labels are exposed and debunked through situational irony since, ultimately, his reasons for coming to Red Rock and ending up at Minnie's Haberdashery are established and known more than any of the other characters' motives or intentions with the exception of Ruth.

Nonetheless, Warren is labeled as "sneaky" and a liar by other characters throughout the story, especially when racial tension remains high and significant. When Mannix calls out Warren's Lincoln letter as a fake, resulting in multiple people laughing at Ruth's naiveté, Ruth's response is not a condemnation of Warren's action but a racist allegation against all Black people:

"Well, I guess it's true what they say about you people. Can't trust a fuckin' word comes out of your mouth." Dismissing Warren's justification for having it as an assurance of his safety against racist whites, Ruth fails to empathize, understand, or forgive, responding: "Call it what you want. I call it a dirty fuckin' trick." The image and stereotype of the Black "trickster" is named and openly reinforced. Ruth's serious expression marks his unconscious racism as he had been the most progressive in his respect for Warren but is now equally suspicious of him.

The same racist stereotype is made when Warren tells Smithers that he had met his son when Smithers's son was pursuing the bounty on Warren's head. Warren claims to have raped and killed him for hunting him, resulting in Smithers screaming, "You're a goddamn lie!" and Mannix injecting claims that Warren is lying and sneaky. While it is never discovered whether Major's tale of Smither's son is true or one used for Warren to murder the racist Smithers in the name of self-defense, the ambiguity is one that allows the antagonism to remain. The characters' reading of Warren reflects the supposed "antics," stereotyped actions of tricking, lying, and being sexually dangerous, first constructed in minstrelsy and melodrama (Hartman, 1997). However, the blatantly racist stereotypes also call it out and reveal how the labels to demonize Black people were placed on them in the first place, reaffirming the bodily politics and pleasures of terror that stemmed from chattel slavery. White reaction and anger to death at the hands of those who are Black reveal the incommensurability to the gratuitous violence experienced by Black individuals. Roche (2018) argues that the human relationships along racial lines emerge in such scenes, which we read as consistent with anti-Blackness interpretations of the positions of the human and slave. Thus the alleged unconscious racism revealing itself signals continued power relations and exposes postracial sentimentalities as deceptive.

In addition to the stereotypical representations, Warren is deprecated as a fungible commodity and an object. His infamous story of escaping a war camp is juxtaposed against the deaths of "Southern youth, farmers' sons, cream of the crop." Mannix argues that Warren's life was not worth the violence inflicted on the (white) men, dismissing and downplaying any of the previous gratuitous violence inflicted on slaves. Additional examples of Warren's/the slave's devaluation are affirmed in the context of Warren's right to earn a living ("Eight thousand dollars is a lot of money for a n****r"), his physical presence in white spaces (Domergue protesting "that n****r" in the stagecoach), the bounty on his head in exchange for the work (". . . to battle-hard rebs, five thousand dollars just to cut off a n****r's head? That's good money"), and the ongoing degrading of Black Civil War regiments.

In all these examples of portrayal and devaluation, Warren remains outside the state of human.

GRATUITOUS VIOLENCE

Wilderson (2010) reminds readers that the ontological position of the slave has come about from a corporeality "generally dishonored, perpetually open to gratuitous violence, and void of kinship structure" (p. 11). Not only are these all characteristics of Warren, the descriptions of antagonistic relationships between slaves and also between slaves and whites are consistently framed by acts of gratuitous violence. However, conditions of gratuitous violence are not shown or enacted (like in *Django Unchained*) but rather described as an unconscious and an always-present condition for Black people. Roche (2018) concurs that the film shies "away from depicting the violence inflicted on the black characters" (p. 68). While the film minimizes the visualization of such graphic violent images, the film does not shy away from the discursive presence of the condition. Instead, *Hateful Eight* uses dialogue and description to carefully and deliberately construct the antagonistic relationship(s) that fuels race relations in the constant context and state of gratuitous violence.

Scenarios described by others illuminate the outrages and brutality of the antebellum period and the Civil War. Ruth explains his dislike for Mannix's father, who "ran a rebel army to kill and steal emancipated Blacks." Likewise, when Warren asks Smithers what happened to the Black command that Smithers's army captured, Smithers exclaims: "We didn't have the time or the food . . . nor the inclination to care for Northern horses and *least of all, Northern n****rs! So we shot 'em where they stood!* [emphasis original]." Mannix admits to "sacking" multiple Black towns and justifies it by saying, "when n****rs are scared, that's when white folks are safe." In all these instances, the antagonisms in this narrative illustrate the ongoing tension of human/ white against slave/Black, an allegory of the parasitic relationship dependent on the suffering (or fear) of Black people. S. Hartman (1997) traces how in slavery "white culpability was displaced as black criminality" (p. 83). Such violence is a never-ending presence in Warren's existence. Warren's representation of the inherent and inevitable experience becomes an allegory for contemporary Black people still experiencing police brutality, murder, and the prison-industrial complex.

One way that gratuitous violence is aesthetically revealed in this film is through camera work, specifically point-of-view shots and close-up reaction shots focusing on the gazes of characters. As Warren and Bob enter the haberdashery after completing their stable work, attention is drawn to them. Previously, the room was quiet with nearly whispered conversations. When Warren arrives, he brings with him the loud howl of the blizzard. The camera remains on Warren (from the point of Smithers) even after Warren eventually turns around, facing the large, open room and meeting the gaze of Smithers, who moves forward anxiously and stares steadfastly: the first sign of agitation or animation from him since the carriage arrived. The gaze on Smithers lasts approximately seven seconds. Smithers is shown from Warren's vantage point, and the gaze that Warren returns, watching him cautiously, is confirmed by the camera, which now focuses on a close-up, head-on, full-frontal shot of Warren's face. Warren's expression is both contemplative and pained. His silence, expression, and gaze indicate that he is not really listening to Bob, who is directing Warren and cursing at the door. Warren's gaze returns to Smithers twice in the moments after his entrance; Smithers's stare is unrelenting. Though the camera breaks from him, the gaze lasts roughly a minute, leading Mannix to notice Smithers's direct stare and ask: "Do you know that n****r, sir?" Though we know that Warren is gazing back, the gaze is precautionary and inspective of the other guests and their surroundings. The gaze may seem contingent in this instance, but the film is consistent with point-of-view shifts throughout it. We argue that the camera and gaze are the representation of gratuitous violence always present and inescapable for Warren.

Another indicator of the gratuitous violence comes from the dialogue and context facing Warren, for example, his references to his desperation to escape chattel slavery but also the reality of "hillbillies" incessantly "headhunting" him. In telling Smithers about his son's supposed death, Warren points to the violence inflicted on Black individuals as the precursor and justification for his retaliatory actions both against Smithers's son and whites in general. In discussing the political and sociological ramifications of the thinking and treatment that set out the condition of slaves, Warren's commentary serves as a reminder that the only way that Black people can exist is through the necessary and required destruction of white civil society. "And I say, let 'em burn. I'm supposed to apologize for killing Johnny Reb? You joined the war to keep n****rs in chains. I joined the war to kill white Southern crackers. And that means killing 'em any way I can." The calling out of the particular double standard—that the human has thrived at the expense of the slave but that such violence on the part of the slave is forbidden or unforgiving—is made apparent.

The white guests express discomfort with Warren's violence imposed on whites regardless of the gratuitous violence they imposed on the Black population through their role in preserving chattel slavery and the mission to maintain a slave economy. For example, Mannix defends his father, now dead, who ran a rebel militia of renegade soldiers that killed and attempted to steal back emancipated Black people. By Mannix demanding dignity for his father, despite the Confederate's defeat and the nation's morally imperative decision to emancipate slaves, he argues for the "decriminalization of white violence" and presumes it is a "requisite to preserving the public good" (Hartman, 1997, p. 101). Such ongoing antagonisms in the dialogue are never resolved or proven more defensible than others. We argue that the tensions fuel antagonisms and expose the double standard that is parasitic and contrived at the expense of Black people. The quote that best acknowledges the state of anti-Blackness and the vulnerability of Blackness responds to Ruth's stereotypical assertion:

I-I know I'm the only Black son of a bitch you ever conversed with so I'm gonna cut you some slack. But you got no idea what it's like being a Black man facin' down America. The only time Black folks are safe is when white folks is disarmed. And this letter had the desired effect of disarming white folks. You want to know why I lie about something like that, white man? Got me on that stagecoach, didn't it?

Warren reminds Ruth that violence and death is at stake when whites are scared, anti-Black, or simply legitimated by an economy, social institutions, and a legal system that protects them more than those who are Black. Without the use of the letter and its postracial rhetoric, Warren would be dead. Warren's rhetorical question shows the precarious situations of Black people in America, the lack of resolve created by the human condition, and the denial of this condition, which undeniably continues today. Although the quote is written for a post–Civil War setting, it is just as applicable in the context of contemporary America.

REPRESENTATIONS OF WHITE CIVIL SOCIETY

The blizzard in the film is a significant element of the mise-en-scène. Its presence is so relevant that it is almost talked about like an additional character. We find the blizzard and "the mountaintops . . . racialized white," a metaphor for white civil society (Roche, 2018, p. 39). Like white civil society, the blizzard dwells in a condition of anti-Blackness (that intensifies along with the storm), and by occurring, it reveals the entire structure as the source of fear and horror for Black people. In relation to grammars of suffering, including gratuitous violence and the representation of the slave, we argue that

The Hateful Eight unflinchingly structures social antagonisms according to white civil society and the ethical dilemmas that provide its foundation; the blizzard symbolizes the disequilibrium and its natural unrelenting force. In the opening scenes of the film, the landscape of snow, the clouds, and the skyline warn of the foreboding blizzard. A literal whiteness is all-encompassing—on the ground, on trees, even on the statue of a crucifix that the carriage passes. The elements of the storm are hostile and controlling and symbolize an inability to escape. The intentionally created sound design remains persistent throughout the entire film, even through the final scenes. Many quotes represent the persistence and violence brought on by the blizzard: "Blasted blizzard has been on our ass for the last three hours," and "Look, I sure hate to interrupt you all, but we got a cold damn blizzard that's hot on our ass that we're trying to beat to shelter!" Further foreboding, though not centering on the blizzard, includes the image of the white-and-black horses that lead the carriage. The camera pans on their muzzles, at times, each one inching ahead, as they race to reach their destination, representing the racial conflicts that will continue to emerge.

Once they arrive at Minnie's Haberdashery, they are reminded that they "are stuck on the wrong side of a blizzard." Not surprisingly, the growing blizzard correlates with the climactic rise of racial tensions inside and among the individuals inside the haberdashery. Throughout the dramatic, hostile, and intense dialogue that centers on race or the Civil War, pauses notably include the sounds of the storm or the wind and the whipping and whistling between scenes and lines, which add dramatic effect, not to mention that the literal snow bursts inside upon the return of each guest who is forced to go outdoors briefly. When the climatic racial tensions occur—such as the confiscation of weapons, the revelation of the Lincoln letter's inauthenticity, and Warren's and Smithers's various conversations—the camera cuts to the blizzard, showing it at its worst. The blizzard is described as "shit" by O. B., and in the same way, the antagonisms occurring between the characters remain represented by the grotesque ugliness of the winter storm.

SOCIAL DEATH

The Hateful Eight concludes its thrilling and violent sequences through a relatively fast-falling action and resolution that may not provide much resolve for its audience. Yet in this way, *The Hateful Eight* reveals white civil society for what it currently is: inescapable and responsible for the gratuity of violence that keeps Black individuals outside of civil society and assures their social death. No better representation of social death is the impending literal death for both Mannix and Warren, who lay dying together in the film. Although an uncertain, postmodern ending persists because viewers do not see their final breaths, chances of any rescue or change of fate during a snowstorm in the frontier of Wyoming are highly unlikely. We can only assume that they will bleed to death or succumb to their wounds. Even if Warren were capable of escape or survival, the previous conversations reveal that the bounty on Warren's head would only grow after his stay at Minnie's Haberdashery. Thus Warren reminds Mannix prior to hanging Domergue, "We gonna die, white boy. We ain't got no say in that." The line is consistent with the claim "Blacks are on the side of . . . social death . . . Blacks will never be post-Black" (Poll, 2018, p. 91). Warren was always already living in social death, hunted, trapped in the blizzard, and unfazed and prepared for the inevitable defeat that meets him in the end.

This condition of inevitable social death is further represented not only by the title of the final chapter, "Black Man, White Hell," which appropriately describes the state of civil society and Warren's context throughout the film, but also by his acceptance or expectation of gratuitous violence and social death. Furthermore, the final exchange focuses on the symbol of the fabricated Lincoln letter and the words that Warren penned. Mannix reads it aloud, which permits audiences to hear the content for the first time. When considering the context of present race relations, the lines "time is changing slowly . . . We still have a long way to go but hand in hand, I know we'll get there" do not reinforce anti-Blackness and the inevitable social death, but rather speak to liberalism and colorblindness. In short, the letter is the myth of postracial ideals: freedom, access, equality, and its attainability, the ideals of liberal white America. War- ren knows the ideologies will appeal to other whites but confirms the letter as the literal manifestation of a lie. In handing over the letter, its clean, crisp sheet is stained by Warren's and Mannix's bloodied hands, a reminder of the antagonistic and parasitic relationships that serve as a foundation of white civil society. After reading it and complimenting Warren, Mannix crumples the letter and tosses it on the floor nearby; it has served its purpose and reveals the myth of progress in the face of inevitable (social) death.

CONCLUSION

Despite society's claims of inclusivity, Wilderson (2010) argues that "its tech-nologies of hegemony (including cinema) are mobilized to manufacture this assertion, not dissent from it" (p. 24). In light of media's approach to postracial logics, we view *The Hateful Eight* as a significant text precisely because it is not seeking to revise the racism of the past and slavery's contribution to contemporary anti-Blackness. Popular culture can illustrate the dynamics of contemporary anti-Blackness if it comes to terms with and comments on the history of conquest and enslavement that developed the present white civil nation-state grounded in violence.

When compared to *Django Unchained, The Hateful Eight* serves as a better allegory of our times. The film productively revises the past through not just a diverse cast in a traditionally white genre but also the revision of humanistic, postracial assumptions and a counternarrative of anti-Blackness. Indeed, the film does not continue the dangerous facade that upholds the discourse and mediations of postracial ideologies, rather *The Hateful Eight* disrupts them. Given its release after *Django Unchained* and during a time when society embraced the social and political biases of postracial logics and the shifting cultural insights brought about by ongoing Black suffering and Black Lives Matter social advocacy, *The Hateful Eight* serves as an allegory for the racial unrest, anti-Blackness, and social death continuing in alleged postracial times. Undeniably, films can play a significant role in influencing or educating people on the subject of race relations, drawing implications for the role of visual culture in representing racial tensions and conflict and revealing the social myths of racial progress we tell ourselves. Reading films for the persistent messages of anti-Blackness may seem defeating to some, but the recognition of society's ongoing grammar of suffering, disavowal of violence, and the antagonism of human life requiring Black death are claims demanding critical consideration.

NOTE

1. Though this term is uncensored in the characters' quotes in the film, we engage in censorship because the word is highly offensive and used in each context as a racial slur. We support marking the term as evidence of our claims but find it unnecessary to write out or replicate the term's offensiveness in our writing.

REFERENCES

Bradshaw, P. (2016, January 7). *The hateful eight* review—Tarantino triumphs with a western of wonder [Review of *The hateful eight*, directed by Q. Tarantino]. *The Guardian.* https://www.theguardian.com/film/2016/jan/07/the-hateful-eight-review-tarantino-triumphs-with-a-western-of-wonder

Cloud, D. (1996). Hegemony or concordance? The rhetoric of tokenism in Oprah Winfrey's rags to riches biography. *Critical Studies in Media Communication, 13*(2), 115–137.

Corrigan, L. (2019). Decolonizing philosophy and rhetoric: Dispatches from the undercommons [Review of *The undercommons: Fugitive planning and Black study*, by S. Harney, F. Moten, A. P. Gumbs, A. Mbembe, C. W. Mills, & C. L. Warren; *Spill: Scenes of Black feminist fugitivity*, by A. P. Gumbs; *Critique of Black reason*, by A. Mbembe; *Black rights / white wrongs: The critique of racial liberalism*, by C. W. Mills; *Ontological terror: Blackness, nihilism, and emancipation*, by C. L. Warren]. *Philosophy & Rhetoric, 52*(2), 163–188.

Craig, B. B., & Rahko, S. E. (2021). From "Say my name" to "Texas bamma": Transgressive *topoi*, oppositional optics, and sonic subversion in Beyoncé's "Formation." In C. Baade & K. A. McGee (Eds.), *Beyoncé in the world: Making meaning with Queen Bey in troubled times* (pp. 260–284). Wesleyan University Press.

Dunn, T. R. (2016). Playing neoliberal politics: Post-racial and post-racist strategies in "Same love." *Communication and Critical/Cultural Studies, 13*(3), 269–286.

Halualani, R. T. (2011) Abstracting and de-racializing diversity: The articulation of diversity in the post-race era. In M. G. Lacy & K. A. Ono (Eds.), *Critical rhetorics of race* (pp. 247–255). New York University Press.

Haney Lopez, I. F. (2010). Post-racial racism: Racial stratification and mass incarceration in the age of Obama. *California Law Review, 98*(3), 1023–1074.

Hartman, S. (1997). *Scenes of subjection: Terror, slavery, and self-making in nineteenth-century America*. Oxford University Press

Kelsie, A. (2019). Blackened debate at the end of the world. *Philosophy & Rhetoric, 52*(1), 63–70.

Lacy, M. G., & Ono, K. A. (2011). Introduction. In M. G. Lacy & K. A. Ono (Eds.), *Critical rhetorics of race* (pp. 1–17). New York University Press.

Law, M., & Corrigan, L. M. (2018). On white-speak and gatekeeping: Or, what good are the Greeks? *Communication and Critical/Cultural Studies, 15*(4), 326–330.

Love, B. L., & Tosolt, B. (2010). Reality or rhetoric? Barack Obama and post-racial America. *Race, Gender & Class, 17*(3–4), 19–37.

Mukherjee, R. (2011). Bling fling: Commodity consumption and the politics of the post-racial. In M. G. Lacy & K. A. Ono (Eds.), *Critical rhetorics of race* (pp. 178–193). New York University Press.

Nama, A. (2015). *Race on the QT: Blackness and the films of Quentin Tarantino*. University of Texas Press.

Poll, R. (2018). Can one "get out"? The aesthetics of Afro-pessimism. *Journal of the Midwest Modern Language Association, 51*(2), 69–102.

Roche, D. (2018). *Quentin Tarantino: Poetics and politics of cinematic metafiction*. University Press of Mississippi.

Sexton, J. (2010). "The curtain of the sky": An introduction. *Critical Sociology, 36*(1), 11–24. https://doi.org/10.1177/0896920509347136

Sexton, J. (2017). *Black masculinity and the cinema of policing*. Palgrave Macmillan.

Sims, D. (2015, December 25). *The hateful eight* is a gory epic in search of meaning. *The Atlantic*. https://www.theatlantic.com/entertainment/archive/2015/12/hateful-eight-quentin-tarantino-review/421632/

Squires, C. R. (2014). *The post-racial mystique: Media and race in twenty-first century.* New York University Press.

Tarantino, Q. (Director). (2015). *The hateful eight* [Film]. Weinstein Company.

Tierney, S. (2011). Quentin Tarantino in black and white. In M. G. Lacy & K. A. Ono (Eds.), *Critical rhetorics of race* (pp. 81–97). New York University Press.

Watts, E. K. (2015). Critical cosmopolitanism, antagonism, and social suffering. *Quarterly Journal of Speech, 101*(1), 271–279.

Wilderson, F. B., III. (2003). The prison slave as hegemony's (silent) scandal. *Social Justice, 30*(2), 18–27.

Wilderson, F. B., III. (2010). *Red, white & Black: Cinema and the structure of US antagonisms.* Duke University Press.

Wilderson, F. B., III. (2015). Social death and narrative aporia in *12 years a slave. Black Camera, 7*(1), 134–149.

Wilderson, F. B., III. (2020). *Afropessimism.* Liveright.

Wilderson, F. B., III. (2021). Afropessimism and the ruse of analogy: Violence, freedom struggles, and the death of Black desire. In M. Jung and J. H. Costa Vargas (Eds.), *Antiblackness* (pp. 37–59). Duke University Press.

Winters, J. (2018). Rescue US: *Birth, Django,* and the violence of racial redemption. *Religions, 9*(21), 1–15.

Part 5

The Spatial and Social Class
Dynamics of Postrace

Chapter 11

POLICE BRUTALITY WITHOUT RACE

The Postracial Enthymeme's Portrayal of Collective Organizing in *The Public*

WHITNEY GENT AND MELANIE LOEHWING

In a series of public service announcements (PSA) for the American Librar-ies Association (n.d.), Emilio Estevez declared public libraries to be "the last bastion of democracy in action." Distributed in conjunction with the release of his 2019 film *The Public*, the PSAs championed public libraries as "the place where facts live, curiosity is encouraged, and all are welcome." Estevez described *The Public*—a film he wrote, directed, and starred in—as a "love letter" to these all-important spaces of diverse and inclusive community (Morehart, 2018). He articulated the underlying argument the film advances in terms of the "moral imperative for libraries and other public spaces to help the homeless and other populations in need. If you possess a beating heart, that is as close to an inarguable statement as you are likely to hear" (Morehart, 2018). Interviewers were moved by the salience of the film's argument, and they anticipated commercial and public success given its warm reception in early screenings and its all-star cast of Estevez, Michael K. Williams, Alec Baldwin, Jena Malone, Christian Slater, and Gabrielle Union, among others (Peet, 2019). With racially diverse actors and a storyline about everyday people standing together in solidarity against political corruption and police brutality, Estevez imagined that *The Public* would be "more relevant now than it would have been had we made it [in 2008]" when he originally pitched the film to backers (Peet, 2019). Ahead of its release, the film seemed poised to resonate with audiences in the broader context of the Black Lives Matter movement and ongoing demonstrations against police violence.

The Public, however, failed to find its audience. The film struggled to secure a distributor and eventually had only a limited release, and this essay takes its failure as an opportunity to consider what went wrong in the argument it advanced about the importance of the public library as a space for inclusion and community. We contend that *The Public* represents a postracial fantasy— a narrative that advances a colorblind account of persistent disparities and inequities in our society—in order to criticize contemporary phenomena that remain, at their core, racially inflected social issues. The film addresses a wide range of current issues directly, including dialogue about economic inequality, political corruption, climate change, mental illness, addiction, healthcare, police brutality, and homelessness. The one issue it neglects to discuss explicitly is racism, and this is a perplexing silence in a film about a marginalized group in a midwestern city protesting police brutality and public indifference to their suffering given the obvious parallels to the real-world events in Ferguson, Missouri.

What accounts for this omission in a film ostensibly concerned with unjust exclusions, disparities, and discrimination? We explain the film's silence on race in terms of a common enthymematic structure of postracial rhetoric. The enthymeme is a particularly useful concept for understanding the rhetorical form of postracial narratives because it entails a strategic silence wherein a core premise or the claim of an argument is left unstated so that the audience may fill it in for themselves. Our analysis of *The Public* shows how postracial fantasies rely on an enthymematic structure inherent in a commitment to colorblindness by suppressing explicit discussions of race and racism. As a consequence, postracial fantasies inhibit their own ability to promote antiracist action because they leave unarticulated the very inequities they aim to transform. Viewers already equipped to fill in the missing information about persistent racism represent the proverbial choir to whom the film preaches but does not need to persuade; those who do need to be persuaded to oppose racism are also those least able to supply the omitted premises or claims on which the argument relies. This essay joins other scholars' examinations of entertainment media texts to discern postracialism's structures and implications (Bineham, 2015; Enck & Morrisey, 2015; Gomez & McFarlane, 2017; Murphy & Harris, 2018; Thornton, 2011). *The Public* provides a useful exemplar to illustrate the rhetorical shortcomings of the postracial enthymeme, and we proceed by reviewing the scholarship on postracialism and enthymemes, identifying the function of the postracial enthymeme in *The Public*, and exploring potential insights for antiracist efforts that can be gleaned from our analysis.

POSTRACIAL RHETORIC'S PROBLEMATIC ENTHYMEME

Over the last two decades, communication scholars have made sustained and diverse contributions to our understanding of postracialism and its ascent in American politics and culture. K. Ono (2010) sums up postracial-ism as "a fantasy that racism no longer exists," one that "disavows history, overlaying it with an upbeat discourse about how things were never really that bad, are not so bad now, and are only getting better" (p. 227). As proof that the United States has moved "beyond" racism, postracial arguments and texts frequently point to the election of Barack Obama in 2008, suggesting that racism no longer holds anyone back because a Black man was elected president. Postracial narratives shore up the values of meritocracy and indi-vidualism at the heart of the American-dream myth by denying that dispari-ties in opportunity, access, and resources exist across racial categories in a "colorblind" society (Bineham, 2015). Postracism presents an urgent threat to antiracist progress because, as R. A. Griffin (2015) reminds us, it "influences public understandings of racial histories, racial inequality, and interracial coalitions from a pedagogical stance invested in the re/production of white power, dominance, and superiority" (p. 148).

Theories of postracial discourse are varied, but colorblindness ap-pears as a common feature in the many analyses of journalistic and entertainment-media artifacts demonstrating a postracial stance. As J. N. Cobb (2011) explains, "Postracialism . . . asserts that we do not see race any more" (p. 407). This is not to say that race no longer exists; rather, postra-cial colorblindness insists that racial difference no longer matters or that it is racist to notice/speak about difference (Melamed, 2011). In this chapter, we focus on three features of postracialism that are particularly relevant to mediated texts like *The Public*: the depiction of a white hero, the de-nial of systemic racism, and the promotion of individual initiative. The first operates despite an insistence that race no longer matters; the latter two divert attention from racial and systemic differences in order to uphold colorblind ideologies.

First, postracial narratives frequently revolve around white heroes and Black tokens, as is the case in recent films and television shows like *The Blind Side* (2009), *The Help* (2011), *Psych* (2006–2014), *Orange Is the New Black* (2013–2019), and *The Public* (2018) (Bineham, 2015; Enck & Morrisey, 2015; Griffin, 2015; Murphy & Harris, 2018; Thornton, 2011). In telling stories that center the experiences of progressive white protagonists, even as it denies the ongoing significance of race, postracialism implicitly reifies the dominance of white identity, perspective, and experience (Griffin, 2015). Such narra-tives situate Black characters as tokens or as opposites of their benevolent, paternal white saviors (Bineham, 2015; Murphy & Harris, 2018). In doing so, they repurpose or recycle racist stereotypes of the past while simultaneously insisting that racism has been overcome (Mislán & Ashley, 2018).

A second key feature of postracial rhetoric is the denial of systemic racism in favor of portrayals that position racism as an individual attribute or attitude. This is particularly the case in narratives that imagine racism to be an anachronistic attitude of the past that has been fully overcome in the present. T. R. Dunn (2016) describes this feature as a rhetorical strategy of minimization "in which the rhetor deposits legitimate racial discussions within a frame that ends in a moment previous to our own, typically sometime around the 1960s Civil Rights Movement" and thereby "removes racial issues as appropriate subjects of debate, misdirects public attention toward other issues, and characterizes policies against racism as 'out of place'" (p. 273). In this conception of a postracial society, when racism appears, it is the result of bigoted thinking by an individual out of step with the rest of the community.

Finally, postracial rhetoric promotes individual initiative as the only prerequisite for success, thereby diminishing the role that cultural capital and privilege play in rewarding effort unequally. M. E. Triece (2017) explains that "strategic forgetting operates in conjunction with the familiar and formulaic frame of personalization" to downplay racism as a structural feature and recast "success and failure in personal terms, as a result of the hard work/ irresponsibility of individuals, as opposed to white privilege or systemic racism" (p. 251). A society that aspires to be colorblind remains ill-equipped to recognize how larger structural forces establish opportunities or obstacles for individuals dependent on their racial identities. The imperative of colorblindness discourages audiences from taking stock of salient disparities in the resources and privileges afforded to different racial groups. When seeing color is presented as a biased way of viewing the world, those who wish to avoid discrimination are encouraged to ignore difference in circumstances that may be attributed to race (Rossing, 2012).

Taken together, these regressive features of postracial thinking suggest it should be an unpalatable choice for those committed to antiracist work, yet communities continue to promote and support postracial rhetorics and colorblindness in the name of progress. Postracialism may remain rhetorically appealing to some audiences for a number of reasons: the insistence on colorblindness has the feel of a rejection of traditional grounds for discrimination and appears to undercut the rationale for white supremacy by denying that anyone's race matters and asserting that no race can be considered dominant over another. Moreover, colorblindness as an attitudinal stance gestures toward equality as an orienting value for rhetorical action, seeming to insist on treating all audiences and interlocuters the same regardless of their identity. But as the scholarship of postracialism reviewed above convincingly demonstrates, postracialism makes empty promises for reconciliation that it cannot deliver. Contrary to its progressive intentions, colorblindness and postracialism prop up systems of discrimination and oppressive institutions (Enck & Morrisey, 2015; Orbe, 2015). Moreover, postracial fantasies function to excuse white people from an obligation to acknowledge, address, or oppose ongoing racism by discouraging race from entering the public conversation at all (Terrill, 2017).

At what point does the outcome of postracial rhetoric deviate so sharply from its progressive intentions? We argue that the concept of the enthymeme gives us important insight into the ways that postracial fantasies advance arguments that ultimately undermine their own goals. Enthymemes function through collaborative rhetorical construction between rhetor and audience: the rhetor leaves some key part of their argument unstated, and the audience fills in the missing pieces to coconstruct the argument. The enthymeme is a relatively simple rhetorical form that nonetheless offers significant persuasive power, which Aristotle submits as "the primary engine of *rhetorical* proof and *practical* reasoning, that is, the means by which the orator influences the judgments and actions of the audience" (Miller & Bee, 1972, p. 201). Enthymemes may take verbal or visual form. The former often imitates a syllogism but with one premise or the conclusion suppressed. The latter operates through visual signs insofar as "images can cue enthymematic participation in an argument's meaning" (Birdsell & Groarke, 2007, p. 112) by evoking commonly held beliefs in their audience or operating as visual commonplaces, often interacting with verbal arguments to communicate their message (Smith, 2007).

What distinguishes enthymemes from other forms of argument is not simply their incomplete nature but also the type of judgment they prompt from the audience. Whereas dialectical reasoning seeks to determine certainty, the rhetorical nature of the enthymeme situates it in the realm of the probable and plausible. Built on shared social knowledge that the rhetor anticipates the audience already holds, enthymemes prompt practical judgments that move the audiences to action based on communal values and beliefs about what is prudent, good, and virtuous (Walton, 2001). If the rhetor misjudges the audience's beliefs, the enthymeme fails because the process of coconstruction breaks down as the audience is unable to supply the missing information. M. Camper and Z. Fechter (2019) point to precisely this type of enthymematic failure in their analysis of arguments in a campaign opposing stop-and-frisk policing. They find that while advocates believed that supplying the data on stop-and-frisk practices would be enough to support their claim that the community should oppose it as a form of racial discrimination, audiences ended up supplying their own racially biased beliefs about criminality to draw opposite conclusions. Here, the enthymeme failed because the rhetors mistook their perspectives as common knowledge shared by the audience. In this case, the enthymeme was hijacked by unintended racist sentiment; in others, the enthymeme is a strategic choice for giving intentionally racist arguments the appearance of acceptability. M. Jackson (2006) suggests that the enthymeme has assisted some white-supremacist discourse in passing for acceptable argument by leaving the overtly racist premises as the unstated part of the enthymeme. The enthymeme hides the racism underwriting such arguments by relying on the audience to (silently) fill in premises asserting white supremacy to complete arguments against inclusion and equality.

We believe something slightly different is occurring with the postracial enthymeme. Unlike the unintended or overtly racist enthymemes investigated previously, texts like *The Public* seem to be self-constraining because of their reliance on an enthymematic argument that produces radically different messages for audiences depending on whether they are "dupes" or in the know. C. E. Morris (2002) uses this terminology to differentiate the two audiences of the fourth persona, in which the implied auditor of a speech act understands the act differently than those who aren't "in on it." Morris uses the fourth persona to describe the passing of sexually marginalized people as a rhetorical phenomenon, and key to this concept is a subversive enthymeme. Whether one is in the know determines the missing premises they will supply to the enthymeme. The dupes miss the point or are deceived, in this case allowing people to pass and protecting them from potential harm.

The same cannot be said of postracial enthymemes, in which premises or conclusions speaking directly and explicitly about race are left out of the argument in the name of colorblindness. In postracial fantasies, the text may still "wink at" or contain innuendo about issues of race and racism, but the arguments they make for racial justice are limited because race-specific premises or conclusions are suppressed. At first glance, it may seem like this is the same sort of rhetorical strategy that Morris identifies, in which two audiences are addressed simultaneously: those in the know and those to be duped. But silence on issues of race does not give shelter to a marginalized group in postracial enthymemes as it does for passing rhetors in the fourth persona. Instead, these silences ensure that those who are already on board with an antiracist agenda are the only ones who will correctly complete the enthymeme in order to be persuaded of the importance of racial justice. And this is the audience that does not need to be persuaded. The audience whose minds do need to change—those unlikely to see the relevance of race to the disparities or injustices depicted on screen—are discouraged by the postracial enthymeme from addressing race directly as a salient part of the critique.

Estevez himself recognizes how *The Public* operates more through "knowing winks" than overt criticism, even as he identifies progressive social critique as an important aim of the film. In an interview he gave before the film's release, he described the choices he made in staging the space of the library where *The Public* was filmed (Morehart, 2018). While he kept much of the real-world setup of the Cincinnati Public Library intact, he also added his own touches, including "images and quotes by Sojourner Truth, Henry David Thoreau, Reinhold Niebuhr, and Frederick Douglass that would serve as subtle and not-so-subtle Easter eggs connecting many of the sensibilities of the story" (Morehart, 2018). Estevez seems confident that audiences will connect the dots in the way that he intended through these visual and narrative cues, but we suggest that this is a risky argumentative strategy at best.

ENTHYMEMATIC COLORBLINDNESS IN *THE PUBLIC*

The Public tells the story of a group of homeless men who stage a peaceful occupation of the public library in downtown Cincinnati, Ohio, to protest a lack of emergency shelter facilities during a dangerously cold winter season. After a series of homeless people die from exposure on the streets, the group in the library decides they will refuse to leave until the city opens additional emergency shelters, and they barricade themselves in the building. City officials soon escalate the standoff, bringing in riot police and hostage negotiators as the librarians attempt to negotiate between their homeless patrons and the city that wants them out. While Jackson, a Black man, appears to have organized the homeless men in protest, Stuart Goodson, a white librarian (who we eventually learn was formerly homeless), is the film's clear protagonist. Goodson becomes the voice of the protestors and, as the film's hero, leads them out of the library at the end. Despite the ultimate failure of the protest to achieve its initial objective—the men are boarded onto police buses after they leave the library, presumably on their way to jail—the protestors do succeed in generating media attention to the suffering of homeless people and broader public support for their cause. The film advances a postracial message through a series of enthymemes revolving around the themes of equity, organizing, and activism, and our analysis addresses each of these enthymemes in turn.

Equity

The Public uses a mostly visual enthymeme to obscure the racialization of homelessness, presenting images that suggest that its impacts are consistent

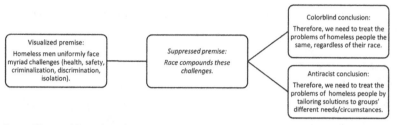

Fig. 11.1. Diagram of the equity enthymeme.

across racial identities. The film never employs dialogue to address the demographics of the homeless people who take shelter in the library, though it does highlight an equal distribution of problems in these men's lives. In most cases, viewers must draw their conclusions about homelessness and race based on the composition of the cast and the issues the characters face. In *The Public*, we are told that somewhere between seventy and one hundred men are occupying the library. Among them, there is clear Black-and-white racial diversity. Neither group visually dominates the screen when we see the men all together.

Viewers meet the four main homeless characters in the men's bathroom early in the film. There are two Black men and two white men. Each of them is addressing his basic hygiene needs: cleaning himself, using the toilets, preparing for the day. The scene appears as an equalizing one. Here, there is no racial majority, and there is no hierarchy. Everyone is, at the beginning of the day, a human just trying to make it through. These characters are friendly. They laugh with one another, offer advice, and show concern for one another in their shared circumstances. They also do not appear to segregate themselves in any way at any point in the film.

Among the characters experiencing homelessness, there also appears to be an even racial distribution of the causes and impacts of homelessness (this is also never explicitly discussed). Addiction is equally Black and white. Mike, the white son of a police officer, is addicted to opioids. Jackson, a Black man, can be seen sipping from a bottle of alcohol that he has snuck into the library. Mental illness is also evenly distributed: George, a Black man, believes he has laser eyes thanks to a government experiment; Caesar, a white man, believes ridiculous stories and offers them as truths to the group. Perhaps most striking, however, is the way the characters talk about criminalization as an inevitability for people living on the street. Race is never mentioned here. In fact, rather than recognizing that Black men are more likely to have negative police encounters than white men, the group associates the length of their rap sheets with the length of their homelessness. When George tells the group he's never been to jail, the response is, "That's 'cause you ain't been on the street long enough." The men list their arrests: nineteen times (ten just for jaywalking), twenty-six times, thirty-two "give or take," and Caesar's fifty-five times—"One time they arrested him for singing in the street." The two Black men in the group make up the middle, not the upper end, of these statistics.

Such a presentation encourages a colorblind lens for understanding the film, homelessness, and interactions with law enforcement. These scenes visually and narratively represent the characters' lives as equally challenging without any suggestion that race might impact their experiences or have contributed to their becoming homeless. Viewers are left to reach their own conclusions. A viewer who approaches the film with a colorblind lens finds an encouragement of that perspective, seeing equity among the homeless men in the library—even if it is a terrible equity. Viewers who are well versed in the machinations of systemic racism are more likely to recognize that an even split among Black and white people in this population is evidence of the disproportionate impact of poverty on Black people. Approximately 13.4 percent of the US population identifies as "Black or African American alone" (US Census Bureau, 2019). Nearly 40 percent of the US homeless population identifies this way (US Department of Housing and Urban Development, 2020). Viewed through a colorblind lens, the injustice is simply poverty; viewed through an antiracist lens, the injustice is both racial and economic. By asking audiences to see for themselves, *The Public* neglects to educate viewers on the racial realities of homelessness and the historical racialization of poverty. Even in a postslavery United States, figures like the "welfare queen" (Hancock, 2004) and influential reports like D. P. Moynihan's (1965) "The Negro Family: The Case for National Action" rhetorically link homelessness and poverty with Blackness in the American imagination. These associations persist despite colorblind denials; postracial enthymemes enable the denial and obscure racial realities.

The equity enthymeme does not just appear at the lower end of the socio-economic spectrum. It does so at the top as well. The police chief, head of the library, and the candidate expected to win the mayoral race are all Black men. The other mayoral candidate, hostage negotiator, and Goodson (supervising librarian and the film's protagonist) are all white men. The distribution of Black and white characters at the top and bottom of the film's power structures suggest to viewers that wealth and power are equally accessible, regardless of one's race. Further, they hear a dismissal of the significance of race in a rare moment of race-focused dialogue in the film. In a scene in which the police chief refuses to endorse Josh Davis, the white candidate for mayor, he defends his choice by saying, "It's not a Black thing; it's a character thing." That Davis's bad character is independent of his whiteness presumably extends to the despicable choices he makes around the library occupation. As the film builds to its climax, Davis tells the hostage negotiator, "No matter how this goes down, we're going to look like the bad guys." Because viewers have been prompted to interpret his actions through a colorblind lens, his villainy appears not as a matter of whiteness, nor is it even necessarily about his relationship to the racial injustices of the legal system. He looks like the bad guy because he has bad character.

A similar logic can be applied to Goodson as the film's hero. While *The Public* visually depicts racial equity, the Black men who organized the protest quickly realize they are in over their heads, admitting that they do not have a plan. They hand the reins over to Goodson, arguing that the police will be more likely to listen to him, and leave him to come up with demands for the city and a plan to lead them safely out of the protest. Goodson is the reason the men stay safe and well fed that evening—he is the film's white hero, saving the ineffectual Black men who started it all. Yet because race has been largely visually neutralized, colorblind viewers will likely see Goodson as a savior rather than a white savior and Davis as merely a villain rather than a representation of white supremacy.

Organizing

To the authors' knowledge, *The Public* is the only fictional US film released in the last twenty-five years to portray homeless people engaging in collective organizing. People experiencing homelessness tend to be portrayed as lonely individuals, occasionally with partners or a close friend but rarely in groups—and never in an organized group working to improve their conditions. One of the primary goals of collective organizing is to amplify the voices of the group and elevate the visibility of its demands. Viewers of this film are faced with enthymemes regarding whose voice gets heard, how those voices are developed, and to what ends those voices speak.

Consistent with the aforementioned theme of equity, viewers are encouraged to understand that the voices of these protestors matter because they are human and not because of any particular identity characteristic. The film regularly points to the First Amendment of the US Constitution as an equalizer. It casts the library as a beacon of knowledge, providing access to information and, in turn, a voice to the voiceless. When Jackson talks about the purpose of the protest, voice is central. "God gave us all a voice," he says. "It's up to us whether we use it or stay silent." Approached through a colorblind lens, these words reinforce a message that everyone has the equal

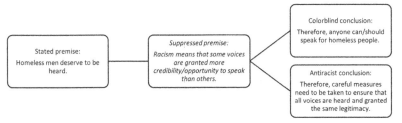

Fig. 11.2. Diagram of the organizing enthymeme.

capacity to speak. Especially when tied thematically to the First Amendment, speech appears as a guaranteed right. Whether one does speak, then, seems simply a matter of choice. This perspective, however, denies systemic racism by obscuring the varying extent to which people's voices get heard. Power relations deeply impact whose voices are privileged in the public sphere and whose remain on the margins, and race and class are two of the major factors that determine this. Because power operates in an intersectional way (Crenshaw, 1989), class does not neutralize this. Poor white people still have white privilege. In order to perceive the irony of Jackson's statement, the viewer must bring with them background knowledge of power, privilege, and access.

The Public provides some minor cues that signal to viewers a connection between race and voice, but it would be easy to miss them or to misunderstand them. Jackson speaks of the protest as an expression of "Black prophetic fire" and fears that the police and public will just understand the protestors as "crazy n****s." He is the only character in the film who uses explicitly racialized language, however, and he never connects his ideas about race to the present protest. This creates an opportunity for viewers to see Jackson's concern about race as a part of his character but not as a reason for the group's organizing. Similarly, there are minor visuals in the film that suggest to viewers that there could be something racial about these protests. For example, George is seen reading a book in the Slavery and Emancipation section, and a quotation by Frederick Douglass adorns the entrance to the room where the protestors gather. These moments are fleeting; one almost has to be looking for them in order to notice.

If Jackson is to be believed, the ultimate goal of the night's protest is to be heard. "We got their attention, right?" he asks. And in the film's final scenes, he declares, "They ain't never going to forget what we did here tonight. Ain't never going to forget us." The protest, however, does not appear to have achieved anything. The men are led out of the library nude, either in handcuffs or hands up in surrender, to a bus that is ostensibly taking them to jail. This, too, is equalizing. All the protestors are displayed in their most vulnerable states—on the coldest night of the year. They are reduced to "bare life" (Agamben, 1998) regardless of the color of their skin. None of the news coverage of the event discuss the race of the protestors. In fact, the protestors' voices are not even correctly represented in the media: for most of the film, the occupation is presented as a hostage situation rather than a protest. The protestors do not receive housing or shelter. They strip down, make a display of nudity that cannot appear on camera, and head off to receive their punishments. But they do it all together, in solidarity, singing. For a colorblind viewer, this is a vision of unity and solidarity. The protestors, Black and white, use their voices, even if they are misheard. An antiracist viewer may note that if they are to be remembered, it will not be for their "Black prophetic fire."

Cause

The ambiguity around the film's enthymemes is perhaps most significant when audiences consider the cause around which its protestors are rallying. The film's opening credits roll over a hip-hop song that references tearing down (presumably Confederate) monuments as it declares, "We go to war for a little peace." Police show up to address the library's occupation in force, wearing riot gear with a battering ram at the ready. Their militarization suggests that this is, in fact, some kind of war. Their display conjures memories of the massive police responses to Black Lives Matter protests. Still, somehow, it is not clear whether this is a film about race. Viewers are told that the protest is about a lack of available shelter during one of the coldest nights of a Cincinnati winter. When asked, "What are they protesting?" a library employee answers simply, "freezing to death." Because the homeless men are not protesting on the basis of race or about race, the police response does not have to be perceived as racialized. There are no mentions of Black Lives Matter, of Ferguson, or of the loss of Black lives at the hands of police even as a militarized police force appears on screen.

Throughout *The Public*, characters nod at racially motivated police violence, but they never name it. Davis, the aforementioned prosecutor-turned-mayoral candidate, is unsympathetic to the plight of the homeless people occupying the library and actively misrepresents their intentions to the media. In the mayoral race, Davis depicts himself as the "law-and-order" candidate. Particularly attentive viewers might connect this to the racist rhetoric of the forty-fifth US president, for whom "law and order" meant squelching the rights of Black- and brown-skinned Americans, particularly as they protested racial injustice. Colorblind viewers may miss this or may

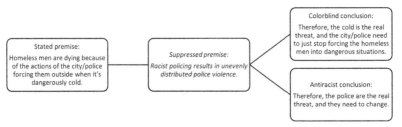

Fig. 11.3. Diagram of the cause enthymeme.

understand law and order to be universally enforced because there is no explicit mention of racial difference. Further, when Davis discusses his campaign with a manager, the two decide they need "something besides another embarrassing unarmed police shooting" to put him in the spotlight. There is also no mention of race in this conversation. The film's producers leave viewers to fill in the blanks around the shootings, but they do nothing to encourage them to see those as "embarrassing unarmed police shootings [of Black people]." The library protest offers this opportunity to Davis; by setting these events up as something *other than* an unarmed police shooting, the filmmakers create conceptual difference between racialized police brutality and what is happening in the library.

Police brutality, racialized or not, does not even appear as a reason the protestors are organizing. Apart from noting the number of times many of them had been arrested, there is no discussion among characters about police. When the protestors "negotiate" with police, Goodson sends Davis to lay coatless on the street for five minutes to experience the cold himself. There are no demands regarding police despite frustration that the protest was being falsely depicted as a hostage situation. Instead, excessive police force appears as a *response* to the protest. The excess does elicit a comment from the head of library, whose frustration with Davis and the hostage negotiator bubbles over: "Do you people know how to do anything without the use of excessive force? This is a public library for god's sake." What matters here is that while police brutality is visible in the film, it is not the issue the filmmakers suggest is worthy of advocacy.

This seems to be the case for a variety of social issues in the film that are depicted but left unresolved. At various points, the characters discuss problems from broad-reaching concerns, like climate change, to local issues of political corruption in their city and a lack of resources for their communities. Neither their discussions nor their one attempt at collective organizing leads to any clear sense of solution to these problems. In the end, the homeless men's occupation is successful not because it accomplishes any of their goals but because they manage to escape the library safely without the police using excessive force against them. It feels like a victory, but for what cause? We, the viewers, are left with just as much uncertainty as the protestors: What did we just watch, and why? The postracial enthymeme and its inherent silences rob the film's core message of clarity, leaving audiences with a confusing model of collective organizing to emulate.

CONCLUSION

In this essay, we've offered *The Public* as an exemplar of the enthymematic structure at the heart of postracial fantasies. We believe the enthymeme is a particularly useful concept to understand the rhetorical mechanics of postracial fantasies because it illustrates how the orienting value of colorblindness works counter to the potentially progressive aims of postracialism. It is the postracial embrace of colorblindness that permits a film such as *The Public* to tell the story of a racially diverse group of homeless men collectively organizing to protest discrimination and police violence without directly engaging the issue of racism. Unfortunately, the film's ability to advance an argument for meaningful social change suffers as a consequence.

We can imagine fans of the film objecting: "But this wasn't a movie about race; you're reading that into a story about homelessness." That's precisely why the postracial enthymeme needs to be identified where it is used and critiqued for its potential rhetorical effects. One cannot talk meaningfully about injustice in the United States—about poverty, discrimination, police brutality, hunger, and homelessness—without also talking about race and taking stock of how ongoing racial inequality heaps these harms disproportionately on Black Americans. To take race out of the discussion of homelessness is to misunderstand its causes and consequences in ways that perpetuate the exclusion and suffering of Black Americans. Postracial fantasies aim for equality through colorblindness, but they end up perpetuating inequality by making racial injustice invisible and therefore beyond critique and resolution.

Our analysis has identified the specific manifestations of the postracial enthymeme in *The Public* as it appears in three forms: in an argument about equity, another about organizing, and a final argument about the cause around which the public should rally. In each case, the enthymematic suppression of the specifics of ongoing racial inequality among homeless men leads to fatal ambiguities about what precisely we see unfolding on screen and how we should understand similar dynamics in the real world. The postracial enthymeme obscures the racial dimensions of the causes and solutions to homelessness, the distribution of power within institutions and societies, the purpose of collective organizing, and the appropriate approaches to initiating social change. In doing so, it relies on the viewer's preexisting beliefs about the status of racial injustice and forfeits the opportunity to change those beliefs, explain their persistence, and pursue effective solutions. This doesn't only hinder efforts to overcome racism; it also holds communities back in resolving all social issues compounded by racial injustice by artificially constraining their understanding of those issues and their potential solutions.

Two additional themes from the film implicate the broader consequences of postracial fantasies and merit additional investigation. The first is the theme of clear vision as a remedy to social injustice. In *The Public*, we see this theme recur as characters have a change of heart and begin to see the world more clearly. This type of revelatory transformation is best exemplified in the film when the protestors allow the police into the library. Seeing them naked and vulnerable, the police finally understand that the homeless men present no danger, and thus they do not merit being treated with the excessive force of the SWAT team. The protesting men's only safe escape from the library is secured when they help the police see them for who they really are. They are allowed to leave, singing "I Can See Clearly Now" as they file out of the library and onto the bus waiting to take them to prison. The men have accomplished none of their original goals: their voices weren't heard, they did not turn the library into an emergency shelter, and they have not received the support of the city to allow them to live without fear of violence or danger. Yet they sing that their dark moment has passed, they more clearly understand the challenges ahead, and they are on their way to a brighter future, implying that it is through clarity of vision that the problems they face finally have the potential to be solved. This implicit message is part of what makes the film's postracial fantasy so dangerous: having presented a vision of the world where race does not register as a meaningful topic of discussion or explanation for injustice, it ends by suggesting that adopting such a vision— cleansed and clarified by the colorblindness at the heart of postracialism—is the preferable outcome of collective action for social change. Moreover, the lack of explicit discussions of race is not the only troubling absence in this film: while families make up a significant portion of the homeless population in the United States, homeless women and children are entirely invisible in this film. In fact, the film struggles with representing women at all; every character in power and all the protestors appear to be male.

Finally, it should come as no surprise that a film titled *The Public* also advances a vision of how that body is constructed and who counts as a member of the public. One way this occurs is through the use of "the public" as a synecdoche for the library. The homeless characters do not refer to "the library"; it is always "the public." This choice invites viewers to understand the library as a hallowed institution collectively owned by the people of Cincinnati, including the homeless people currently occupying it. It also imbues the public (as a term for a body of people) with the values the film associates with the library—access, equality, and belonging. "The public" is a space where virtually no one is turned away, where everyone is free to pursue their own interests, and where everyone has equal standing uncomplicated by their race (and also gender, class, sexuality, or any other identity). In the context of a postracial fantasy like this film, we get a vision of "the public" that actually delegitimates the ongoing work for creating an inclusive community by pretending that it already exists. Such narratives render exclusions based on race invisible, which also negates the impetus to identify and challenge such exclusions and deflects attention from the project of forging alliances based on solidarity across racial difference. *The Public* thus presents a dangerously misleading dream of a postracial world. It is a dream—or a nightmare—in which collective organizing is destined to fail because of the postracial fantasy.

REFERENCES

Agamben, G. (1998). *Homo sacer: Sovereign power and bare life.* Stanford University Press.

American Libraries Association. (n.d.). *New PSAs from Emilio Estevez.* http://www.ala.org /advocacy/emilio-estevez-psas

Bineham, J. (2015). How *The blind side* blinds us: Postracism and the American dream. *Southern Communication Journal, 80*(3), 230–245.

Birdsell, D. S., & Groarke, L. (2007). Outlines of a theory of visual argument. *Argumentation & Advocacy, 43*(3), 103–113.

Camper, M., & Fechter, Z. (2019). Enthymematic free space: The efficacy of anti-stop-and -frisk arguments in the face of racial prejudice. *Argumentation & Advocacy, 55*(4), 259–281.

Cobb, J. N. (2011). No we can't! Postracialism and the popular appearance of a rhetorical fiction. *Communication Studies, 62*(4), 406–421.

Crenshaw, K. (1989). Demarginalizing the intersection of race and sex: A Black feminist critique of antidiscrimination doctrine, feminist theory and antiracist politics. *University of Chicago Legal Forum, 1989*(1), 139–168.

Dunn, T. R. (2016). Playing neoliberal politics: Post-racial and post-racist strategies in "Same love." *Communication and Critical/Cultural Studies, 13*(3), 269–286.

Enck, S. M., & Morrisey, M. E. (2015). If *Orange is the new black,* I must be color blind: Comic framings of post-racism in the prison-industrial complex. *Critical Studies in Media Communication, 32*(5), 303–317.

Gomez, S. L., & McFarlane, M. D. (2017). It's (not) handled: Race, gender, and refraction in *Scandal*. *Feminist Media Studies, 17*(3), 362–376.

Griffin, R. A. (2015). Problematic representations of strategic whiteness and "post-racial" pedagogy: A critical intercultural reading of *The help*. *Journal of International and Intercultural Communication, 8*(2), 147–166.

Hancock, A. (2004). *The politics of disgust: The public identity of the welfare queen*. New York University Press.

Jackson, M. (2006). The enthymematic hegemony of whiteness: The enthymeme as antiracist rhetorical strategy. *Journal of Advanced Composition, 26*(3–4), 601–641.

Melamed, J. (2011). *Represent and destroy: Rationalizing violence in the new racial capitalism*. University of Minnesota Press.

Miller, A. B., & Bee, J. D. (1972). Enthymemes: Body and soul. *Philosophy & Rhetoric, 5*(4), 201–214.

Mislán, C., & Ashley, R. R. (2018). Black(er)face and post-racialism: Employing racial difference and "progressive" primitivism online. *Communication Culture & Critique, 11*(2), 247–264.

Morehart, P. (2018, March 1). Actor and filmmaker tackles the library response to homelessness. *American Libraries*. https://americanlibrariesmagazine.org/2018/03/01/newsmaker-emilio-estevez/

Morris, C. E. (2002). Pink herring & the fourth persona: J. Edgar Hoover's sex crime panic. *Quarterly Journal of Speech, 88*(2), 228–244.

Moynihan, D. P. (1965). *The Negro family: The case for national action*. US Department of Labor.

Murphy, M. K., & Harris, T. M. (2018). White innocence and Black subservience: The rhetoric of white heroism in *The help*. *Howard Journal of Communications, 29*(1), 49–62.

Ono, K. (2010). Postracism: A theory of the "post"- as political strategy. *Journal of Communication Inquiry, 34*(3), 227–233.

Orbe, M. (2015). #AllLivesMatter as post-racial rhetorical strategy. *Journal of Contemporary Rhetoric, 5*(3–4), 90–98.

Peet, L. (2019, March 2). Emilio Estevez, back in the library with *The public*. *Library Journal*. https://www.libraryjournal.com/?detailStory=Emilio-Estevez-Back-in-the-Library-with-The-Public-ALA-Midwinter-2019

Rossing, J. P. (2012). Deconstructing postracialism: Humor as a critical, cultural project. *Journal of Communication Inquiry, 36*(1), 44–61.

Smith, V. J. (2007). Aristotle's classical enthymeme and the visual argumentation of the twenty-first century. *Argumentation & Advocacy, 43*(3), 114–123.

Terrill, R. E. (2017). The post-racial and post-ethical discourse of Donald J. Trump. *Rhetoric and Public Affairs, 20*(3), 493–510.

Thornton, D. J. (2011). *Psych's* comedic tale of Black-white friendship and the lighthearted affect of "post-race" America. *Critical Studies in Media Communication, 28*(5), 424–449.

Triece, M. E. (2017). Whitewashing city spaces: Personalization and strategic forgetting in news accounts of urban crisis and renewal. *Journal of Communication Inquiry, 41*(3), 250–267.

US Census Bureau. (2019). *Quick facts*. US Department of Commerce. Retrieved April 5, 2021, from https://www.census.gov/quickfacts/fact/table/US/PST045219

US Department of Housing and Urban Development. (2020). *The 2019 annual homeless-ness assessment report to Congress*. https://www.huduser.gov/portal/sites/default/files /pdf/2019-AHAR-Part-1.pdf

Walton, D. (2001). Enthymemes, common knowledge, and plausible inference. *Philosophy & Rhetoric, 34*(2), 93–112.

Chapter 12

PITTSBURGH'S POSTRACIAL HILL DISTRICT?

Mediated Challenges to Governmental Discourses about the Hill District in *Fences* and Steve Mellon's "A Life on the Hill"

NICK J. SCIULLO

The Hill District ("the Hill") is a historically Black community bordering downtown Pittsburgh, Pennsylvania, that has been the center of the city's Black life. The Hill is often thought of as a vibrant Black neighborhood of the early and mid-twentieth century, but its roots as a Black cultural center extend much further back to stories of the American Revolution, escaped enslaved people, a Little Haiti, and a burgeoning Black middle class composed of freedmen (Gaw, n.d.). Like many Black cultural centers, it experienced a boom in population and business from the 1940s to the 1960s but has more recently struggled with a decreasing population, high poverty, and poor access to educational and health resources.

There are multiple Hill Districts in the public imagination, as there are with many neighborhoods in major metropolitan areas. There is the Hill of Black culture and Black business. There is the Hill District of blight and crime. There is the Hill of nearby Duquesne University and PPG Paints Arena that is on the cusp of urban renewal. There is the Hill District that is already renewed. And this is to name but a few. Neighborhoods are spaces of contestation, negotiation, and interaction. The Hill is no different.

The Hill is the site of a contested narrative about Blackness and the postracial that has been forged by a diverse range of discursive stakeholders, including the city of Pittsburgh's various politicians and bureaucrats, Hill District residents, and multimedia creators. Naturally, the stories these groups craft about the Hill often emphasize or deemphasize different strands of thought, objectives, and realities. This chapter argues that the City of Pittsburgh's attempt through official governmental discourses to rebuild the Hill into a "natural and healthy community" through postracial discourse obscures a much more complex reality that is countered by mediated texts (City of Pittsburgh, n.d.). This language itself raises questions about what might be unnatural or unhealthy about a historically Black community and expresses a larger postracial imperative to rebuild Black communities on white terms. While official discourses about Pittsburgh and the Hill stress greenspace, community, healthcare opportunities, and a burgeoning technology sector, the Hill District's story is much more complicated and more accurately reflected in recently released mediated texts that center Black life.

The Hill District and competing visions of development, redevelopment, and success are significant because of the Hill District's history, but these competing forces of history and history preservation verses new construction and redevelopment as well as historically Black and immigrant neighborhoods verses white-led developers are also common in Pittsburgh. The East Liberty neighborhood seems lost to redevelopment. Homestead has been radically changed and is now home to a major shopping district complete with a Dave & Buster's, but other than preserved parts of the Homestead Steel Works, there is not much to remind people of Homestead's industrial, immigrant, and Black past (Machosky, 2022). The Strip District, which was a major location for trade in foodstuffs, is now as trendy and popular as it has ever been and continues to get more expensive every year. The South Side was largely an eastern European immigrant neighborhood, but after several arsons in the 1980s, the neighborhood experienced redevelopment too and Carson Street is now anchored by a Holiday Inn Express and an Urban Outfitters.

Cities are unique places of racial construction. While some scholars note the construction of the racial state (Derickson, 2014), others focus exclusively on the city and other substate geographical sites as locations of racial construction (Avila & Rose, 2009; Derickson, 2014). Regardless of the spatial focus, cultural geographers and other communication scholars of space have long noted the relationship between race and space (Allen et al., 2019). G. D. Squires and C. Kubrin (2005) argue urban space is racialized by a wide range of practices that produce disparate outcomes across a range of quality-of-life issues, usually resulting in Black people lagging behind their white cohabitants. Neighborhoods, such as the Hill District, are a functional unit of segregation in which "the geographical decomposition clearly points to municipalities and their equivalents as the central organizing units in the new structure of metropolitan segregation" (Farrell, 2008, p. 489). Indeed, the

Fig. 12.1. Clyde Hare's 1950s *View of Downtown Pittsburgh from the Hill District* from the Carnegie Museum of Art collection (accession number: 85.4.89).

Hill represents a unique example of the complex ways postracial ideology is culturally produced at the nexus of space, place, and racialization.

"Postracialism," of course, is a contested concept, but it is often used to signal a time in which race no longer matters, to challenge the Black-white divide, and to signal a hopeful course for the world (Bobo, 2011). I use the term "postracialism" to denote the first two understandings, which I further understand to indicate the exclusion of race from discussions of political and social life—that is, under the regime of postracialism, there is no need to discuss race because racial problems have been solved or are being solved. The ideology of postracialism is culturally produced through a variety of speech acts, media texts, and popular discourses (Chen et al., 2015).

Postracial discourses focus on the present, often ignoring the past and the legacies of historical injustices. Put another way, postracialism allows public memory to minimize and simplify past racial strife (Russell, 2019), thus making mention of racism the problem more than its minimalization or simplification. J. Rossing (2012) argues postracialism is "a belief that positions race as an irrelevant relic of the past with no viable place in contemporary thought" (p. 45). Indeed, postracialism is dangerous because it denies the memory of structural racism and Black suffering since slavery and renders commentary on race as antithetical to the ways in which people might constructively communicate about racial difference.

Since scholars argue that we must visualize racism to resist it (Mitchell, 2012), postracialism actively undermines our collective capacity to address the enduring realities of racial inequality, discrimination, and anti-Black violence. As I will demonstrate below, this is evident in the postracial discourse Pittsburgh city leaders employ with respect to the Hill, which makes reforming historical racial inequalities difficult because they deny the visuality of race and its effects on communities and politics. Race exists even if individuals claim they "do not see color" or that it "doesn't matter" (Capehart, 2014).

Postracialism is also spatially rooted since space itself is imbued with racial ideologies (including postracialism). As many scholars have demonstrated, urban space, since the 1980s, has been rhetorically reimagined by neoliberal city planning popularly called "gentrification" (Feldman, 2016). Gentrification is a deeper expression of postracialism since it proposes that we understand the management of space beyond the question of race and specifically in terms of market value and exchanges that actively reduce matters of race to statistical techniques of biopolitical statecraft (Craig & Rahko, 2016). Blackness, within this neoliberal imaginary, is reduced to dehumanized economic metrics tracked against other ethnic groups (e.g., crime, unemployment, health, incarceration rates, etc.), which establishes a pretense for gentrified-urban-renewal policies. Gentrification policies, however, are often predatory and have the effect of dislocating Black people from historically Black urban communities since they ultimately make these spaces unaffordable (McElroy & Werth, 2019). Understood this way, postracialism is not antiracist, but rather racist and a product of "racism's violent spatialization" (Feldman, 2016, p. 293). Geography, through the practices of real-estate cartography, rhetorically marks space in racial terms so that, as in the case of the Hill or Chicago's Cabrini Green, attempts to improve, rebuild, or revitalize neighborhoods always occur in spaces marked by Blackness.

In this chapter, I offer a reading of two 2016 texts on the Hill: Denzel Washington's movie adaptation of August Wilson's (1985) play *Fences* (first performed in 1983), set in the Hill in 1957, and *Pittsburgh Post-Gazette* writer Steve Mellon's ten-part multimedia story "A Life on the Hill" (2016) on Sala Udin, a Hill District resident, famous Pittsburgh city councilman, community activist, and friend of August Wilson. My analysis demonstrates how mediated texts can challenge the postracial discourses of city planners through visual and textual rhetoric. *Fences* and "A Life on the Hill" paint a much different picture of Pittsburgh than the city's postracial discourse suggests, although *Fences* does offer a main character, Troy, who, despite his many flaws, is relatable and certainly complicates postracial desires. These texts critique these discourses by providing a visual rhetoric of the city's history that is rife with racial conflict, discrimination, subjugation, and violence even as they humanize the Hill, thus offering opposition to the techno-economic understanding of the neighborhood advanced by developers. While the Hill is much different than it was thirty or seventy years ago, ignoring this racial history erases the Hill and replaces it with a postracial utopia that, while certainly aspirational, denies the neighborhood's complicated past, the cultural memory of residents inside and outside of the neighborhood, and the story of Black struggle and perseverance that makes the Hill a remarkable and interesting neighborhood.

C. Squires (2014) argues, "Media discourses and imagery help us to map the contours of change in society's understanding of race" (p. 2). Those media discourses span television, radio, film, advertising, online communication, literature, newspapers, theater, and more. If media can help map society's understanding of race, then media may also be understood as both supporting and critiquing various understandings of race. Postracial rhetoric increased substantially with the election of Barack Obama as president of the United States in 2008, expanding far beyond a focus on Blackness to also include Latinx, Asian, and other populations (C. Squires, 2014). The ideas that Obama's election ended racism and signaled that Black and multiracial populations had "made it" circulated widely after 2008 and 2012 to the effect of denying racial discrimination as a barrier for success (Craig & Rahko, 2021). Thus *The Greater Hill District Master Plan* (2011), *Fences*, and "A Life on the Hill" are all captured in this era of postracialism in which, E. K. Watts (2010) argues, "postracialism enunciates the demise of race" (pp. 216–217). Nothing could be further from the truth, however.

THE TWO HILL DISTRICTS

For the purposes of this analysis, there are two Hill District narratives. One is that of a vibrant, multicultural, and inclusive neighborhood that is primed for redevelopment. The other is a neighborhood riven by racial unrest, discrimination, and the fight for civil rights, anchored by Black radicalism. Official sources like the City of Pittsburgh, economic development agencies, and occasionally the ever-optimistic columnist created the first narrative— the narrative of the Hill as a multicultural neighborhood of the future. The more political, violent, and troubled Hill District has been created by activists and artists seeking to not forget the neighborhood's troubled history to center Black experience in the story of a historically Black neighborhood. This is to argue nothing about the notions of the Upper Hill District and

Lower Hill District, which is an arbitrary division, that displaced residents and was pushed by developers who had vested monetary interests in various redevelopment initiatives (Papazekos, 2022).

It makes sense that governmental and nongovernmental actors would seek to erase race under various attempts at postracialism and multiculturalism because doing so advances an image of the neighborhood that benefits these actors. The more people that move into, invest in, spend money in, and discuss the virtues of the Hill, the more these actors benefit from business and tax revenue. These messages are also amplified by media that have a stake in access to these politicians and business leaders. Media are important for social control and are often used by social institutions to promote the narratives those institutions want (Fabregat & Beck, 2019). This is especially true in discourses that promote and obscure racial identities (Fabregat & Beck, 2019). Political and economic objectives to promote the neighborhood and obscure racial identities find willing reception in media that are often eager to help local partners.

The language of the City of Pittsburgh is one of cleaning up, brightening, and emphasizing multiculturalism. Brightening, lightening, and whiteness are commingled metaphorically to denote positivity and to be opposed to darkness and Blackness, which are considered negative (Gallagher, 2014; Marshall, 2020; Sciullo, 2015). Councilmember R. Daniel Lavelle, whose district includes the Hill District, opens *The Greater Hill District Master Plan* with a letter that describes "envisioning a brighter future" (Master Plan Management Committee, 2011, p. iv). This comment is innocuous enough, but it suggests a dismal past and makes no mention of the tremendous history of the neighborhood. The *Master Plan*, despite community involvement, "outlines a set of guidelines for developers and investors to follow," which makes no mention of residents past or present, nor does it do much to emphasize the racial identities that have and that continue to call the Hill District home (Master Plan Management Committee, 2011, p. iv). Lavelle closes the letter with a promise for a "vibrant future," ignoring the neighborhood's storied and vibrant past (Master Plan Management Committee, 2011, p. iv). Indeed, the words "history," "past," "Black," and "African American" do not appear in his opening letter, suggesting that, whatever else the *Master Plan* purports to do, it is not interested in the neighborhood's racial dynamics, racial history, or racial struggles.

The Pittsburgh visitor's authority, VisitPITTSBURGH (n.d.), promotes this deracialized Hill as well. It notes that the Lower Hill gives breathtaking views of the city skyline, which is true enough, but the Hill is not important and not worth visiting because of its views alone (and indeed there are many better places to view the city skyline including from Mt. Washington and the North Side). The urban cityscape is a site of racial configuration, one that can be articulated as both racialized and postracial—that is, "space, place, and landscape are not just the stage for, but the mode of, operations of power, inextricably connected to class, capital, gender, and race" (Cleary, 2015, p. 93). Thus one must be attuned to representations of space and place to understand how race functions. The focus on city views is a postracial discourse that literally directs the eye away from the neighborhood in which one finds oneself and its residents toward other parts of the city and other residents (corporations and city and county offices mostly). The Hill is a place not to see the Hill, but rather to look away and see the city of Pittsburgh. This both erases the Hill in favor of the city of Pittsburgh and understands the Hill as serving other parts of the city or the city *writ large*. The function of the Hill District is neither cultural nor historical, but rather solely a vantage point to view business. The Hill's history does not matter because the direction for visitors is to not look at the Hill, to move through its streets, to communicate with its people, but rather to use the Hill to look elsewhere. The Hill's history as a Black cultural center is abandoned in favor of the tourist and real-estate potential of Pittsburgh's cityscape.

This does not mean that Black history does not factor into the *Master Plan*, although much of that discussion occurs in the relatively short first chapter, but rather that, in an era of postracialism, Blackness is set aside as an artifact more than a lived experience. As an example, the report names the African American Cultural Legacy as a program initiative, and the phrase appears on all relevant pages describing the initiative, but the phrase appears nowhere in the body of that section. This suggests that the African American cultural legacy of the Hill was not a major consideration when developing the 144-page *The Greater Hill District Master Plan*. The omission of race is glaring.

The narrative is not simply buried in a report that many Hill District residents are unlikely to read but also continued on the City of Pittsburgh's homepage where the city articulates a hope to build the Hill into a "natural and healthy community" as if there was something unnatural about the historically Black community (City of Pittsburgh, n.d.). The residents did not create the food desert in the Hill (Dubowitz & Wagner, 2019), did not fail to attend to city-owned infrastructure, like roads and sidewalks (Giammarise, 2016), or let weeds on publicly owned property tower ten feet (O'Neill, 2017). If the Hill is unnatural and unhealthy, the city is to blame.

The problem is not so much with having hope for a new Hill District, but rather that postracialism erases the important history of the Hill and its residents, which has not always been so hopeful and has often been depressing and conflict-ridden. This is not an argument to condemn the Hill or those that hope to recreate or revive it. This is an argument, however, to challenge the smooth rhetoric of postracialism that denies this history through platitudes, dreams, and optimism. It is impossible to understand a place without understanding its troubled history, and the city's postracial discourses that deny the troubled history of the Hill pervert our understanding of the neighborhood's struggles.

RESISTING POSTRACIALISM

The Hill District has received critical media attention as both the subject of August Wilson's *Fences* and the 2016 movie adaptation of the same name, as well as in Steve Mellon's ten-part multimedia story published by the *Pittsburgh Post-Gazette*. These two texts highlight the struggles of Hill District residents to be heard, feel included, and thrive. In this way, they both resist the deracialized and dehistoricized vision of developers as well as humanize a population often missing from official rhetoric about the neighborhood. Consistent with J. Melamed's (2008) understanding of race radical literature, the texts under exploration in this chapter disrupt official rhetorics of governmental power by reconfiguring race as a generative challenge to neoliberal postracial imaginaries. Popular media can both reinforce and challenge widely held beliefs. As M. Gurevitch and M. Levy (1985) argue, media can collectively be thought of as "a site on which various social groups struggle over the definition of social reality" (p. 19). While it is true that media framing can favor elites (Gamson, 1992; Kellner, 1990), elite media discourses are not the only frames to understand society and are not always ideologically successful. Extending the work of C. Ryan, K. M. Carragee, and C. Schwerner (1998), which argues that "news media ... represent critical arenas of social struggle," I argue that all media, including popular films and newspaper coverage, represent critical arenas of social struggle that can challenge postracialism (p. 166).

One of the dangers of postracial discourse is that it obscures history, ignoring how important the difficult parts of history are to the present. Media can obscure this history as well or enliven discussion of that history. August Wilson (2005) was especially aware of this argument: "Blacks in America want to forget about slavery—the stigma, the shame. That's the wrong move. If you can't be who you are, who can you be? How can you know what to do? We have our history. We have our book, which is the blues. And we forget it all" (p. 15). Wilson presciently argued against the postracialism that would come to be a major current in US racial thinking especially after Barack

Fig. 12.2. Irene Kaufmann Settlement's May 1940 *The Cities Neglect* from the University of Pittsburgh Oliver M. Kaufmann Photograph Collection of the Irene Kaufmann Settlement, 1912–1969. (identifier: 7812.201389.IKS).

Obama's election. S. Koprince (2006) notes that *Fences* is a play of deep historical understanding, which is consistent with Wilson's own belief about the importance of Black history. Wilson's awareness of the dual character of remembering and forgetting positions him to be a special critic of postracialism, a view in which history is often ignored. Of course, much of Wilson's work was a reaction to the colorblindness of theater casting (Burbank, 2009), which ignored the lack of Black representation in theater, thus we ought not to read him only as a critic of the theater establishment he worked in and against but also an early critic of postracialism especially concerned with the ways in which we remember Black history.

Wilson's *Fences*, in both its play and movie adaptation, represents a 1950s Hill District that is dirty, tense, violent, and troubled. Much like Irene Kaufmann Settlement's photograph entitled *The Cities Neglect* (1940), which portrays, in black and white, a Hill District street strewn with trash, a stray dog, people only sparsely present, and an ironic Clean Quick box of soap chips positioned just to the left of the trash piled on the street, the 2016 film adaptation of *Fences* emphasizes loneliness and dirtiness. The film's aesthetic is faithful to Wilson's original play as the set design is sparse, the colors muted, and the lighting dark, and there is a focus on character development. There is something hopeless about the film that echoes the despair of the Hill's residents who seem largely forgotten.

Denzel Washington's adaptation of *Fences* reflects a prevailing mood of disillusionment evident after the culmination of the Obama presidency. The film taps into this energy and revives the centrality of the struggles of Blackness, anger, racism, and economic difficulty, all of which directly challenge the City of Pittsburgh's postracial discourses that consciously ignore the legacies of structural racism of America evident in the Hill's racialized past. Moreover, *Fences* appeared after the emergence of Black Lives Matter and reflects a deeper ethos of disappointment with Obama's policies and his reluctance to rhetorically embrace the problem of racial inequality, much less his own Blackness. As E. Logan (2014) argues, "Postracialism demanded also that Obama downplay the significance of racism. His candidacy after all proved that the bad old days of 'real racism' were in the distant past and that the nation had achieved remarkable progress with regard to race. With this imperative, Obama readily complied" (p. 663).

Wilson's tragic protagonist, Troy Maxson, represents a figure of Blackness whose visceral dissatisfaction with structural racism and his economic disempowerment offer a commentary on the failures of the Obama presidency to deliver on much of what Black America hoped for. The film's embrace of Wilson's themes offers a direct rebuke to the Obama-era postracial ethos for they suggest that despite the presence of a Black man in the White House, the struggles of Blackness continue to be erased as a priority of the state. Indeed, the reemergence of Maxson thirty years after the play's original 1985 debut serves as a reminder of the way race still shapes the opportunities and life chances in America. Troy is also a relatable character that an audience can understand, which exposes the multivalent critical capacity of *Fences*. He is human, and his struggles almost intuitively make sense. This humanity challenges modern actors who are concerned with the neighborhood and the city but not the residents by reminding them that people make up the Hill. His struggles also bring up a range of issues that the City of Pittsburgh and developers would rather ignore—economic struggle, racism, illness, anger, and more.

The 1950s Hill of *Fences* illuminates a much more complex Hill District than present-day pronouncements would have one believe. Aside from the human trauma of living under racial and economic inequality, there are also material concerns related to homes in permanent disrepair—a far cry from the shining glass facade of the PPG Paints Arena. The fences of *Fences* are both metaphorical and real. Troy Maxson is trying to build a fence around his property, and it is not clear if he is trying to keep people out or keep his family in. In the film, Bono, Troy's friend, makes the point explicitly: "Some people build fences to keep people out . . . and other people build fences to keep people in. Rose wants to hold on to you all. She loves you" (Wilson, 2016, p. 85).

Yet Troy reacts with hostility to this seemingly innocuous information, suggesting that whatever the fences are for, they are a source of struggle. Troy has a reason to keep the world out. It is a world that has done him wrong, having been passed over to play professional baseball. He also has a desire to keep his family in because they never seem to be living up to what he wants. As he beckons death to challenge him in an angry, drunken shouting match with personified Death, he wakes the neighbors: "See? I'm gonna build me a fence around what belongs to me. And then I want you to stay on the other side. See? You stay over there until you're ready for me" (Wilson, 2016, pp. 108–109). This task is obviously futile, yet Troy is headstrong and defiant until the end. His fence will keep Death away even though the audience has a sense early on that he is dying behind that fence. The fences metaphor would also have resonated both in the 1980s and 2010s for residents of the Hill and those familiar with it. Fences abound, as do vacant lots, half-constructed material projects, and all those objects that appear in the play and movie: lumber, sawhorses, and home-improvement waste. The scene of the play and movie both remind one of parts of the Hill.

The fences are metaphorically about the barriers society puts around us and about those we put around society (Gantt, 2009). This is a starkly different world than that the City of Pittsburgh imagines with greenspaces, pedestrian-friendly throughfares, and interpretive signage. Moving through the Hill, one does not have the sense of openness the *Master Plan* suggests, but rather notes roads filled with potholes, cracked sidewalks, overgrown grass and shrubs, and vacant lots abounding. That is not a condemnation of the Hill, which has suffered from inadequate economic opportunities for its residents, poor access to city services and healthcare, and disregard by municipal authorities. Troy Maxson's troubles are both external and internal. His lack of luck as a professional baseball player seems equally attributable to the racism of the day and his poor attitude. His struggles with his family seem a result of not only his tough-love approach and adultery but also the economic pressure put on the family. Overcoming such struggles are prominently featured in Wilson's plays, leading S. G. Shannon (2004) to argue that Wilson is as much a theorist of struggle in Black life as anything else. Although Troy remains convinced that he is constantly being bested or missing opportunities due him, he remains indefatigably a warrior hero "do[ing] battle while contending with demons from [his] private and collective past" (p. 112).

Troy is cut off from his neighborhood (Noggle, 2009), a difference from the inclusive and multicultural Hill District official discourses promote. This is, of course, to say nothing about the way the Hill is cut off from the rest of the city, like many Black neighborhoods in Pittsburgh that only seem important as spaces for economic redevelopment, like East Liberty or Homewood. While Troy is a product of the 1950s and one need not argue that the 1950s are like the 2020s, something about Troy managed to register with audiences in the 1980s and 2010s, suggesting that the isolation Troy experiences—forced and not—resonate in more modern times. Wilson's constant revision of *Fences* produces an increasingly flawed character (Fishman, 2000), which aside from making Troy interesting, also evokes sympathy and anger, two common emotions that resonate with us all. Although, there are many reasons to dislike Troy, including his harsh treatment of his son Cory, as when he yells at Cory, "N****r! That's what you are! You just another n****r on the street to me!" (Wilson, 2016, pp. 120–126). Despite this, parents, at least, appreciate the conflict with children as an important commonplace—that difficulty between a child becoming an adult and their own person and the emotional challenges that brings to parents and other caregivers who provide for them. Wilson's plays focus on such relatable experiences that underscore the spectrum of Black life and bring new understandings to Blackness. Wilson, in an interview, argues:

Here in America whites have a particular view of blacks, and I think my plays offer them a different and new way to look at black Americans. For instance, in *Fences* they see a garbageman, a person they really don't look at, although they may see a garbageman every day. By looking at Troy's life, white people find out that the content of this black garbageman's life is very similar to their own, that he is affected by the same things—love, honor, beauty, betrayal, duty. Recognizing that these things are as much a part of his life as theirs can be revolutionary and can affect how they think about and deal with black people in their lives. (Lyons & Wilson, 1999, pp. 2–3)

One wonders what Wilson would have thought of *The Greater Hill District Master Plan* and about all the official discourses of improvement and betterment. Would this be a clear effect of taking Wilson's plays seriously and understanding that Black life means as much as white life and therefore Black neighborhoods deserve the care that white neighborhoods receive? Or would Wilson understand the City of Pittsburgh and other actors as simply imposing white values on a Black community without any understanding of the socio-historical importance of the Hill District in its successes and failures? Troy is a timeless character, whose life experience resonates with white and modern audiences, yet the official discourses about the Hill seem to ignore stories like Troy's.

Wilson's concern is that the audience member can fail to develop a sense of self-worth by denying the past (Lyons & Wilson, 1999), yet that is exactly what the City of Pittsburgh and urban developers do. It is difficult, then, to understand the Hill because the Hill's past is denied. Troy understands this history and its impact on the present in a moment of self-reflective thought that, while deeply flawed because he uses it to justify his adultery, still highlights the centrality of memory to one's sense of efficacy: "I done locked myself into a pattern trying to take care of you all that I forgot myself" (Wilson, 2016, p. 94). The City of Pittsburgh has forgotten itself with its postracial identity, and the city suffers through the suffering of its forgotten residents. Any redevelopment or beautification project in a postracial regime then, in a sense, becomes worthless because it denies the past, and more importantly, it works against the self-worth of residents, which is emboldened by embracing the past. Wilson would likely be disappointed by the current situation in the City of Pittsburgh's treatment of the Hill.

Yet August Wilson would likely have been pleased with the movie adaptation of *Fences*. The movie uses sparse props, maintains a darkness that evokes the city of Pittsburgh in the 1950s, and foregrounds Troy's struggles with anger. Most notably, it stays true to his artistic vision in retaining the centrality of Blackness. The fence, Troy's baseball bat, and Troy's bravado all feature prominently in the movie adaptation. The stage of Wilson's play was also minimalist, which focused attention on the characters and their struggles with themselves and each other. Denzel Washington's square-jawed anger evokes, in the viewers, the dogged determinism—what some have called an ideology of "going down swinging"—of Troy's character (Letzler, 2014). The swinging metaphor evokes Troy's past baseball success, signaling that this past is never far from Troy and is indeed central to his character. As Troy tells Rose: "You can't afford a call strike. If you going down, you going down swinging" (Wilson, 1985, p. 69).

Steve Mellon's ten-part series "A Life on the Hill" represents a different mediated approach to challenging official discourses about the Hill District. It focuses on the life of Sala Udin, an activist and city councilmember with a story as complex as the Hill itself. Mellon's story is broken up into ten chapters, each illustrated by local art students in the Hill. There are a couple of things that make the text remarkable. One is that it focuses so clearly on the Hill, which usually makes few long-form appearances in media. Second, it is a story that centers Black activism and not Black crime, Black poverty, or the promises of new development. Third, it is illustrated by local students, whose paintings give the story a depth and warmth, even if some of the paintings suggest tragedy.

Sala Udin grew up in the Hill struggling with all the temptations young life breeds, including gambling and pornography magazines. He struggled with an overbearing and abusive father, discrimination at school, poverty, and social isolation, and he eventually fled his house to New York (Mellon, 2016c). Perhaps unremarkably, Udin's story is not included in the official discourses of the Hill despite the obvious involvement of current city councilors. It is a story of the Hill that is not a welcoming postracial paradise, but rather a racially charged danger zone. Sagar Kamath's accompanying illustration portrays a vibrant but lonely Hill District with only Black figures: four in the street and four in a second story apartment. Only one car is on the road. No businesses appear to be open. While the illustration is colorful, the scene is bleak. Doors and windows are all closed, a clear reference to the boarded-up storefronts that one finds in the Hill.

Udin's story takes him around the country as he works in several social-service jobs and charts a course of Black radicalism. When he returns to Pittsburgh and eventually runs for city council, losing once before winning, he offers up a progressive voice (Mellon, 2016a). The illustration by Cole Gradeck that accompanies chapter 8 shows Udin at a podium surrounded by other Black individuals. No white person is in sight, which represents a hard cry from the multicultural and inclusive community official discourses now suggest the Hill is. This was 1995, and the Hill still struggles with racial segregation. Yet the illustration also centers Black life in the Hill, a necessary anecdote to official discourses that ignore it. Udin would go on to challenge police violence regularly, including the tragic case of Jonny Gammage in 1995, which bears a startling similarity to George Floyd's death some twenty-five years later (Mellon, 2016a).

It seems that with every success Udin has, he suffers a crushing defeat as well, suggesting that, aside from whatever failings he might have as a person, Pittsburgh simply had trouble embracing Black progressive politics. Of course, this also seems eerily connected to Troy's perception of major league baseball failing to embrace him because of his Black excellence. Udin was labeled a "voice for the oppressed," and Mellon (2016a) suggests this is why he did not run for mayor—Pittsburgh was not ready for a Black mayor and has not had one since Udin's time on council.

Udin delivered a eulogy at August Wilson's 2005 funeral, where he said that Wilson "gave us the reality of where we've been and how we got there" (Mellon, 2016b). Wilson as a chronicler of Black experience lived on in 2005, clearly affecting Udin. Udin would then go on to "identify the body of his youngest son," Patrice, twenty-four hours later (Mellon, 2016b). Udin's Hill District was not a postracial neighborhood, but rather one where his Black friends and kin where dying—some from natural causes and others from violence. The painting that accompanies chapter 9, by Sagar Kamath, depicts Sala Udin sitting alone on a bench at night. There is no one around, and the woods in the painting echo the police responding to reports of gunfire from the woods that lead them to discover Patrice's body in his car. Here, again, we have competing images of isolation, including Udin's isolation from democratic politics and his isolation after losing his son and Troy's isolation from major league baseball and increasing distance from his family as he engages in an adulterous affair and succumbs to alcoholism. To be sure, Troy's and Udin's stories are different, but similar themes pervade them.

Steve Mellon's story of Sala Udin brings to life the violence, crime, poverty, and struggle of Black families in the Hill, as well as their fights to make the city of Pittsburgh more livable for Black people. The power of this multimediated storytelling with local magnet-school students providing illustrations, numerous pictures from the *Pittsburgh Post-Gazette*'s archive, and Mellon's long-form prose is that they present a more complicated story than the few hundred words one might get for a traditional news story. The story is visually and verbally stunning and does not shy away from Udin's struggles or, by extension, the difficulties of Black Hill District residents. It also centers Blackness, which is unusual and certainly not keeping with official discourses that obscure that Blackness by generic platitudes or ignoring it. It would be difficult, one imagines, to center Blackness in a traditional news story and certainly difficult and costly to print so many pictures and illustrations. By including young artists, Mellon also brings the Hill's struggles to younger readers, challenging official discourses, which rarely invovle younger people's views, and helping younger readers who likely have little knowledge of the Hill's history. This should not go unrecognized because, while these students' parents are inundated with governmental discourses, the students involved in this project experience a different narrative, one that runs counter to official pronouncements and flashy promotional material and reports. Thus Mellon's series and the movie adaptation of *Fences* both critique postracial discourses for an audience that may have only grown up in times of these postracial ideologies. Troy and Udin are representative of the relatable, flawed, Black individuals official discourses have ignored. They directly challenge the popular

notion that a Black presidency could ever compensate for the way America
has continually stifled and failed Blackness from slavery through Jim Crow
and now to predatory gentrification. Raising awareness of the Hill's racialized
past both encourages alternative understandings of the Hill advanced by official discourses of economic development and multicultural understanding.

CONCLUSION

Black media can counter mainstream media narratives (Williams, 2020).
August Wilson's play and the 2016 movie adaptation along with Steve Mellon's series create a counternarrative to investor-centric, ahistorical, and
postracial narratives of life in the Hill, one that is neither postracial nor
completely without hope. These texts offer powerful visual, textual, and auditory challenges to the redeveloping, brightening, and improving language of
the City of Pittsburgh and other governmental and nongovernmental actors.
By telling a more complete story of the Hill, these creators push back against
the idea that a historically Black neighborhood is now in or poised to be in
some postracial renaissance. Whatever renaissance one might want, it cannot
happen without appreciating the Hill's difficult history—of which Sala Udin
and people like Troy Maxson are a part. One need not forget this history or
ignore Black residents to devote city resources to the Hill, where decades of
neglect have already caused the current crisis. These counternarratives also
emphasize the importance of Black history to modern struggles against racial violence and racialized forgetting, urging us to remember history even
when it is troubling.

    As another Black Pittsburgher, J. E. Wideman (2002), has written about
memory, it is an "atemporal medium in which all things that ever have been,
are, or will be mingle freely, the space that allows us to bump into relatives
long dead or absent friends or children unborn as easily . . . as we encounter
people in our daily lives" (p. xi). And, as S. Hall (1990) argues, "Far from being
grounded in a mere 'recovery' of the past, which is waiting to be found, and
which, when found, will secure our sense of ourselves into eternity, identities
are the names we give to the different ways we are positioned by, and position
ourselves within, the narratives of the past" (p. 225).

    That memory has been excluded from official discourses as well as the
positioning of Black Hill District residents, which promotes a postracial
vision for the future. Yet this history, Black history, can and does resonate
loudly in the work of August Wilson and Steve Mellon. Some may read these
counternarratives as reasons the Hill should be improved, but doing so denies

the transformative potential of countering postracial narratives with those that are historical and those that address the systemic problems of racial and economic inequality. As such, these counternarratives should not be pushed aside and relegated to the footnotes. Popular culture can offer cultural resources for remembering what the Hill postracial discourses are ignoring.

REFERENCES

Allen, D., Lawhon, M., & Pierce, J. (2019). Placing race: On the resonance of place with Black geographies. *Progress in Human Geography, 43*(6), 1001–1019.

Avila, E., & Rose, M. (2009). Race, culture, politics, and urban renewal. *Journal of Urban History, 35*(3), 335–337.

Bobo, L. D. (2011). Somewhere between Jim Crow & post-racialism: Reflections on the racial divide in America today. *Daedalus, 140*(2), 11–36.

Burbank, S. (2009). The shattered mirror: What August Wilson means and willed to mean. *College English, 36*, 117–129.

Capehart, J. (2014, December 29). The fallacy of a "post-racial" society. *Washington Post.* https://www.washingtonpost.com/blogs/post-partisan/wp/2014/12/29/the-fallacy-of -a-post-racial-society/

Chen, Y., Simmons, N., & Kang, D. (2015). "My family isn't racist—however . . .": Multiracial/multicultural Obama-ism as an ideological barrier to teaching intercultural communication. *Journal of International and Intercultural Communication, 8*(2), 167–186.

City of Pittsburgh. (n.d.). *The Greater Hill District master plan.* https://pittsburghpa.gov /dcp/hill-district

Cleary, E. (2015). Here be dragons: The tyranny of the cityscape in James Baldwin's intimate cartographies. *James Baldwin Review, 1,* 91–111.

Craig, B. B., & Rahko, S. E. (2016). Visual profiling as biopolitics: Or, notes on policing in post-racial #AmeriKKKa. *Cultural Studies ↔ Critical Methodologies, 16*(3), 287–295.

Craig, B. B., & Rahko, S. E. (2021). From "Say my name" to "Texas bamma": Transgressive *topoi,* oppositional optics, and sonic subversion in Beyoncé's "Formation." In C. Baade and K. A. McGee (Eds.), *Beyoncé in the world: Making meaning with Queen Bey in troubled times* (pp. 260–284). Wesleyan University Press.

Derickson, K. (2014). The racial politics of neoliberal regulation in post-Katrina Mississippi. *Annals of the Association of American Geographers, 104*(4), 889–902.

Dubowitz, T., & Wagner, L. (2019, March 30). Pittsburgh's Hill District is losing more than a supermarket. *Pittsburgh (PA) Post-Gazette.* https://www.rand.org/blog/2019/04/pitts burghs-hill-district-is-losing-more-than-a-supermarket.html

Fabregat, E., & Beck, T. J. (2019). On the erasure of race in control culture discourse: A case study of Trayvon Martin's role in the Black Lives Matter movement. *Social Identities, 25*(6), 759–774.

Farrell, C. (2008). Bifurcation, fragmentation, or integration? The racial and geographical structure of US metropolitan segregation, 1990–2000. *Urban Studies, 45*(3), 467–499.

Feldman, K. P. (2016). The globality of whiteness in post-racial visual culture. *Cultural Studies, 30*(2), 289–311.

Fishman, J. (2000). Developing his song: August Wilson's *Fences*. In M. R. Elkins (Ed.), *August Wilson: A casebook* (pp. 161–182). Garland.

Gallagher, A. J. (2014, March 10). *Metaphors of colors: Black and white*. Metaphors in American Politics. http://www.politicalmetaphors.com/2014/03/10/metaphors-of-colors-black-and-white/

Gamson, W. (1992). *Talking politics*. Cambridge University Press.

Gantt, P. M. (2009). Putting Black culture on stage: August Wilson's Pittsburgh cycle. *College English, 36*(2), 1–25.

Gaw, M. (n.d.). *The Hill District: A melting pot at the turn of the century*. Marin Theatre Company. https://www.marintheatre.org/productions/august-wilsons-gem-of-the-ocean/the-hill-district

Giammarise, K. (2016, December 6). Hill District residents say Lombard Street has been neglected. *Pittsburgh (PA) Post-Gazette*. https://www.post-gazette.com/local/city/2016/12/07/Hill-District-residents-say-Lombard-Street-has-been-neglected/stories/201611280002

Gurevitch, M., & Levy, M. (1985). Introduction. In M. Gurevitch & M. Levy (Eds.), *Mass communication review yearbook* (Vol. 5, pp. 11–22). Sage.

Hall, S. (1990). Cultural identity and diaspora. In J. Rutherford (Ed.), *Identity: Community, culture, difference* (pp. 222–237). Lawrence and Wishart.

Kellner, D. (1990). *Television and the crisis of democracy*. Westview.

Koprince, S. (2006). Baseball as history and myth in August Wilson's *Fences*. *African American Review, 40*(2), 349–358.

Letzler, D. (2014). Walking around fences: Troy Maxson and the ideology of "going down swinging." *African American Review, 47*(2–3), 301–312.

Logan, E. (2014). Barack Obama, the new politics of race, and classed constructions of racial Blackness. *Sociological Quarterly, 55*(4), 653–682.

Lyons, B., & Wilson, A. (1999). An interview with August Wilson. *Contemporary Literature, 40*(1), 1–21.

Machosky, M. (2022, March 17). *Visionaries are betting on Homestead's future*. NEXT Pittsburgh. https://nextpittsburgh.com/city-design/investors-are-banking-on-homesteads-ongoing-revival/

Marshall, L. (2020, August 21). *Is saying "dark" to mean "bad" an offensive, racist metaphor?* Teaching Traveling. https://www.teachingtraveling.com/metaphor-darkness-as-bad/

Master Plan Management Committee. (2011). *Greater Hill District master plan*. Sasaski; Stull & Lee. https://apps.pittsburghpa.gov/redtail/images/10497_Greater_Hill_District_Master_Plan_2011.pdf

McElroy, E., & Werth, A. (2019). Deracinated dispossessions: On the foreclosures of "gentrification" in Oakland, CA. *Antipode, 51*(1), 878–898.

Melamed, J. (2008). The killing joke of sympathy: Chester Himes's *End of a primitive* sounds the limits of midcentury racial liberalism. *American Literature, 80*(4), 769–797.

Mellon, S. (2016a). A life on the Hill: Chapter 8. *Pittsburgh (PA) Post-Gazette*. http://newsinteractive.post-gazette.com/life-on-the-hill/#chapterEight

Mellon, S. (2016b). A life on the Hill: Chapter 10. *Pittsburgh (PA) Post-Gazette*. https://newsinteractive.post-gazette.com/life-on-the-hill/#ChapterTen

Mellon, S. (2016c). A life on the Hill: Chapter 2. *Pittsburgh (PA) Post-Gazette*. http://news interactive.post-gazette.com/life-on-the-hill/#chapterTwo

Mitchell, W. J. T. (2012). *Seeing through race*. Harvard University Press.

Noggle, R. (2009). ". . . if you live long enough the boat will turb around": The birth and death of community in three plays by August Wilson. *College English, 36*(2), 58–73.

O'Neill, B. (2017, August 30). A park's great view of Pittsburgh obscured by neglect. *Pittsburgh (PA) Post-Gazette*. https://www.post-gazette.com/opinion/brian-oneill/2017/08/30/robert-e-williams-memorial-park-herron-hill-park-pittsburgh-hill-district-pwsa-reservoir/stories/201708300034

Papazekos, T. (2022). Power play goal: Analyzing zoning law and reparations as remedies to historic displacement in Pittsburgh's Hill District. *Georgetown Journal on Poverty Law and Policy, 29*(3), 407–430.

Rossing, J. P. (2012). Deconstructing postracialism: Humor as a critical, cultural project. *Journal of Communication Inquiry, 36*(1), 44–61.

Russell, J. C. (2019). *Visceral whiteness: Public memory and (dis)comfort in "post-racial" narratives about slavery and civil rights in America* [Doctoral dissertation, Georgia State University]. ScholarWorks. https://scholarworks.gsu.edu/communication_diss/96/

Ryan, C., Carragee, K. M., & Schwerner, C. (1998). Media, movements, and the quest for social justice. *Journal of Applied Communication Research, 26*(2), 165–181.

Sciullo, N. J. (2015). Richard Sherman, rhetoric, and racial animus in the rebirth of the bogeyman myth. *Hastings Communication and Entertainment Law Journal, 37*(2), 201–230.

Shannon, S. G. (2004). August Wilson on a century of Black worklife. *New Labor Forum, 13*(2), 111–121.

Squires, C. (2014). *The Post-racial Mystique: Media and Race in the Twenty-First Century*. New York University Press.

Squires, G. D., & Kubrin, C. (2005). Privileged places: Race, uneven development and the geography of opportunity in America. *Urban Studies, 42*(1), 47–68.

VisitPITTSBURGH. (n.d.). *Must see Pittsburgh views*. https://www.visitpittsburgh.com/blog/must-see-pittsburgh-views/

Watts, E. K. (2010). The nearly apocalyptic politics of post-racial America: Or, "this is now the United States of Zombieland." *Journal of Communication Inquiry, 34*(3), 214–222.

Wideman, J. E. (2002). *The Homewood books*. University of Pittsburgh Press.

Williams, A. (2020). Black memes matter: #LivingWhileBlack with Becky and Karen. *Social Media + Society, 6*(4), 1–14. https://doi.org/10.1177/2056305120981047

Wilson, A. (1985). *Fences*. Penguin.

Wilson, A. (2016). *Fences* [Screenplay]. Squarespace. https://static1.squarespace.com/static/5a1c2452268b96d901cd3471/t/5b95da684d7a9cece57cb18b/1536547438707/FENCES+Script.pdf

ABOUT THE CONTRIBUTORS

Maksim Bugrov is a lecturer and the assistant director of forensics in the Department of Human Communication Studies at California State University, Fullerton. He completed his bachelor's degree in communication studies at California State University, Fullerton (2013) and earned his master of arts in communication studies at California State University, Fresno (2016).

Byron B Craig (PhD, Indiana University) is an assistant professor in the School of Communication at Illinois State University. Dr. Craig's research focuses on race, racism, and citizenship in American democracy. His work has appeared in journals such as *Cultural Studies ↔ Critical Methodologies*, *Journal of Religion and Communication*, and the *Journal of the Scholarship of Teaching and Learning* as well as in edited volumes such as *The Gig Economy: Workers and Media in the Age of Convergence* (Routledge, 2021) and *Beyoncé in the World: Making Meaning with Queen Bey in Troubled Times* (Wesleyan University Press, 2021). Dr. Craig is also a fellow with the American Democracy Project and faculty fellow and chair of the Committee on LGBTQIA+ Policies and Initiatives at Illinois State University.

Patricia G. Davis is an associate professor of communication studies at Northeastern University. Her research and writing foreground issues of race, memory, identity, and representation. Her work has been published in *Rhetoric Review*, *Text and Performance Quarterly*, *Social Media + Society*, *Rhetoric and Public Affairs*, *Southern Communication Journal*, *Feminist Media Studies*, and the *Journal of International and Intercultural Communication* as well as in multiple edited collections. Her book *Laying Claim: African American Cultural Memory and Southern Identity* (University of Alabama Press, 2016) received multiple awards from the National Communication Association. She is currently writing a book on the history of elite Black civic and political discourse centered on Black women's public presentation.

Peter Ehrenhaus (PhD, University of Minnesota) is professor emeritus of communication at Pacific Lutheran University. His research concerns cultural memory as a site of struggle in conditions of cultural trauma with particular focus on the legacies of America's Vietnam War and the nation's history of white-on-Black race violence and race lynching. His work has been published in *Argumentation and Advocacy, Communication Education, Communication Monographs, Critical Studies in Media Communication, Journal of Communication, Journal of International and Intercultural Communication, Quarterly Journal of Speech,* and *Western Journal of Communication* as well as in various edited collections.

Whitney Gent (PhD, University of Wisconsin—Madison) is an assistant professor in the School of Communication at the University of Nebraska, Omaha. Her research on rhetorics of homelessness and poverty, advocacy, policymaking, and public deliberation has appeared in journals, including the *Quarterly Journal of Speech, Howard Journal of Communications, Communication and the Public, Evidence & Policy,* and *Annals of the International Communication Association.*

Christopher Gilbert is associate professor of English in communication and media at Assumption University. His work looks at the role of humor in cultural politics as well as comic responses to controversy and conflict. It appears in a variety of leading journals in the fields of rhetoric and humor studies as well as in his 2021 book *Caricature and National Character: The United States at War.* Beyond academia, Chris is an avid road cyclist, an abecedarian guitarist, and a drawing enthusiast.

Oscar Giner is a dramatic poet who has been working in the American Southwest and in his native Caribbean for over four decades. He is a professor at the Herberger College of Design and the Arts and the Barrett Honors College at Arizona State University. With coauthor Robert L. Ivie, Giner has written book chapters and articles that have been published in China, Poland, and Slovenia. He has also published *Hunt the Devil: A Demonology of US War Culture* and has completed a new book, *After Empire: Passage to Democracy.* Giner has translated the only surviving text of the Mayan theater, the *Rabinal Achí,* as a guest artist of the Institute of American Indian Arts in Santa Fe, New Mexico. He recently translated, acted, and directed *Summer, Summer* by Myrna Casas at the off-Broadway Cherry Lane Theatre in New York.

J. Scott Jordan, PhD, is a cognitive psychologist who studies the neuroscience, psychology, and philosophy of cooperative behavior. Jordan is chair of the Department of Psychology at Illinois State University, where he is also a distinguished university professor. With over 150 publications, he regularly contributes to Sterling's Popular Culture Psychology series and other outlets to reveal connections between pop-cultural narratives, psychology, and the realities of lived life. Examples include *Exploring the Hidden Kingdoms of Assumption: Interview with Christopher Priest on Black Panther, Culture, and the Art of Changing Minds* (Black Panther Psychology) and *The Welcoming Spiderverse: Finding Your "Self" in a Web of Others* (Pop Mythology). He has published a peer-reviewed, scientific song about the "self" ("It's Hard Work Being No One), which received a positive review in *Discover Magazine*. He is a comember of the *WGLT Psych Geeks* podcast and has appeared on the *bodyselfmind* podcast. He is co-organizer of ReggieCon, a virtual comic-book-convention panel series that celebrates diversity and heritage months during the academic year. He also produces the *Dark Loops Productions* channel on YouTube, where he hosts discussions of lived life, science, art, the humanities, and all things pop culture. He is also extremely proud of his international comic book collection.

Euni Kim is a doctoral student in the Department of Communication at the University of Utah, which rests on Shoshone, Paiute, Goshute, and Ute tribal lands. Her work lies at the intersections of rhetoric and critical theories of race and representation. She adopts an interdisciplinary approach to all her work, frequently drawing from Asian American studies, film and media studies, and critical cultural studies. She is currently researching how people of color negotiate instances of racialized and gendered violence in terms of their own racial identities.

Melanie Loehwing (PhD, Indiana University) is associate professor in the Department of Communication at Mississippi State University. Her research on rhetorics of homelessness and poverty, public-sphere theory, advocacy and protest, and visual rhetoric has appeared in journals including the *Quarterly Journal of Speech*, *Philosophy & Rhetoric*, and *Enculturation*. She is the author of *Homeless Advocacy and the Rhetorical Construction of the Civic Home* (Penn State University Press, 2018).

Jaclyn S. Olson is a PhD candidate in the Department of Communication Studies at the University of North Carolina at Chapel Hill. She received her

MA in communication at Villanova University. Her research explores the melancholic function of anthems in the American imagination, particularly in moments of perceived national crises. Her published work can be found in *Rhetoric Review.*

A. Susan Owen (PhD, University of Iowa) is professor emerita of communication studies and African American studies at the University of Puget Sound. Her critical-media-studies research of film, television, and photography focuses on female characterizations in action-adventure, war, science fiction, and apocalyptic narratives; representations of race violence since Reconstruction; and representations of traumatic memory. She is coauthor of two books and has published in *Critical Studies in Media Communication, Journal of Homosexuality, Journal of Popular Film and Television, Quarterly Journal of Speech, Rhetoric and Public Affairs, Text and Performance Quarterly,* and *Western Journal of Communication.*

Stephen E. Rahko (PhD, Indiana University) is an assistant professor at Illinois State University. Dr. Rahko's research focuses on the challenges posed by the intersection of capitalism and race for American democracy. His work has appeared in journals such as *Cultural Studies « Critical Methodologies, Electronic Journal of Communication, Journal of the Scholarship of Teaching and Learning* as well as edited volumes such as *The Gig Economy: Workers and Media in the Age of Convergence* (Routledge, 2021) and in *Beyoncé in the World: Making Meaning with Queen Bey in Troubled Times* (Wesleyan University Press, 2021). He is also the editor of the *Journal of the Scholarship of Teaching and Learning.*

Nick J. Sciullo is an assistant professor of communications at Texas A&M University—Kingsville. His research focuses on rhetoric and cultural studies applied to Black radicalism, debate and argumentation, and law and the humanities. His work has appeared in *Review of Communication, Communication Teacher, Communication Education, Argumentation & Advocacy, Canadian Journal of Communication,* and *Rhetoric & Communications* along with many other peer-reviewed journals and law reviews. In 2021, he was awarded the Dean's Award for Outstanding Scholarly Productivity from the College of Arts & Sciences at Texas A&M University—Kingsville. He has been awarded the Top Paper Award by the Argumentation and Forensics Division of the Southern States Communication Association three years in a row. In 2020, he was awarded the Article of the Year Award by the Argumentation and Forensics Division of the National Communication Association.

In 2016, he earned the Outstanding Dissertation Award from the Critical and Cultural Studies Division of the National Communication Association. He received his PhD in communication from Georgia State University and his JD from West Virginia University.

Arthur D. Soto-Vásquez is an assistant professor of communication at Texas A&M International University. He studies the relationship between digital media, popular culture, and identity making. His first book is entitled *Mobilizing the Latinx Vote: Media, Identity, and Politics* (Routledge, 2020). His current projects cover US Latinx political identity, misinformation, influencers, and consumer culture. He has presented his research at the University of Oxford, the Università degli Studi di Milano, and the International Communication Association. He received his PhD from the American University and is from El Paso, Texas. He is an active Rotarian and board member of the Laredo Film Society.

Erika M. Thomas (PhD, Wayne State University, 2011) is an associate professor and the codirector of forensics in the Department of Human Communication Studies at California State University, Fullerton. She teaches and researches in the area of rhetorical theory and criticism, using critical/cultural theories to examine media representations. Her work has been included in *Reimagining Black Masculinities: Race, Gender, and π*ublic Space (Lexington Books, 2020) and in the journals *Women & Language* (2018) and *Relevant Rhetoric* (2017).

INDEX

Page numbers in bold refer to illustrations.

Rodgers, Richard, 46
Rosselló, Ricardo, 56
Rossing, J., 241
Ruff, Matt, 103
Ryan, C., 246

Saludos Amigos, 142
San Francisco 49ers, 83
Sánchez, Luis Rafael, 42
Sanchez, Sonia, 106
Sanders, Bernie, 100
Schama, S., 54
Scheer, Gene, 92
Schleier, M., 30
Schwerner, C., 246
Schwerner, Michael, 165
Scott, A. O., 162
Screen Actors Guild, 161
1776 (Edwards), 54
Sexton, J., 199, 201
Shakespeare, William, 46, 54
Shakur, Tupac, 35, 49–50
Shannon, S. G., 249
Shelby County v. Holder, 5
Shirley, Don, 76, 77
Silva, Ellen, 82
Silva, K., 86
Sinatra, Frank, 82
Singh, Lilly, 32
1619 Project, 63
Slater, Christian, 221
slavery/enslavement, 5, 53, 163, 175, 203, 207, 208–11, 239, 246; chattel, 201–2, 204, 212–13; laughter and, 117–18; legacy of, 28, 103, 216, 241, 254; sentimentalizing of, 164; social death and, 201–2, 208–11, 214–15; white control of the Black gaze, 170
Sloop, J. M., 185–86
Smith, S. M., 173
social change, 10
social death, 201–2
social justice, 9, 62
Song of the South, 140
sonic episteme, 87–88

Soo, Phillipa, 54
Sound of Music, The, 46
South Pacific, 46
Spielberg, Steven, 71
Spillars, H., 201
Spivak, G. C., 194n2
Squires, C. R., 69, 83, 88, 123, 200, 243
Squires, G. D., 240
St. Johns Church, 96
Stallworth, Ron, 161–63, 165, 169–71
"Star-Spangled Banner," 82–83, 86
Stoler, A. L., 193
Stone, Emma, 186
stop-and-frisk policies, 225–26
Stowe, Harriet Beecher, 67
"Strange Fruit" (Holiday), 168
Student Nonviolent Coordinating Committee (SNCC), 172
Students for Fair Admissions v. President and Fellows of Harvard College, 5
Sturken, M., 172, 182
suburbia, media portrayal of, 30–31
Sugino, C., 28, 38
Swinton, Tilda, 186
symbolic violence, 21–57

Taíno, 43
Tarantino, Quentin, 199–216
taste communities, 17n3
Taylor, Breonna, 9, 99, 111n1
"Ten Crack Commandments" (Notorious BIG), 49
theory of catharsis, 47
theory of the subaltern, 194n2
"Thesis of the Philosophy of History" (Benjamin), 3
This Is Us, 31
"This Land Is Your Land" (Guthrie), 87, 92
Thomas, Jonathan Taylor, 149
Thompson, Tessa, 152
Thoreau, Henry David, 227
Tierney, S., 205
Till, Emmett, 174
Till, Mamie, 174
Time, 168

Printed in the United States
by Baker & Taylor Publisher Services